Guns and Roses

GUNS AND ROSES

The Untold Story of
Dean O'Banion,
Chicago's Big Shot Before Al Capone

ROSE KEEFE

Cumberland House
Nashville, Tennessee

Published by
Cumberland House Publishing, Inc.
431 Harding Industrial Drive
Nashville, TN 37211-3160

Cover design: Gore Studio, Inc.
Text design: John Mitchell

Library of Congress Cataloging-in-Publication Data
Keefe, Rose.
Guns and roses : the untold story of Dean O'Banion, Chicago's big shot before Al Capone / Rose Keefe.
p. cm.
Includes bibliographical references and index.
ISBN 1-58182-378-9 (pbk. : alk. paper)
1. O'Banion, Dean, 1892-1924. 2. Criminals—Illinois—Chicago—Biography. 3. Organized crime—Illinois—Chicago—History. I. Title.
HV6248.O33K44 2003
364.1'092—dc22

Printed in Canada
1 2 3 4 5 6 7—09 08 07 06 05 04 03

For my parents, Don and Bev Keefe,
and also for Bill Helmer, a North Sider at heart

CONTENTS

Acknowledgments

Good men must not obey the laws too well.
— Ralph Waldo Emerson

Much of what has been written about Dean O'Banion is either a distorted version of what little is known about him, or complete fiction that described the type of person he *must* have been.

No wonder this book took ten years to write.

Locating those who knew the real O'Banion sixty years after his death was not an easy undertaking. But time had left three people still alive to tell the tale when I was looking to hear it, and they deserve most of the credit for shattering the misleading mask and revealing the man behind it:

E. Barnett worked for the North Side Gang as a delivery man and booze hauler from 1921 until 1924. Through a chance meeting in eastern Canada in 1988, I snagged him for a long interview and found him to be most generous with his time and memories. "The best boss I ever had," was how he remembered O'Banion. "If I had trouble or needed money, he listened to me."

Louise Gentle of Maroa, Illinois, went to school with the young Dean from 1897 until 1901. She provided the rare class photograph that appears in this book and spent an entire afternoon reminiscing about O'Banion and the Maroa of his day. Louise passed away recently at the age of 108. She is both missed and remembered.

H. J. Pitts used to patronize O'Banion's flower shop at 738 North State Street. Fifteen years old in 1924, he was so traumatized by O'Banion's murder that he began carrying a gun himself. He was kind enough to grant a telephone interview in 1995 and share his memories of both "Mr. O'Banion" and the North State Street area during the early Twenties.

There are others who didn't know Dean O'Banion personally yet still contributed so much to this book in terms of personal expertise, research materials, family stories, and just plain moral support:

Bill Helmer, without whom . . . not. Bill's faith in this project and insistence that the North Siders needed in-depth book coverage of their own were just as invaluable as the collection of news clippings, books, and photos that he placed at my disposal. Our association began as mutual researchers and evolved into a true friendship. Thanks, Bill.

The O'Banion relatives, namely M. Klever and J. Lindau Jr., fantastic people who took time to speak with me about a great-uncle they had only heard about. This story about the real Dean O'Banion is as much for them as for future students of Chicago criminal history.

Bob Koznecki, whose grandfather Frank was a cousin to O'Banion friend and successor Earl "Hymie" Weiss, for the family stories about the most enigmatic North Sider.

Richard Kaufman, who was generous with memories of his grandfather, O'Banion associate Julian "Potatoes" Kaufman.

Mark and Anita Lewis, for information about their colorful relative, O'Banion bodyguard Louis Alterie.

Others who deserve special mention are John Binder, Chicago crime historian and writer who cheerfully let me take advantage of his considerable expertise on the subject of the Chicago outfit; Sister Mary Clare McGrath of Holy Name High School, for providing access to Dean's school records; Julie Satzik of the Archdiocese of Chicago, for the church records; Susan Karren of the National Archives, Great Lakes Region, for supplying copies of the Sieben Brewery court proceedings and other federal cases involving the North Side Gang; Richard Lindbergh, whose excellent *Chicago Ragtime* was my Bible when it came to understanding the Chicago of Dean's youth; Mark

LaVell, Mary Huff, Mike Duffy, Sarah Simard, Mario Gomes, Richard Tilden, and the staff of the Chicago Public Library.

Special thanks to Bob Gentle and Gwen Clifton from Maroa, and to Eddie Holtsclaw for locating and sharing O'Banion's childhood letter to his mother.

Last but not least, thanks to Ron Pitkin at Cumberland House for his enthusiasm about this long-overdue project, and my editor, John Mitchell, for his assistance in preparing the final manuscript for publication.

PROLOGUE

Chicago, November 10, 1924

THE WILLIAM F. SCHOFIELD FLOWER SHOP at 738 North State Street stood in an area that struggled for working class respectability in the midst of urban, moral, and social decay. To the Northwest, centered around Oak and Cambridge Streets, was Little Sicily, or Little Hell, a Sicilian immigrant colony where murders routinely went unsolved and the honest poor shared soot-blackened dwellings with pimps, thieves, Black Handers, and other criminal agents who found the area a ripe place in which to operate. A short distance south of Schofield's stood the Levee, Chicago's infamous red-light district, which once housed more than five thousand prostitutes in resorts with brazen names like the Bucket of Blood and the Sappho. A 1912 "closure" brought about by church and civic groups had merely installed the same women in massage parlors, hotels, and dance studios.

A few blocks north of the shop, in the vicinity of the Newberry Library, a Bohemian community flourished, an employment-free haven where rebellious sons and daughters slept all day, painted or devoured obscure poetry at night, and argued for Communism in dimly lit lounges such as the Black Cat and the Dill Pickle Club. Those families and blue-collar workers living in the rooming houses, apartment buildings, and small homes around 738 North State Street could only hope that the current boundaries remained impenetrable.

Tragedy and infamy did occasionally hit the neighborhood. Few could forget the murder of six-year-old Janet Wilkinson by child molester Thomas Fitzgerald in 1919. Both killer and victim had lived in the same apartment building at 114 East Superior Street, causing parents to view their neighbors with a fearful suspicion that took a long time to subside.

Since Fitzgerald's hanging on October 27, 1919, things had been comparatively quiet, but the feeling persisted that it was only a matter of time before something even worse happened. The 1920 advent of nationwide Prohibition had made booze-related violence a new source of worry. Bootleggers' battles were front-page news in 1924. Lurid accounts of hijacked liquor shipments (sometimes resulting in murdered drivers), gang wars, and even death by rotgut poisoning all suggested that human life had assumed less value than a bottle of recut Scotch.

George Calder, Harvey Beilgard, and Anthony Pfirschy, teenage schoolboys from Holy Name Parochial School at State Street and East Chicago Avenue, were worrying more about their homework load than the next big drama as they hurried north on State that brisk November day. The noon bell had rung minutes previously, and they were on their way home for lunch. When they reached Schofield's, they paused, attracted by a window display of goldfish in flower-ringed bowls. All three pressed their faces to the glass for a better look.

Suddenly, the shop door swung open with a crash and three men ran out. The first man, whom Harvey Beilgard observed to be young and wearing a blue suit with a gray hat, knocked the boy to the pavement. Sprawled on his back, he only saw the legs of the second runner. The third pushed down George Calder, who noted that his assailant was older than the other two and wore a dark suit, brown overcoat, and brown hat.

Anthony Pfirschy fared no better. As he later told it, "One [of the men] brushed against me so hard that I was knocked down. Getting up, I saw this man stick something in his pocket that resembled the handle of a water gun."

The shaken schoolboys rose to their feet and looked through the window again. Peering beyond the lazily swimming fish, they saw a man lying on the floor in front of a refrigerated glass showcase. Not daring to investigate further, Calder and Beilgard ran back to the school to summon help. Anthony Pfirschy, motivated by curiosity or valor or both, followed the fleeing men, who had turned onto Superior Street.

"When I got to the corner," he later recalled, "I saw them get into an automobile parked at the alley just west of State Street. A woman was at the wheel of the car; she held the doors open for the men as they hurried up and pushed one another into the automobile." He described the car as an Overland-style model, with long, nickel-plated bars at the back. The woman, he said, wore a black veil and brown coat with a fur collar.

While Pfirschy watched, the woman started the motor, backed out onto Superior Street, and drove west. At Dearborn, she turned south and vanished from sight. Two cars that had been parked nearby drove away as soon as her vehicle disappeared. The boy did not notice, or failed to mention, that four more automobiles had swung into obstructing positions on State Street as soon as the trio exited the shop, blocking traffic and preventing pursuit of the woman's car. Once the coast was clear, they tooted apologetically at the infuriated midday drivers and went their separate ways.

Calder and Beilgard, in the meantime, had gone to the school office and alerted two priests, Father Morrison and Father O'Brien. The clergymen hurried to the shop, where they found a handful of badly shaken employees clustered around the fallen man. One look at his multiple gunshot wounds confirmed that he was beyond medical help. Bending over him, they began to administer the last rites.

They were still praying when acting Captain Daniel Murphy of the Chicago Avenue station arrived in response to a telephone message that there had been a "shooting" at Schofield's. After pushing through the crowd that had assembled outside, Murphy and his men joined the small group around the victim. The policemen made a positive identification at once despite the bloody and bruised features. Doubtlessly they shuddered as they did so, knowing that this was no routine homicide.

The dead man was Dean O'Banion, gang leader and bootlegging boss, whose territory encompassed all of Chicago's North Side from Madison Street to the city limits near Evanston. His gang included more than two hundred hard-bitten hoodlums who, at his bidding, had terrorized North Side voters the week before into handing traditionally Democratic wards to the Republicans. O'Banion's connection with the Johnny Torrio–Al Capone Gang from the South Side had increased his power and influence, although there had been rumors lately that Torrio and Capone, as well as the Genna brothers of Little Italy, had wanted him out of their association and in his grave. O'Banion's followers, on the other hand, were fiercely loyal to him, and Murphy had little doubt that more bullet-riddled bodies would appear on the coroner's table in the coming months, maybe even years.

O'Banion, who ran the flower shop with William Schofield as his legitimate front, had been struck by five bullets in the head, neck, and right chest cavity. A sixth had missed and shattered the glass showcase, where it buried itself in the wall beyond a stunning display of American Beauty roses. A pair of florists' shears lay inches from the corpse's left hand. Murphy learned that before the assassins came calling, the gangster had been preparing floral tributes for the upcoming funeral of Mike Merlo, president of the Unione Siciliana (Sicilian Union), who had died of cancer on November 8.

Captain Murphy had been a Chicago citizen, never mind a cop, long enough to know that O'Banion's murder would never be solved, at least not officially. Gangland was always its own judge, jury, and executioner, with some cases resulting in multiple casualties. The impact of O'Banion's death would set a new precedent in terms of bloodshed; it would later be described as the opening shot in the "Bootleg Battle of the Marne."

Regardless of an investigation's futility, the motions still had to be gone through. Murphy telephoned the detective bureau. Because of the case's explosive nature, Chief of Police Mike Hughes and Captain William Schoemaker took charge of it. They were joined by Assistant State's Attorneys John Sbarbaro, who also ran the undertaking establishment where O'Banion's body was later delivered, and William McSwiggin, whose suspicious death in the company of gangsters over a year later would lead to rumors of underworld connections.

The best witness was the shop's black porter, William Crutchfield, who had been sweeping up front when the killers arrived. He told the police that two of them had been Italians: "short, stocky, and rather rough-looking." The third, he said, had been "tall, well-built, well-dressed, smooth-shaven, wore a brown overcoat and brown hat. He might have been a Jew or a Greek."

O'Banion, he said, had emerged from the work area at the rear of the shop and approached the trio with his right hand extended, saying cheerfully, "Hello, boys . . . you here for Merlo's flowers?" Assuming that his employer knew them, Crutchfield, after seeing the well-dressed man shake O'Banion's hand, picked up his broom and went into the workroom. About fifteen minutes later, gunfire erupted, sending most of the employees running out the delivery door into the alley in terror. Crutchfield looked back out into the shop when the shooting ceased, and saw the three visitors making a hasty escape.

While witnesses were being rounded up and questioned, coroner's physician Dr. Joseph Springer arrived. He concluded from the location of O'Banion's wounds that death had been instantaneous, and noted that three of the fatal bullets had been "dum-dummed," or deliberately disfigured to create a larger wound. He also saw the grip of a .45 automatic army pistol protruding slightly from the gangster's hip pocket. It looked as if he had tried to draw it, perhaps sensing at the last minute that his time had come. Springer found, in addition to $575 in cash, an extra clip of cartridges in the same pocket. O'Banion had always been ready and willing to defend himself, but for some reason he had relaxed his guard for the visitors. It was a rare carelessness that cost him his life.

After Dr. Springer concluded his examination, the body was removed to Sbarbaro's mortuary at 708 North Wells Street. Policemen then went to the O'Banion home at 3608 North Pine Grove Avenue, a spacious twelve-room apartment he had shared with his wife, father, and stepmother. Mrs. Viola O'Banion, a young woman of twenty-three, was there alone. When the officers told her gently that they wanted to speak with her about Dean, she guessed at once the reason for the visit.

"Is he dead? Tell me!" she sobbed. After answering some delicately worded questions, she left the apartment and went to a relative's house.

Chief of Police Morgan Collins, a staunch anti-gang crusader who had assumed office after the 1923 election of reform mayor William Dever, merely stated the obvious when he called the killing the result of an underworld vendetta. "The woman theory does not stand up well," he said, countering a love triangle suggestion, "nor does the political angle. [It had been hinted that a recent interest in politics had concerned certain factions already in office.] I believe the shooting was the result of someone being 'shorted' in an alcohol deal." He detailed O'Banion's suspected involvement in a few underworld battles of the past year, and dramatically concluded, "I had expected him to be killed, and so had he."

Collins's statement was more than just a piece of good press copy. By November 1924, Dean O'Banion had generated enough animosity against himself to make his murder inevitable.

One enemy was Davy Miller, prizefight referee and one-time pugilist who, with his brothers Hirschie and Max, had a minor bootlegging operation on the West Side. He had been shot in the stomach by O'Banion the previous January during an altercation in the LaSalle Theatre, and survived merely by chance. He said, "I might as well admit that I'm glad he's dead. But I'm also glad that my family had nothing to do with it." Hirschie and Maxie Miller echoed his sentiments. The three brothers were released after providing alibis.

Another leading suspect was Domenic "Libby" Nuccio, leader of the small Gloriano Gang. On November 4, during the city elections, O'Banion had attacked Nuccio in front of a polling station at Wells and Division Streets because the latter had disobeyed orders to direct all votes to the Republican ticket. Nuccio, whose record dated back to 1917 and included arrests for burglary, larceny, carrying concealed weapons, and suspicion of murder, denied knowing anything about the shooting, and lacking evidence to the contrary, the police let him go.

The detective bureau learned that O'Banion had been planning to build a small community outside Connorville, Illinois, where he had recently looked at a spread of several hundred acres. Rumor hinted that he was going to center the fledgling settlement around a country club offering protected gambling. "It was this plan," suggested the *Herald and Examiner*, "that brought a certain coolness into his relationship with [Johnny] Torrio, who hitherto had been a fast friend. In O'Banion's new plan, Torrio saw his prestige as 'king of gambling' about to slip."

Johnny Torrio was, naturally, questioned. A short, dapper figure, Torrio presented a sharp contrast to the hulking, slovenly dime-novel gangster, but his menace laid in his ability to command such characters. A graduate of New York's bloody Five Points Gang, Torrio supervised the lion's share of bootlegging, gambling, and prostitution on the South and West Sides. He looked and behaved like a genteel businessman, and was known as somewhat of a diplomat who preferred peace over bloodshed. But as his recent association with O'Banion was examined, it became evident that the murdered gangster's behavior would have infuriated a saint, and Johnny Torrio was no Peter or Paul.

There was, for instance, the police raid on the Sieben brewery the previous May, in which both Torrio and O'Banion had been arrested. Underworld gossip had it that O'Banion had known of the raid beforehand but, resentful of Torrio's gangland supremacy, refused to tip him off. Torrio had been arrested once before for violation of the Volstead Act, and a second conviction carried a mandatory prison term. To add insult to injury, O'Banion had allegedly sold his now worthless share of the Sieben to Torrio for half a million dollars. The humiliation, financial loss, and blatant treachery on O'Banion's part might easily have turned Torrio's feelings from friendly to murderous.

Torrio, however, only had glowing words to describe his deceased partner. He said that he and O'Banion had been close friends—only last Sunday he had placed an order with him for ten thousand dollars' worth of floral decorations for the Merlo funeral. For some reason, the assistant state's attorneys accepted this costly order as proof of unsullied friendship, and let him go.

Another suspect was Al Capone, alias Al Brown, Torrio's second in command and fellow Five Pointers alumnus, who had a few more years to go before he became the quintessential American gangster. A husky young hoodlum with steel gray eyes and three scars gouged into the left side of his face, Capone explained that he, too, had placed a flower order with O'Banion, this one for an eight-thousand-dollar rose sculpture. Mention of a huge purchase worked the same magic as it had for Torrio, and Capone was released.

The police also talked to Angelo Genna, one of six Sicilian brothers who had built a lucrative alcohol-cooking industry in the slums of Little Italy. Angelo, the family enforcer, had owed O'Banion money, and trouble supposedly erupted when the North Sider tried to collect. Both gangsters had volcanic tempers when crossed, and no one doubted that a clash would have left one of them dead. Genna, who had been responsible for at least two violent killings, pleaded ignorance. Like Torrio, Capone, and the other suspects, he could not be linked conclusively with the murder.

Captain Schoemaker knew that the case was hopeless, but went through the motions with remarkable diligence. He questioned not only O'Banion's known and suspected enemies but also his friends in the faint hope that one of them might be angry or grief-stricken enough to say something.

Earl "Hymie" Weiss, O'Banion's best friend and second in command, gave Schoemaker an accurate idea of what kind of help he could expect from that quarter. The wiry, dark-eyed young Pole's answers were sullen and useless. When Schoemaker finally asked point-blank, "If you knew anything about this murder, would you tell me?" Weiss replied, "Well, to be frank, I guess I wouldn't."

Weiss, everyone knew, was merely playing a waiting game. "There'll be more murder," predicted a veteran detective. "More murder, and it will come quick." He was right. Once Weiss embarked on a revenge campaign, over six hundred gangsters would die in the ensuing war.

Only one O'Banion aide talked: "Two-Gun" Louie Alterie, the slain gangster's bodyguard and Man Friday. Alterie, a loudmouthed extrovert who, with "Dapper Dan" McCarthy, handled the North Side Gang's union rackets, brandished his twin maple-handled pistols and publicly challenged O'Banion's slayers to a duel at the corner of State and Madison Streets, commonly referred to as "the world's busiest corner."

Most smirked at Alterie's flaky challenge, but Mayor Dever, notorious for his anti-gang stance, was not amused. Alterie's outcry prompted him to declare all-out war against the underworld. He ordered that every known gunman be arrested on sight. Later he urged the police to shoot to kill any hoodlum who resisted arrest. No officer went that far, but the rash order hinted at the gangster hysteria that the city, and later the nation, was about to plunge into.

Who ordered O'Banion's murder has never been a mystery. It was a joint effort by the Torrio–Capone and Genna factions to eliminate a long-standing threat. The inconvenience he caused them, however, paled in comparison with the bloody assaults launched by his followers, led first by Hymie Weiss, then Vincent Drucci, and finally George "Bugs" Moran. Torrio and the Gennas were the earliest casualties, leaving Al Capone the chief target from 1925 on. Capone's subsequent four-year struggle with the North Siders almost tore Chicago apart, and left the scarfaced gangster in constant fear for his life. He lamented once, "If I'd known what I was getting into, I'd never have left the Five Points outfit in New York." He might also have thought twice about the wisdom of killing O'Banion.

The North Side Gang leader's murder was a momentous event in the annals of Chicago crime. It inspired the most lavish gangster funeral ever witnessed in the city up until then. It also led to the gang war that gave Chicago the violent reputation it is still trying to live down. As the catalyst for such a bloody chapter in the city's history, O'Banion acquired a macabre celebrity in death. He is remembered more for his passing than anything he ever did while alive.

Although it is a popular assumption that O'Banion became someone only after the last of his lifeblood seeped into the shop floorboards, research denies this. Between 1920 and 1924, Dean O'Banion was a major gangland power, raking in hundreds of thousands of dollars a year from his bootlegging, gambling, and union interests. He enjoyed the hospitality and protection of politicians who sought his election-day support. While Al Capone was still a bouncer at the Four Deuces nightspot, O'Banion was an underworld force to be reckoned with, having fought in the newspaper circulation wars and belonged to the safecracking ring headed by the legendary Charles Reiser. Chief Collins, believing that few big "scores" would take place without the North Sider's knowledge or active participation, had a standard response to any news of such: "Find Dean O'Banion." Upon first hearing about O'Banion's murder, he congratulated Chicago on the death of its "arch criminal."

The notoriety of Dean O'Banion and Chicago's other Jazz Age gangsters, such as Terry Druggan, Frankie Lake, and Spike O'Donnell, has been eclipsed by that of Al Capone. Few think about that decade of bathtub gin, saucy Charlestons, and hot, shrieky jazz without recalling its most famous criminal. Gangster movies, old and modern, almost invariably feature Capone or a character modeled on him. The reasons for his fame would take an entire book to explore in depth; suffice it to say that Alphonse Capone is an American icon. With his bootlegging fortune, scarred features, and blood on his conscience, he has come to represent everything that was dangerously wrong with Prohibition. Ignorance about his predecessors is more than understandable; as the first gangster to achieve nationwide (later worldwide) celebrity, Capone's name overshadowed those who were giving Chicago a wild reputation long before he arrived from New York in 1919.

If Capone represented the birth of organized crime in Chicago (a concept introduced by Torrio but maintained by Capone, who became Chicago's first "Big Fellow" since Mike MacDonald), O'Banion symbolized the feudal system that existed until Capone forced almost everyone under his banner. A professor lecturing at Yale in the 1960s paralleled the O'Banion era with the twelfth century and its internecine warfare among the English barons. Like the chieftains of old, each gang with an established territory had little respect for permanent boundaries and were relentless and bloody in both defending their rackets and muscling in on someone else's. Like his contemporaries, O'Banion wanted no part of anyone else's master plan, a rebellious and isolationist policy that made him a liability.

When Prohibition became law, presenting the underworld with a gold mine, Torrio told everyone that the maximum benefit could be attained only if all the gangs united and refrained from hijacking, bombing, murder, and other acts of aggression. It was sound business advice but O'Banion was loath to relinquish his independence and the wild, opportunistic streak that a lifetime in Chicago had instilled in him. Torrio, a genuine advocate of peace, diplomacy, and plenty for all, was not motivated merely by resentment over personal slights when he sanctioned O'Banion's death. He was at his wits' end. O'Banion was too powerful to be ignored. His refusal to fall in line for the common good made it necessary that he die.

O'Banion was once called "the most storied gangster in Chicago history." The description reveals more than the writer might ever have intended. Because little was known about his life out of the spotlight, stories were created to fill the void. Most of them were outright fiction; others were the exploits of other gangsters that were attributed to O'Banion. By various accounts he was a thwarted aspirant to the priesthood, a sick joker who enticed people into firing clay-packed shotguns, and a diehard Irish patriot with a fierce hatred for Italians. Careful research has painted a new picture that contradicts the current image. He was neither saint nor Satan but exhibited traits of both. He was a powerful gang boss who cracked skulls as brutally as any of his henchmen on election-day campaigns, yet supported entire North Side slums with his charity. He had few gangster allies but inspired such fanatical loyalty among his own men that in avenging his death they were prepared to incur their own.

Stripped of legend and rebuilt with solid facts, the Dean O'Banion story is that of an Illinois farm boy who rose to underworld greatness in Chicago. He used the city's times of crisis (the Irish-Sicilian clashes on the Near North Side, the newspaper circulation wars, during which he slugged for William Randolph Hearst, and later Prohibition) to strengthen his standing and acquire useful contacts. Along the way, he met and worked with other key players in Chicago crime: safecracking genius Charles Reiser, Jewish gang boss "Nails" Morton, "Kiss of Death" girl Margaret Collins, the bellowing hypocrite Mayor William Hale Thompson, and of course Capone, Torrio, the Gennas, et al. From this viewpoint, his life contains some sociological and historic interest. Chicago did not create its most famous gangster, Al Capone; it was Capone who altered Chicago to his specifications. O'Banion, on the other hand, was a complete product of the city. Following his exploits is as much a stroll through the memory of old Chicago as a study of its most storied gangster.

Guns and Roses

1

Maroa Boyhood

FRED BUCKMEYER WAS SHAKEN, but not surprised, to find a body buried in a snow bank off Nottingham Road on the chilly morning of February 21, 1924. A former motorcycle policeman, he knew that it was there, on the isolated plains of the city's southwestern limits, that gangsters routinely dumped the corpses of gunmen, beer runners, and other underworld denizens who, for one reason or another, no longer had a purpose or place in the current hierarchy.

Daylight brightened the Eastern skyline, allowing Buckmeyer to see the bullet holes in the dead man's skull. One was ringed by powder burns, indicating that the gun had been pressed against his head when fired.

Arriving police officers found a card in his pocket (along with $190 and a gold watch, ruling out robbery as a murder motive) that identified him as John Duffy of 1216 Carmen Avenue. Subsequent investigation revealed him to be a Philadelphia native wanted in his home city for suspected murder. Chicago had not been a taming influence; he had shot his bride of eight days to death only hours before his own body was found. An opportunist (and a foolish one at that), he had peddled beer on a freelance basis in territories claimed by ruling gangsters, and tried to profit from the Miller–O'Banion feud by going to Hirschie Miller and offering to kill O'Banion for ten thousand dollars. His ambition had gotten him a skull full of .38 slugs and a one-way ride to gangland's outdoor mortuary.

John Duffy's slaying was similar to that of "Big Steve" Wisniewski, whose riddled corpse was found in July 1921 on a dusty side-road outside Libertyville, Illinois, just north of Chicago. Underworld gossip had it that prior to his murder, he had tried to fatten his income by stealing a truckload of O'Banion liquor and selling it himself. If the story were true, Big Steve had little time to enjoy his dangerously gotten gains before gunmen seized him in a Valley saloon, hustled him into a car, and exacted a grisly payment for the stolen booze.

Some detectives blamed the killing on the Druggan–Lake Gang, with whom Wisniewski had clashed three weeks earlier. The Polish bootlegger had beaten up boss Terry Druggan after the latter threatened him for looting a liquor storage depot the gang had already marked for a raid. Others suspected O'Banion's North Siders. O'Banion himself was a liberal hijacker of liquor trucks bound for government warehouses, more for the sport than the need for stolen riches, but did not tolerate similar encroachment directed at himself. Seven times he had been quizzed by the state's attorney's office after the same number of gangsters he had obviously disliked had turned up dead. Chief Morgan Collins would later attribute no fewer than twenty-five underworld murders to O'Banion.

A witness later reported seeing a dark-colored Studebaker slow to a halt in that stretch of Nottingham Road during the predawn hours of February 21. Several men got out, carrying something between them. They deposited their load onto the prairie snowbank, hurried back to the car, and drove leisurely away.

The witness was not close enough to observe, or was too frightened to mention once he realized the significance, that one of the men carrying John Duffy's body through the snowdrifts had walked with a heavy limp.

Heads turned regularly at the sight of the black Cadillac as it drove down Main Street. Although it had been arriving every Memorial

Day for the last three years, it was still greeted like the Eighth Wonder. In Maroa, Illinois, a farming community of approximately twelve hundred people, such a luxurious car was a rarity. Those standing close to the curb as it passed could smell, and even catch a glimpse of, the floral arrangements heaped in the back seat.

It was Memorial Day 1924, and a former Maroa native was making a yearly pilgrimage to his birthplace. Nothing outwardly indicated that he had once been a part of small-town life; the price of the Cadillac was more than most Maroans earned in years.

Maroa, like any other community, would have welcomed the idea of a former resident achieving a degree of celebrity. Mark Twain had focused interest on Hannibal, Missouri, and Woodrow Wilson had put Staunton, Virginia, on the map. But few Maroans would have embraced the kind of notoriety that this returning resident was capable of bestowing on them.

The Cadillac slowed down at the lower end of Main Street, where the town cemetery stood. It was a small tract of land separated from the road by a waist-high stone wall. Three tire-worn driveways led into the cemetery, one at either end of the wall and a third through the center. The driver directed the car through the center opening, halting after going about a hundred yards. The door swung open, its sleek black surface catching the sun, and a man climbed out. He wore an expensively tailored but conservative suit, had dark blond hair that was slicked back and parted on the left, and maintained a youthful appearance that belied his thirty-one years. Of short stature, and stout without being fleshy, he also walked with a pronounced limp.

Leaving the car, he approached a red granite stone with a sloping top bearing the inscription "MOTHER." On its face was the engraving "EMMA O'BANION 1868–1898." He had bought the monument to replace the old wooden one, which had almost rotted away.

It marked the gravesite of his mother. She had died of tuberculosis in 1901, when he was nine years old. (Although the age on the stone—thirty—was correct, the birth and death dates were not.) Later that year, his father had taken him and his brother to Chicago, altering the course of his life forever. If the O'Banions had remained in Maroa, he might have become a farmer, a barber like his father, or gone to work in the town cigar factory. Chicago made Dean O'Banion into something else.

He took the fragrant wreaths, crosses, and bouquets, all lovingly constructed in his Chicago flower shop, out of the Cadillac and carried them to Emma O'Banion's grave, where they were grouped for maximum visual effect. He worked until the gravesite had been transformed into a feast of color. When finished, O'Banion took a few limping steps back and viewed his handiwork.

He often told his Chicago friends and colleagues that it comforted him to return to Maroa every year and adorn his mother's grave. He also enjoyed revisiting his childhood haunts and talking to old schoolmates and neighbors. He knew that his reputation preceded him but rested assured that the townspeople, many of whom had known him during his youth, would be selective about what they believed.

After spending a few hours at the grave of the person whose death had changed his life forever, O'Banion drove back into town, where he had a room at the Hotel Orlando. On the street he encountered George Waller, a former classmate who was now president of the Bank of Maroa. During their conversation, which lasted the better part of two hours, O'Banion made a request that Waller never forgot.

Over forty years later, Waller recalled, "He told me to let him know if anyone from Maroa was in a Chicago hospital." O'Banion wanted to send fresh flowers every day, but he would have been only too happy to pay the medical bills if asked.

"There was a lot of good in him," Waller said firmly, expressing the opinion of most Maroans. "Without anyone to look after him, he just got to hanging around saloons after he moved to Chicago."

The next day, Dean O'Banion left the rural tranquility of Maroa, where he was fondly remembered as Charles and Emma O'Banion's mischievous but good son, and drove back to Chicago, where a lucrative gambling and bootlegging business and the fealty of two hundred thugs awaited him.

Like most of his life, Dean O'Banion's origins are shrouded by legend. Crime historians and even his contemporaries called him "the Irishman," and the December 1924 edition of the *Literary Digest* claimed that he had been born in Ireland, but in reality his closest connection to the Emerald Isle was through his maternal grandfather, who had immigrated to the United States in the mid-nineteenth century. The surname O'Banion is not even Irish in origin; it is a derivative of the Welsh surname Ab'Einion, which belonged to a noble family in Cheshire circa 1046. The Ab'Einions were ruling class, with manors and estates in Sussex (Esmondum), Essex (Geddy Hall), and Berkshire (Englefield). They also gave the literary world one of its greatest talents, John Bunyan (1628–1688). Between the sixteenth and eighteenth centuries, many family members, their power diminished, went to Ireland, where they settled in County Kerry and changed their surname to O'Banane or O'Bunyan. Others emigrated directly from Wales to the New World.

Another myth started in a full page feature covering the news of O'Banion's sensational death. A *Herald and Examiner* reporter, eager to create a Chicago legend, named the gangster's birthplace as the corner of Chicago Avenue and Wells Street. The idea of a young man who was born, attained power, and died in Chicago, his life a testimony to the city's wilder side, was as romantically appealing as the jolly, apple-cheeked-but-deadly Irishman concept. Depending on which authority one believed, Dean O'Banion was either an unruly immigrant or a true-blue Chicago boy gone wrong.

The truth was not quite so dashing. Dean Charles O'Banion was born on Friday, July 8, 1892, in Maroa, Illinois, some 150 miles southwest of Chicago. He was the third child—his immediate predecessor had died in infancy—and second son of Charles and Emma O'Banion.

His birth commanded more attention in Maroa than it would have had it occurred in Chicago, where 1892 was a progressive and memorable year. The University of Chicago was established, and the elevated railway system, affectionately known as the "el," commenced service. The commuter trains that clattered along the el tracks, shaking the steel grids supporting them, were initially steam-powered, and did not switch to electric power until 1897. Telephone lines connected Chicago to New York and Boston for the first time, a feat few Chicagoans could appreciate, as approximately seventeen people per thousand in the city owned telephones. Although it was not realized at the time, serial killer Dr. H. H. Holmes was courting his eleventh victim, Emeline Cigrand. On December 6, he locked her in a walk-in vault in his Englewood "Murder Castle" until she perished from asphyxiation. O'Banion would acquire headlines of similar magnitude in Chicago, but not for another thirty years.

O'Banion's father, Charles, a barber by trade, came originally from Lincoln, Illinois, where his family had settled after migrating from their Kentucky homestead. His mother, Emma Brophy, was the Chicago-born daughter of an Irish immigrant father and American mother. She had been only eight months old when, in October 1871, the Great Chicago Fire leveled the city, killing about three hundred people and leaving over a hundred thousand homeless. When Chicago was reincorporated under general law, the Brophys were among the first returning residents.

Charles and Emma married in Chicago on May 19, 1886, when he was nineteen and she a mere fifteen, and moved to Maroa the following year, where his parents resided. John P. O'Banion, Charles's father, was a police officer serving on the small town force. Charles plied razor and scissors in the town barbershop and bought a two-story saltbox house in the north end of Maroa, near what is today Route 51.

On September 5, 1887, Emma gave birth to their first child, a son, whom they christened Floyd. He grew into a husky, rugged boy who also went by the nickname "Jock." Dean Charles was born five years later. Daughter Ruth completed the little family in August 1894.

Maroa was connected to the nearby, larger town of Decatur by a dirt road that turned perilously muddy in the spring, so in its isolation, the little community became remarkably self-sufficient. Between 1892 and 1910, Maroa boasted two furniture stores, three grocery outlets, four small hotels, three restaurants, and a dry-goods shop, to name a few. Women strolling along Main Street were drawn to the lavish displays in the millinery shop window, and a men's clothing store offered the male residents both work clothes and Sunday best. The drugstores doubled as soda fountains and were a common refuge during the scorching Illinois summers. A cigar factory employed many of the townspeople and sent a refreshingly bitter tang into the country air. A livery stable and blacksmith shop took care of the horses that were so essential for both transportation and work in the fields.

When in need of recreation, Maroans visited the photograph gallery or attended the weekly dances held in a lodge hall above a grocery on Main Street. Like most towns, Maroa had a saloon, this one in conjunction with a bowling alley.

It was in this casually paced, proudly independent small town atmosphere that Dean O'Banion spent his first nine years. He later viewed them as the happiest time of his life.

As a boy, O'Banion's appearance belied his hyperactive, mischievous nature. He was shorter than average, fair-haired, and had inquisitive brown eyes. His round face grinned brightly and easily. When it suited him, he could charm with a vengeance. This last talent came in handy in the wake of innumerable pranks and stunts that scandalized his elders.

He was an incurable showoff, and safety ranked low on his list of personal priorities. Once he fell and broke his arm after trying to walk on a pair of stilts that defied the courage of his friends. One boyhood comrade, Ralph Moore, recalled sixty years later that Dean had been "a real daredevil, who had to do everything best." Another friend, George Kincaid, remembered him as "always full of the devil and having fun." A nasty streak sometimes surfaced beneath the naughty charm: one morning, on the way to the Maroa public school on Locust Street, he kicked the lunch pail out of Ralph Moore's hand and laughed when the contents spilled onto the road.

Mrs. Louise Gentle, aged 101 when interviewed in 1993, a lifelong Maroa resident who was in Dean's class from Grades One through Four, remembered vividly one time when she personally experienced his destructive mirth. Being the daughter of the town doctor, she often wore better clothes than the other children and exuded an air of comparative privilege. One day she came to school wearing a new pair of white leather shoes, of which she was quite proud. Dean noticed her pleasure and decided to take her down a notch.

"He came up to me in the schoolyard," she recalled, "and scraped his dirty shoes over mine, nearly ruining them. I don't remember what I did about it; I suppose I must have cried." She did not remember him as being inordinately destructive but admitted that schoolteacher Antoinette Slovik would not have tolerated any nonsense while the children were in her charge. She reminisced, "I can still picture him now—short, with a round little face." Referring to a newspaper variation of his name, she added, "I don't know why he was called 'Dion' in the papers. We only ever knew him as Dean."

Dean, who also went by the nickname "Brinigan," did enjoy tamer pleasures, such as playing in the woods and fields outside the town. Whenever he and his friends had a few pennies between them, they hightailed it to one of the drugstores and had homemade ice cream sundaes and root beer floats at the soda fountains. Summers brought county fairs, autumn the harvest and all the ensuing excitement. Plenty of conventional outlets existed for his youthful energy, although they were less interesting than wrecking shoes and tempting fate with stilts.

Although life was simpler in the American towns of the late nineteenth century, it was also a lot more precarious. Tuberculosis, pneumonia, and influenza were deadly and common. Tuberculosis was perhaps the most dreaded, because the killing process was slow; with symptoms that dragged on for months, sometimes years, it gradually robbed the sufferer of all vitality. In the final stages, the afflicted lost most of their body weight, expectorated blood and lung tissue, and collapsed with a burning fever. If such facilities were available, patients went to a TB sanitarium, but most had to make do with living in a tent during the summer months, taking in badly needed fresh air. These measures were merely palliative, as there was no known cure, and death eventually came as a friend. Known also as the white plague, TB accounted for 188 deaths per 100,000 Americans in the early 1900s, making it the country's leading cause of mortality.

Soon after the birth of little Ruth, Emma O'Banion contracted the disease. According to Louise Gentle, when Mrs. O'Banion became too weak to manage household chores, Charles's sister Lee moved in to do the housework and take care of the children. She entered a tuberculosis sanitarium, an austere location where her children were not permitted to visit, due to fears of contagion. Dean tried to compensate for the separation by writing to her frequently. His letters, which were later saved by the doctor who treated Emma O'Banion, were touchingly chatty and embellished with childish drawings. One, dated February 9, 1900, reads as follows:

> Dear Mamma,
> I love you awful well. At school I have only got a lock box and two tablets and a book and a book to write things in that Miss Hill puts on the board and a box of pins and a pen and a pencil and a ruler and bell that says Dr. Bell's Pine Tar Honey on it.
>
> I have only used five pages in my tablet. Tomorrow it will be colder weather. I will draw a picture now (followed by a pencil drawing of a little girl).
>
> Dean O'Banion
>
> *(Next to his signature is a self-portrait, depicting himself smiling and holding his hands playfully over his eyes.)*

Despite the assistance and bed rest, she finally passed away in 1901. The exact date is not known, as no death certificate was filed; reporting of vital statistics did not become mandatory until January 1, 1916.

The loss staggered Dean, who had been deeply attached to his mother. At nine years old, he had long since passed the age where fantasy could persuade him that she might one day come back. He was painfully aware that the separation was permanent, and lack of psychological or spiritual counseling (child psychology would have had no adherents or practitioners in small-town Maroa; also, the O'Banion family was Catholic, and the community churches were all Protestant) made him deal with the loss in an unhealthy and far-reaching manner.

Experts on the subject agree that at age nine, children begin to internalize a sense of justice and fair play. They realize that right and wrong exists on a universal level as opposed to a personal one, an acceptance that marks their first step toward becoming a law-abiding adult. Emma O'Banion's death interrupted her son's absorption of this principle. Angry and grieving, he perceived a world that would take his mother from him as an unjust place, and turned his back on it. Right and wrong, for him, would be determined on the basis of his personal belief system. Sometimes his sense of justice would tally with the norm, but more often it would not.

Dean O'Banion, along with Ralph Moore, George Kincaid, Louise Gentle (born Louise MacCain), and the other students in the Grade Four class of 1901, posed for a school portrait at the end of the year. Dean sat in the front row. Dressed in short pants with suspenders, dark stockings, and a striped shirt, he sat with his hands at his sides, studying the camera with a wry half-smile. He looked sober, as if mulling over something unpleasant.

It was his last school year in Maroa. Charles O'Banion had decided to move the family to Chicago, where his in-laws still lived.

The innocent years were over. The hard times—and the legend—were about to begin.

Charles, who had genuinely doted on his wife, also took her death hard. He made his young family the focal point of his life. When Emma's parents expressed a wish for him and the children to relocate to Chicago, he agreed. He felt that the children needed their grandparents at such a difficult time, and that it might be best if they moved away from an area so full of memories of their mother. He had their best interests at heart, and likely never realized how deeply disturbed Dean was.

He sold his house and gave up his barbering business, and in the summer of 1901, he, Floyd, and Dean boarded the Illinois Central train to Chicago. Ruth O'Banion continued to reside in Decatur with her aunt Lee, who married a prominent widower, Volney Barber, in 1903. In 1910 she and her guardians moved to Coldwater, Kansas, where Barber became owner of the Coldwater Telephone Company. On December 31, 1915, she married George Roy Stewart, a local widower eighteen years her senior, and had three children. She remained in Kansas the rest of her life.

For Floyd and Dean, accustomed all their lives to sleepy Maroa, the prospect of Chicago, with its theaters, parks, and crowded streets, must have been exciting. Floyd anticipated finding a job, and Dean wondered about a new school and new friends.

Charles O'Banion had the best of intentions when he took the boys out of their rustic birthplace and transplanted them in the huge, clamorous, ever-changing metropolis that was turn-of-the-century Chicago. But had he known at the time what fate awaited his younger son there, he would never have left Maroa.

2

LITTLE HELLION

MRS. O'BANION'S PARENTS, THE BROPHYS, lived in the vicinity of a North Side district long noted for its violence and disregard for law and order. Centered around Kinzie and Erie Streets, it had originally been an Irish immigrant community called Kilgubbin. As was the case with most immigrant colonies, the outlaws had overshadowed the honest, hardworking element. *The Chicago Times* observed in August 1865:

> At the head of a list of squatter villages of Chicago stands Kilgubbin, the largest settlement within its limits. It has a varied history, having been the terror of constables, sheriffs, and policemen. . . . It numbered several years ago many thousand inhabitants of all ages and habits, besides large droves of geese, goslings, pigs, and rats. It was a safe retreat for criminals, policemen not venturing to invade its precincts or even cross the border without having a strong reserve force.

The Irish came to Kilgubbin in the early 1800s with more than just dusty carpetbags and proud, independent spirits. They brought political ideologies and cultural beliefs that soon made their presence known in Chicago, for better or worse.

One Irish trait that Chicago law enforcement agencies found frustrating was their refusal to cooperate during crime investigations. Centuries of oppression under the British had taught the Irish to be wary of the police, and they were long accustomed to righting wrongs privately. They were also selective about what they considered outlawry. Crimes against Americans were viewed as natural reactions to the prejudice and discrimination their new home had shown them.

Their deep reverence for informal, silent governments also made outsiders nervous. As one English observer in Ireland noted uneasily, "There are in fact two codes of law in force and in antagonism: one the statute law enforced by judges and jurors, in whom the people do not yet trust, and the other a secret law enforced by themselves."

The unofficial governors were leaders of secret societies such as the McManus, who combated British tyranny with terrorism. They were ruthless and violent, and routinely exploited those who sought their help, but as far as the Irish were concerned, at least they were sons of Erin. In Chicago and every other American city where a Kilgubbin might be found, the Irish people obeyed the laws and edicts set down by the McManus and scorned the American equivalents. In New York, the McManus succeeded in planting some of its representatives in Tammany Hall, the city's powerful political machine, reinforcing the Irish people's faith in its might and influence. It was in many respects similar to the Mafia but preceded its Sicilian counterpart in America by several years.

The publican-politician, an Irish mainstay back home, found an equally strong niche in America. Saloons were the places where politics were discussed, anti-British plots hatched, and other important decisions made that affected the Irish community, and the saloonkeeper was the central figure. With the same faith that the religious obeyed their priests and pastors, saloon patrons respected and bowed before the man who quenched their thirst. His ability to direct their votes on election day gave him clout with grateful politicians. In America, where Irish origins did not impede one's political aspirations, the saloonkeeper's position often evolved into public office and his popular title became "Boss." Few, however, abandoned their original trades entirely. One New York wag said that the surest way to break up a Tammany Hall meeting was to open the door and yell, "Your saloon's on fire!"

The boss's relationship with his fellow Irish was not solely one of exploitation; he used his influence to get wayward sons sprung from jail or find a newly arrived immigrant a job. He also gave his people a voice in a system that preferred to ignore the concerns of immigrants. But when he began using the bloody talents of local criminals to further his political machine's interests, he acquired a menace that bound his constituents to his will almost as strongly as their sense of tradition had previously.

The gangs that terrorized Kilgubbin and Chicago's other immigrant colonies found work on election day slugging anti-boss voters, kidnapping stubborn election judges who challenged repeat voters, fixing ballots, and even stealing ballot boxes in areas hostile to the boss. They became election day fixtures in Chicago, brandishing weapons and strutting like roosters in front of policemen whose fear of boss retaliation kept them from interfering. Many of them were mere adolescents whose loyalty had been bought with money, clubhouses, and sports tickets. The mutually parasitic relationship between the criminal and the politician made citizens sincerely doubt whether theirs was indeed a government for the people.

When it was founded circa 1840, Kilgubbin was a respectable settlement, a Catholic haven for Irish newcomers to Chicago. Time and poverty led to its decline, and by 1865 it was little more than a thieves' warren and source of cheap housing for destitute families. When the Great Chicago Fire of 1871 destroyed its shops and shanties, cheap wooden tenements of not much greater quality were erected in their place. Because of the mud (Chicago was built on poor, marshy soil), the streets were elevated four to eight feet, creating dark underground tunnels that sheltered dirt-poor families, smugglers hiding contraband, and criminals fleeing police detection.

Most of the Irish abandoned the area by the 1870s, giving way to an influx of Swedish immigrants who earned it the new name of "Swede Town." The latter stayed until around 1890, when the Sicilians started moving in. Then Swede Town underwent a grim name change, becoming "Little Hell."

By 1901, when Charles O'Banion and his sons arrived, it was no longer merely an ostracized community but a world unto itself. Little Hell had a crime rate higher than that of any other part of Chicago, including the infamous red-light district to the south. Policemen patrolled it only in twos and threes. Vendors' carts selling vegetables, fruit, and suspicious-looking meat packed the dirty streets. Vagabonds slumbered in alleys, where they were joined during sweltering summer months by families seeking relief from indoor temperatures of as high as 116 degrees. Battered newsstands shivered and swayed on windy street corners. Garbage, dumped in the gutter and rarely collected, gave the air a sickly sweet odor. The buildings, mainly shops, cheap rooming houses, and factories, were grime-coated and had smashed windows and sagging porches. All day and well into the night, the area reverberated with the screams of children, pealing of church bells, clatter of the elevated train, shouts, curses, and often the bark of a revolver or muffled explosion of a Black Hand bomb. A huge gashouse by the river belched orange flames that turned the night skies a hellish red, partly accounting for the name Little Hell.

Vice prevailed as strongly as poverty. The once fashionable section between Oak and State Streets now contained numerous whorehouses, saloons, dance halls, massage parlors, and gambling dives. Old, regal hotels such as the Revere, the Clarendon, and the Regis were used for disreputable purposes. Sections of Wells and LaSalle Streets contained houses where girls in silk kimonos and filmy negligees sat at brightly curtained windows and called saucily to men passing in the street below.

A shaky environment where neighbors neither knew nor trusted each other made a sense of community impossible. For every family scrambling to remain decent, there were dozens of thieves, prostitutes, and tramps. Regular moral precepts and common decency went by the wayside. When an actress died in a Little Hell rooming house, her estranged husband, reading of her death in the papers, slipped into the funeral parlor where her body awaited a pauper's burial and pried a diamond and gold filling from one of her teeth.

The inhabitants of Little Hell had contact with the world beyond its limits mainly through the social agency and the police. Both links were futile. No one trusted the social agency, with its barrage of caseworkers who offered the direction to a better life but not the means. The law, symbolized by the "copper," the "wagon," and the "can" (jail cell), was an oppressive force to be thwarted at every turn. Few things in Little Hell were so hated as the sight of a blue uniform. Once, someone approached nineteenth-century gambling boss "Big Mike" MacDonald for a two-dollar donation. When MacDonald asked what it was for, the collector explained that funds were needed to bury a policeman. MacDonald yanked a fistful of bills from his pocket and declared, "Good. Here's ten dollars. Bury five of 'em."

Church figures, normally a source of comfort in desperate times, met with hostility. A group of theological students once held a meeting in Washington Square, in front of the Newberry Library, and tried to offer solace and inspiration to their downtrodden audience. Hecklers responded with shouts of "I'll give God five dollars to strike me dead this minute," and "If you believe in your God so much, let's see you drink this bottle of carbolic." When one determined preacher asked how many were ready to come to Jesus, the audience laughed, hooted, and groaned.

The transience and harshness of tenement life left Little Hell worlds away from Maroa in more aspects than merely distance. The O'Banion boys, accustomed to living in a placid, close-knit environment, would find this to be one of many unsettling features of their new home.

Charles O'Banion and his sons moved into a Little Hell tenement near the Brophy home. Their exact addresses for 1901–03 are not known, because they were either between residences or simply overlooked when the city was canvassed for its annual directory.

Charles found a job in a plant manufacturing calcimine, a solidifying wash applied to walls and ceilings. Floyd elected to take out a working certificate and join his father in the same trade. Dean went to parochial schools and was enrolled in catechism classes. Although his parents were Catholic, he had never attended church in Maroa and consequently had never been baptized. Grandmother Brophy was horrified, and persuaded Charles to shun the free public schools in favor of paying tuition at a Catholic-run institution.

She was determined that religious education, regular church attendance on Sunday, and eventual baptism would fortify her grandson against a violent, Godless world.

When not in school, Dean was a newsboy, running through the streets waving one paper over his head like an ink-stained banner and carrying a stack of others under his arm. Newsboys of that period did not have an easy job; they tangled with juvenile gangs out to rob them of their earnings and battled each other over choice street corners. O'Banion, small but tough, never backed down from confrontations. In Maroa, no childish brawling was ever allowed to progress to the point of injury, but Chicago had a harsher code of ethics. Many times Dean came home with a black eye or bloody nose.

Learning to fight was a necessity. The O'Banion family's arrival in Chicago coincided with a terrifying rise in North Side crime. For reasons never explained to anyone's satisfaction, the number of policemen on duty in the area had decreased by half over a ten-year period while the local population continued to rise. Hold-up and burglary gangs set forth each night when darkness fell, robbing every pedestrian and unprotected building they could find. Herbert Asbury later painted a grim picture of the situation in *Gangs of Chicago*:

> Sometimes the footpads stripped their victims, tied them to lamp posts, and cut shallow slits in their flesh with razors and knives. They broke into stores and residences, held sex orgies and drinking parties on the lawns and porches of private homes, and pursued every woman they saw. If they caught her, she was dragged into an alley and raped. If she attempted to defend herself, she was beaten, in many instances fatally.

The problem was not confined to the poorer regions. On the late afternoon of January 12, 1906, the socially prominent wife of a printing-plant owner left her home to sing at a funeral. Her raped and mangled body was found the next day in a trash heap on Belden Avenue. Frightened families left their North Side residences to take shelter in downtown hotels, and some left Chicago entirely. Those who remained barricaded themselves in their homes after dark and armed themselves. Strangers who rang doorbells or went down alleys risked being shot by paranoid householders, causing utility companies to limit meter readings. The terror began to abate only after citizens groups organized protective associations and hired private detectives to patrol the streets and escort women to their destinations. Recalling this violent period fifteen years later, O'Banion told E. Barnett, a friend who drove a liquor truck for him, that he'd carried his first gun while accompanying his grandmother on an excursion. He did not elaborate as to whether he had opportunity to use it or if his grandmother had even known that he had it on him. All he would say was, "I never had trouble, ever."

One of the most disturbing aspects of the crime wave was that many of the perpetrators were as young as the teenaged O'Banion. Foremost among the growing breed of juvenile terrorists was the Formby Gang, whose leader, Jimmy Formby, had murdered a streetcar conductor in 1904. Another member, seventeen-year-old Bill Dulfer, had once held up a saloon and, on impulse, killed two men with randomly fired shots. "I didn't even aim to hit 'em," he boasted afterward. "Just held a gun in each hand and let go. I saw 'em fall—that was all I wanted." When arrested, he insisted on being tried on the murder charge. "I'm a killer, not a robber," he asserted proudly.

In 1906 the *Chicago Tribune* deplored the situation. The editor commented, "It is not unusual for a boy six years old to be arrested for a serious offense. Boys who should be at home learning their ABC's are often found with cheap revolvers and knives."

The editorial went on to state that in one police precinct alone, about sixty boys under age sixteen were arrested for serious crimes every month. It concluded, "Chicago is terrorized by . . . criminals who have helped make the name 'Chicago' a byword for crime-breeding throughout the country."

It would be wrong to assume that all youth gangs were as homicidal as the Formbys. Most were mischievous but not really destructive. Gangs had their greatest following among culture-shocked immigrant children, for whom the attraction was understandable. Rather than stay with their large families in crowded cold-water tenement rooms or be whipped by Old World elders who demanded strict obedience, they played stickball, shot dice for pennies, and engaged in minor acts of mischief, such as riding streetcar bumpers, shoplifting in dime stores, and swiping fruit from vendors' carts. For every gang that posed a genuine menace, there were dozens that remained local nuisances.

The police took a wary stance regarding youthful congregations, seeing them as potential criminal units in embryonic form, and dispersed them on sight. In doing so, the force inadvertently created its own headaches. Cops became the common enemy, and anyone who successfully spooked their horses, knocked them down, or otherwise assaulted them gained local hero status.

For years, the ruling gang in Little Hell had been the Market Streeters, so named because their hangouts were in the Market (now Orleans) Street area. Their political connections were brazenly displayed each election day, when they used guns and knives on voters opposing their patron and tossed their bloodied victims into water troughs while policemen, aware of their powerful backing, looked on helplessly. These violent acts of service to the local boss gave them immunity in their other nefarious dealings, and few if any gang members ever went to trial for their actions.

Nearly every gang recruited or tolerated a juvenile entourage. They assisted the adult members, ensured the gang's future, and even took the rap for crimes committed by their elders, knowing that their age would guarantee them a minor sentence for a transgression that could send an adult to prison for years. The Market Streeters had their youthful counterpart in the Little Hellions. These boys ran errands, carried weapons, and, during burglaries, squeezed into entrances too narrow to accommodate a man. On election day they proudly followed their mentors into battle, carrying extra weapons and compounding the injuries of already fallen victims. Their specialties included knocking down drunks to steal their money, breaking into shops after closing to raid cash registers, and looting warehouses of anything that the Market Streeters might be able to fence. They routinely fought other local gangs with a ferocity that belied their youth.

Much of the gang fighting in Little Hell resulted from ethnic rivalries. Since 1890, when they arrived to answer a call for cheap labor, Sicilians (mostly immigrants from Palermo, Alta Villia, Milicia, Bagheria Vicari, Cimminia, Termini-Imarezi, and Monreali) had dominated the area in terms of population, and their presence met with resistance from the Irish and Swedish die-hards who had not moved elsewhere. The local struggle was examined in a document titled "The Dark People Come," which illustrated the general contempt that was felt for the Sicilians not only in Little Hell but the neighborhoods that bordered it. The author wrote:

> I interview Pastor ——— of Chicago's largest Swedish church at the corner of Elm and Sedgewick, to learn why he opposes the intention of the Lincoln Park Commission to put a playground there. "This is *our* neighborhood, a *Swedish* neighborhood," he explains. "The Dark People have come further south in the ward. If a playground is put in our neighborhood, these people will come live in our neighborhood. . . ."

He also offered an illustration of how the prejudice filtered from parents down to their children:

> The Sicilian girls, timid and shy, come to Seward Park. They run to an empty swing. Two Swedish girls jump in, pushing them away. "Get out. Dagoes. Dagoes. You can't play here." It is the same at the sand piles and the "shoots." It is the same on the beaches. After the playground has been open several months, I pass one day and see a colored girl by the gate. She is talking earnestly to the Sicilians. "Sure you can go in. You got as much right to dem swings as anybody. I'm gwine right in now and show you—you come along." They follow Mattie, the colored girl, who seizes the first empty swing in spite of protesting pushes from Swedish girls. The Sicilians look scared and defiant, but they get into a swing. Their Americanization has begun.

When the gangs of boys settled their differences, they used sticks, stones, garbage can lids, and anything else capable of doubling as a weapon. A battle planned in advance always had a few combatants armed with knives or guns. A popular weapon was a shotgun loaded with rock salt, which, when fired, embedded salt fragments in the target's skin and on occasion tore out eyes.

As the boys grew older, girls joined territory as a source of contention. Sicilian youths pursued young women outside their ethnic group because they had few options for romance; a chaperon system forbade Sicilian girls over the age of twelve to mingle with boys or even go out on the streets unless accompanied by a female relative. Their brothers, left to their own devices, found outlets for their adolescent passions in the less confined Irish and Swedish girls. Irish girls were particularly receptive because they were lonely, too, as Irish men preferred to establish themselves financially before getting married, and in the slum's precarious economic climate, such a goal might take years to reach. Because the Sicilians had fewer reservations about youthful marriages, mixed couples were a common sight—and a regular target for gangs of possessive Irish boys. The man would be beaten up, the shaken woman advised to "start seeing white men."

Parents did little to discourage the violence, as Sicilians were generally regarded as being criminal by instinct. The Black Hand terror that gripped Chicago at the turn of the century originated in Little Hell and the Sicilian community around Taylor Street. Although it was commonly linked with the Mafia (a misconception that its practitioners did nothing to discourage, finding the accompanying fear value beneficial), the Black Hand was not an organized criminal unit, but a collection of small gangs who made a living extorting money from frightened Italians. These predators tended to target more affluent members of the Italian/Sicilian neighborhoods. Each campaign of terrorism started with a letter that might be eloquent and chillingly courteous, or crude and marked with drawings of skulls and daggers, depending on the literacy of the particular gang sending it. Some bore the ink impression of a handprint, which gave the practice its name. All demanded money and warned that refusal could bring on the annihilation of the victim and his or her family, too.

Mrs. Joseph Lupo of Little Italy was one recipient of a Black Hand letter. Days earlier, she had bought an apartment building for twenty-five thousand dollars, a display of largesse that few Italians in the neighborhood dared to show. Her daughter bought some property as well. The following note was sent to her:

> Place $4,000 in a red handkerchief and put it with $4,000 from your daughter. Place it at the west end of the Chicago Avenue Bridge at midnight Thursday. We

> have looked at your new building on Park Avenue and have found a nice spot where a bomb could do a great amount of damage if you don't obey. Don't notify your son in law, Marino Modeni.

Mrs. Lupo ignored the warning and went to Modeni, who swallowed his own fear and informed the police. A trap was set, but the Black Handers, perhaps suspecting such, never showed up.

When the Chicago police traced a Black Hand letter to one Joseph Genite of South Racine Avenue, they raided his apartment and found a cache of shotguns, revolvers, knives, and explosives. The Black Handers' liberal use of bombs made few Italians eager to acquire real estate, and even fewer banks would agree to mortgage it.

Black Handers accounted for several of the killings that took place in Little Hell. The corner of Oak and Cambridge Streets was known locally as "Death Corner" after a mysterious assassin known as the Shotgun Man allegedly gunned down thirty-eight people there within the span of a year. Police investigations invariably proved futile. Inquiries were met with shrugs, vacant expressions, and noncommittal replies like "Me don't know." No one wanted to be the next victim, or to be scorned by their neighbors for informing.

For many, cases like that of Antonio Moreno confirmed the futility of speaking up. Moreno, a day laborer who lived on Cambridge Street, acquired a sizable sum of money and soon began receiving Black Hand letters threatening that his son would be kidnapped if he refused to pay up. He was so worried for the boy's safety that he broke tradition and went to the police. In the meantime, his son was kidnapped. Following police instructions, Moreno paid the next demand for money with marked bills, which were used to track down the kidnappers after the boy was returned.

The "gang" was composed of two brothers who, although prominent in local politics, received lengthy prison terms. Because he had informed in the first place, Moreno required round-the-clock protection for a year afterward. His wife died, supposedly because of her terror over everything that had transpired. His neighbors cleared out of the house where the Moreno family lived, fearing a midnight bombing or worse. The entire affair ended with the Black Hand brothers being pardoned soon after their sentences began and returning to the neighborhood, where they were greeted by a brass band and an entourage of applauding men and boys. Moreno, it was said, lived the rest of his days in terror, never knowing if and when vengeance might be wreaked on him.

From 1901 until the spring of 1904, Dean O'Banion attended the Holy Name School for Boys at 817 North Sedgewick Street. A handsome brick and stone building constructed in 1883 at a cost of forty thousand dollars, it was staffed by the Clerics of St. Viator. In 1904 Archbishop Quigley divided Holy Name parish to form a new parish, St. Domenic's, and the school building was converted into temporary church quarters. The students transferred to a building at Chicago Avenue and Cass Street, formerly the Holy Name School for Girls. The new establishment, offering co-ed classes and staffed by the Sisters of Charity of the Blessed Virgin Mary, opened its doors in September 1904 with an enrollment of 830 pupils. The student population rose so rapidly that by Christmas 1904 the original staff of twelve was increased to seventeen.

While it has been documented that O'Banion attended Catholic schools, it is less certain whether he served as an altar boy at Holy Name Cathedral. Legend asserts that he served under Father Francis M. O'Brien for four years; however, he would not have been eligible for altar duty until January 29, 1905, when the Reverend D. L. MacDonald baptized him, and he left school in 1907, which was presumably the end of his religious activities. So, was O'Banion an altar boy during those two years?

Unfortunately, records pertaining to altar service were not kept, so it is impossible to know for sure. But if Grandmother Brophy was interested enough in his religious immersion to pay tuition at a parochial school, then it is conceivable that she arranged for him to assist at Mass. O'Banion had a fine tenor voice in the tradition of his Welsh-Irish forebears, and he told E. Barnett that he'd sung in the church's boys choir. The progression from choir member to altar boy is not a long one, but whatever the case, he definitely was not the young religious zealot of popular lore. Although he remained a lifelong attendant at Sunday Mass, O'Banion severed all other associations with the church once he left school.

Below are the facts about Dean O'Banion as listed in the school journal:

YEAR	AGE	PARENT	RESIDENCE	TUITION PAID
Sept 1904–05	12	Charles	42 Dearborn Ave	Sept to June
Sept 1905–06	13	Charles	34 Maple Avenue	Sept to June
Sept 1906–07	14	Charles	255 Wells Street	Sept to Jan

According to the record, no tuition was paid for the months of February, March, and April 1907. A notation indicates that Dean was absent for May and June. Perhaps it was at this time that he suffered the accident that crippled him for life.

Charles O'Banion specified during an interview that Dean's limp was the result of a streetcar accident. According to one published account, he was selling papers in the LaSalle Street tunnel when a streetcar ran him down. O'Banion himself confessed to friends that his own foolhardiness had caused the injury. A popular sport among the boy gangs was a free trolley car ride—you jumped onto the bumper while passengers boarded and hung on until the conductor kicked you off or a sudden stop sent you flying. O'Banion and some friends were "bumper riding" one day, and Dean was dislodged from his perch by a sudden jolt as the car came to a halt. He fell to the ground. The car lurched backward and ran over his left leg. Passersby rushed him to the nearest hospital, where an examination revealed that an inch of bone below his left knee had been crushed. An operation saved the leg, but it remained one inch shorter than the other, forever hobbling his gait.

Full-length photos of O'Banion show that he stood with his shoulders listing to the right and hips to the left, striking a figure like the letter S. The deformity was not grotesque, but his uneven legs did cause some curvature of the spine. E. Barnett recalled O'Banion suffering spells of terrible back pain.

His limp, combined with his tendency to cock his head when speaking, left Al Capone biographer Fred Pasley with an "impression of infinite slyness, reminiscent of *le jongleur de Notre Dame.*" The comparison was somewhat harsh. O'Banion was no Douglas Fairbanks, but he did have a round face and ingratiating smile that people other than Pasley found attractive. His persistence in smiling, even under nerve-racking conditions, led a psychologist to later comment on his "sunny brutality." He stood five-foot-four and was slightly overweight, which added to his overall benign appearance. In later years he looked less like a gangster than a plump, good-natured businessman whom life had treated better than most.

Beneath the surface, however, bitterness simmered. In a matter of five years he had lost his mother and home and been crippled for life. Charles O'Banion admitted that Dean was a fighter as a boy "as any kid has to be to get along," but one wonders whether he or Mrs. Brophy detected the submerged hostility. As Dean's life in Chicago unfolded, it would have been extremely surprising if they had not.

3

From McGovern's to the Bridewell

McGovern's Saloon and Cabaret, located at 666 North Clark Street, was the worst sort of dive and attracted a comparable clientele. Any law-abiding citizen brave or foolhardy enough to cross the threshold after dark might find himself under the suspicious scrutiny of "Hot Stove" Jimmy Quinn, king of North Clark Street and its hellish assortment of saloons, bawdyhouses, and robbers' roosts; Mont Tennes, gambling czar, whose life, according to the *Illinois Crime Survey*, would "disclose all there is to know about organized crime in Chicago in the last quarter century"; and "Big Jim" O'Leary, South Side boss, who was still trying to live down the fact that his mother's lantern-kicking cow had allegedly caused the Great Chicago Fire of 1871. The pimp and the thief rubbed elbows over foaming beer mugs, and the cutthroat spent a rare sentimental moment in the company of one of McGovern's painted "hostesses." Scarcely a night went by without two or more tempers erupting and escalating into a free-for-all that would leave the staff mopping blood and glass off the floor until long after closing time.

O'Banion was sixteen when he started working for Bob McGovern, the saloon's ugly-tempered proprietor. McGovern maintained order in his establishment by being as violent as any of his customers. A dedicated woman-hater, he even refused to hire females to clean the floor. "I wouldn't let a female cat in my place," he often boasted. His misogynistic rules did not apply to the prostitutes who cavorted on the stage and entertained men in the upstairs room—they were essential to his business.

O'Banion's job was that of a singing waiter. He slung beer and booze while singing sentimental ballads to the tune of a tin-pan piano. His was a "sobbing" tenor, affecting all the dramatic pauses and intakes that added extra bathos to the popular tearjerkers of the day. When raised in "When Irish Eyes Are Smiling" or "Where the River Shannon Flows," his voice moved many tough characters to tears. Because of his limp, he was popularly known as "Gimpy" O'Banion, a nickname no one used in his presence without courting disaster. Anyone drunk or brazen enough to utter it swiftly found himself on the receiving end of a thunderous beating. Even at sixteen, O'Banion had powerful shoulders and arms. He was never arrested for brawling, but he did come to the attention of local police as a tough kid capable of holding his own.

O'Banion served many familiar faces from his boyhood. He knew Mont Tennes, the racetrack king, from the year that his family had spent at 42 Dearborn Avenue. At 12 years old, he had watched uniformed police officers walk into Tennes's handbook joint at 40 Dearborn to indulge in a unique graft system: Tennes allowed cops to bet on horses without laying down money. It cost them nothing to lose and gave them unlimited chances to take home a small fortune.

His hours outside of the saloon were spent in the company of the Little Hellions, the belligerent gang of aspiring Market Streeters, and under their direction he became a proficient jack-roller. A younger member would lure a drunk to a secluded alley or side street, where O'Banion and the others waited. A bigger boy would then seize their victim around the throat and brandish a gun or knife to quell any resistance, permitting his cohorts to help themselves to money, watches, and other valuables. O'Banion quickly appreciated how easy it was to make in one night three times his paper-tossing or even McGovern's wages. He graduated from participating in thieving ventures to planning them. A natural leader, he guided the gang down a continuous path of thrills and easy money.

Although low on the ladder of criminal pursuits, jack-rolling and petty thievery were the foundations for careers in crime. They whetted the appetite for excitement and fast money, and created dissatisfaction with the few rewards of legitimate work. If their parents forced them to take menial honest jobs, it was not long before tardiness and repeated absences got the boys fired. Running with the gang, drinking and smoking on saloon doorsteps, and entertaining girls in steamy cellar parties was, for them, a greater celebration of life than working long hours for three dollars a week.

Despite his success at it, O'Banion disliked jack-rolling, perhaps viewing drunks as too easy a target, or maybe he rebelled at having to split paltry proceeds with his fellow Hellions. He progressed to solo street mugging. Skulking in shadows and alleys, he waited for solitary strollers to amble within striking range, whereupon he would spring into the light, crack the victim over the head with a blackjack, and then drag the motionless form into the darkness to be fleeced at leisure.

One night on East Van Buren Street, O'Banion laid his blackjack across the skull of a tipsy target . . . and did a double take when confronted by a fellow mugger who obviously had the same intention. The two stared at each other over the fallen victim, until O'Banion invited his rival to do battle or get lost. To his surprise, the young man declined to do either and suggested that they simply split the take fifty-fifty. Dean agreed, appreciating the other's sense of fair play, and in the process made a friend and future business partner.

The mugger with Solomonic wisdom was Lou Greenberg, a shrewd Jewish youth also destined for underworld celebrity. Greenberg later allied with the Capone gang, but for the next fifteen years he and O'Banion both worked and played together.

Young criminals like O'Banion and Greenberg found no shortage of mentors. Bob Duncan's saloon on State Street was a favorite hangout for both. They listened with rapt attention as Duncan, long heralded by the Chicago press as the "King of the Pickpockets," bragged about how easily he could fix things with the police. For a price, he guaranteed "dips" a cop-free area in which to operate. For a greater price, he arranged for a crooked officer to remain in the chosen vicinity to lull victims into a false sense of security. His saloon had been a popular stopover for thieves and fences since the 1890s, and both O'Banion and Greenberg made contacts there that would later prove useful.

One of the earliest, and most profound, influences on O'Banion was Hot Stove Jimmy Quinn, boss of the Forty-second Ward and a politician with a dubious past and present. His nickname stemmed from a memorable burglary he committed as a youth. One night he and some companions broke into a store and backed up a horse and wagon to the rear door to maximize the take. After almost everything that could be fenced had been carried off, Quinn spied a brand-new stove and decided to add it to the pile. He grabbed it without waiting for help, not stopping to think that it might recently have been in use, and nearly burned all the skin off his palms.

Quinn operated a haberdashery as a legitimate front, but to make a real living, he took over the vice operations on North Clark Street. Bitten by the political bug after appreciating how public office could allow him to protect and further his illegal interests, he became city sealer during one of Carter Harrison II's five administrations. He understood the value of gang support and cultivated the friendship of O'Banion and his fellow Hellions. It was through Quinn's example that O'Banion became a hard-core burglar. The passion for stealing remained with him for the rest of his life.

It was at McGovern's that O'Banion met his other important influence. Eugene Geary was a regular patron, and one that the staff dreaded seeing come through the door. An October 1920 Chicago Crime Commission bulletin later described him as "a protégé of the late 'Moss' Enright and a leader of the gunman school, developed in 'Canaryville,' the toughest section of the Stockyards district . . . known to the police as one of the most dangerous men in Chicago—a man killer, quick on the trigger of the pistol he carried, and who gloried in the unsavory reputation he had earned through his exploits as a labor slugger, gangster, and all-around 'bad man.'"

No one could forget the night he wrecked Polack Joe's Vestibule Café near Twenty-second and State because of a song. He and a menacing entourage had staggered into the place demanding whiskey and Irish ballads, the latter of which he was passionately fond. The terrified waiters plied him with both until he fell asleep. One of his men then called out for a livelier tune. It was a huge mistake.

According to one newspaper report, "Before the first verse had been sung, Geary was awake and raging. He picked up the cash register and flung it through the mirror. He sent a chair flying after the running bartender and then proceed to wreck the joint."

Dean O'Banion was Geary's favorite waiter at McGovern's. When the younger man raised his voice in singing "Mother Machree," the Neanderthal Geary sobbed into his beer. The two struck up a friendship with a marked teacher-student aspect. Geary taught O'Banion better marksmanship with a pistol, including the art of ambidextrous gunplay. In all likelihood, O'Banion returned the favor by assisting his mentor as a strongarm whenever Geary encountered resistance in his cigar-sales business.

Gene Geary was one of Chicago's earliest racketeers. In the slang of the day, a "racket" was the use of physical intimidation or political pressure to squeeze protection money out of merchants. Saloonkeepers, shop owners, even chestnut vendors had to buy protection from personal and property damage. Once in a while the deal included buying inferior goods peddled by the racketeer. The system resembled the Black Hand modus operandi, but the racketeers prided themselves on being above outright blackmail. In their eyes, a service and sometimes product in exchange for the forced tribute squared things. The fact that the merchant had little choice but to comply did not even enter the equation.

The barrel-chested, pig-faced Geary conducted his business by wandering into cigar stores, looking over the premises, and approaching the owner/operator. Planting his meaty hands on the counter, he would ask where the dealer got his wares. The answer would scarcely be given before Geary interrupted with the wonderful news that he had a better cigar to offer. Like a proud parent, he would draw a few samples from a coat pocket and hold them up for the dealer's inspection.

They were made of dried broccoli wrapped in cabbage and cigar paper. He sentimentally called them "Gene Geary's Own," and as far as the shop owners were concerned, he could have kept them. They stank terribly, gave off a pungent black smoke, and crumbled apart, but the dealer bought them, or else.

If the merchant did state in no uncertain terms that he was not interested, Geary became more congenial. Elbow on the counter and leaning forward in an intimate fashion, he would cheerfully describe a fellow dealer who had also been hesitant. The man had finally relented, he added, but only after intense persuasion.

"You shoulda seen it," Geary would chortle. "I nearly killed the guy."

Geary was not an educated man, but he knew enough gruesome adjectives to offer a terrifying description of the stubborn dealer's injuries. Even the hardest cases usually cracked at that point, and Geary would saddle him with several boxes of the bogus cigars. He always left with the hint that nothing would displease him more than poor sales.

Now assured of a new customer who would be too frightened to go to the police, Geary would wander on to the next victim, using the previous one as a "reliable reference." It usually worked, but Geary was quick to fall back on his talents as a labor slugger if need be.

This systematic brand of extortion grew in Chicago by leaps and bounds. In 1928, long after Geary stopped practicing his trade, law officials estimated that racketeering cost the city $136 million in lost wages and taxes. A "racket court" was set up in 1929 to deal exclusively with the problem, and its caseload was constantly full.

Geary and O'Banion became close because in some respects, they were cast from the same mold. They loved indulging in reckless, oddball stunts and had senses of humor that bordered on the macabre. But O'Banion was gleefully aware that he was kicking dirt in the law's face, while Geary remained immersed in a private, maniacal world of his own. Many years (and an estimated eight murders) later, legal and medical authorities recognized his homicidal insanity and put his shooting and racketeering days to an end.

Charles O'Banion, despite his later insistence to the contrary, must have been painfully aware of the direction his younger son's life was taking. If not, the winter of 1909 was a reality check. Seventeen-year-old Dean broke into a drugstore and stole some postage stamps as well as (according to legend) a bottle of perfume for a girlfriend. A passing policeman grabbed him as he was leaving and dragged him to the station, where an interrogation took place. Years later, O'Banion would recall its details to E. Barnett and other friends with laughter.

A burly officer demanded to know why O'Banion had stolen the roll of stamps. The teenager replied without blinking an eye that he wanted to write to his mother.

"Where's your mother?" the cop asked.

"In heaven. She's dead."

"Then what the hell did you want these stamps for?"

With a grin, O'Banion replied, "Well, it would take a whole roll to get a letter to her now, won't it?"

The cop was not amused, nor was the judge before whom he went on a burglary charge. He received a six-month sentence in the Bridewell.

Its official name was the House of Correction, but the ancient building was commonly called the Bridewell or Bandhouse. Constructed during the Civil War to detain Confederate prisoners, it now held juvenile delinquents, drunks, petty thieves, and other offenders whose crimes were not severe enough to warrant imprisonment at Joliet Penitentiary.

Reformers had long been concerned about conditions at the Bridewell. The structure was in an advance state of decay, and the inmates were housed in such close quarters that disease was rampant. Each dank cell had been built to hold two prisoners but contained as many as four or five, and had no toilet facilities save an open bucket that was emptied each morning into an outdoor cesspool. The ramshackle bunks were covered with dirty, lice-infested blankets. A tin cup wired to the bars provided the only source of drinking water, as no sinks or faucets were in any of the cells.

Upon arrival, O'Banion, like other new prisoners, was led by a guard to a large, bleak reception room, where he gave a clerk his age, date of birth, birthplace, and length of sentence. The clerk gave him a work assignment. He and the others then submitted to a search for contraband. A cold-water bath and issuing of a prison uniform followed.

According to the Illinois census of 1910, taken while O'Banion was still incarcerated, he was one of the youngest prisoners in the Bridewell; most of the men (and the one woman) were in their late twenties and early thirties. O'Banion worked as a shoemaker, and the youngest of his co-workers was five years his senior. Young inmates, new to the prison system, were free to mingle with the experienced criminals, learning from them and frequently being victimized by them.

Mornings at the Bridewell began at sunrise. The prisoners washed their faces in a communal trough (once a week there was a group shower) and ate a breakfast of watery oatmeal without milk or sugar, two slices of bread, and a tin of weak coffee. They worked in forced silence at their assigned duties all day, breaking only for lunch and dinner. Lockup came after the evening meal.

Defiant prisoners quickly became familiar with the "hole," a dark, airless basement cell, and a bread and water diet. Guards also responded to provocation, either real or fancied, with their clubs.

If authorities assumed that these harsh measures were enough to scare first time offenders into a law-abiding existence, they were wrong. Out on the street, prison time was a recognized and valued proof of one's toughness. Released inmates were graduates, albeit not of the Harvard or Yale variety. They had served their apprenticeships in the saloons and streets, and the Bridewell record marked them as determined criminals.

O'Banion was jailed again in 1911, when he received a three-month sentence for carrying concealed weapons. He'd initially been arrested for fighting, but a search at the police station yielded a revolver and other weapons, all secreted in his clothing. These two jail terms, served before his twenty-first birthday, constituted his only time behind bars. The next time he faced a judge, Dean O'Banion was no longer a rebellious young hoodlum but an underworld king with enough money and power to make the occasional court appearance little more than a farcical waste of time.

Chicago was experiencing one of its coldest winters on record when, on the night of February 15, 1913, twenty-five-year-old Floyd O'Banion came into the family residence at 1363 Cleveland Avenue, complaining of feeling ill. He was feverish and had trouble breathing. The family nursed him for five days. On the sixth, they were forced to call in a doctor, who diagnosed lobar pneumonia. He arranged for Floyd to be admitted to Alexian Brothers Hospital on February 21.

Floyd O'Banion was young, but eleven years of working as a painter and inhaling crude paint fumes had weakened his lungs and affected his vitality. Despite round-the-clock care, he slipped into a coma and died at 5:45 P.M. on February 25. A quiet burial took place two days later at Mount Carmel Cemetery in Hillside, southwest of the Chicago city limits.

Little is known or remembered about Floyd O'Banion today. A newspaper story published in the 1960s recalled the O'Banion family's Maroa years, and asserted that Floyd had run off to join the navy some time before the migration to Chicago. Since he was only fourteen in 1901, this is unlikely. When providing history for the death certificate, Charles O'Banion indicated that Floyd had been a painter since his arrival in Chicago, but the 1910 census listed his occupation as "Teamster." He may have been part of the two-fisted Teamster's National Union, which had been established in 1902, much to the dismay of employers associations everywhere. It had probably been a temporary change of career, brought on by a lull in his regular trade, as he and his father were partners in a longstanding freelance painting business.

No details exist regarding the fraternal relationship between Floyd and Dean. But it is interesting to note that once he became prosperous, Dean visited his mother's Maroa grave every year and replaced its old marker with a finer, more durable stone that exists to this day. Although Floyd's resting place was right next to the Chicago city limits, it did not receive similar attention. Today it is unmarked, one of many faceless resting places in Mount Carmel's oldest section.

4

Wicked City

In the 1670s French trader Pierre Moreau pitched a makeshift tent beside the river Chickagou, a name derived from an Indian word meaning "bad smell." Moreau sold liquor to the Potawatomi Indians in defiance of the laws of New France, thus establishing himself as the territory's first bootlegger. A mutually profitable arrangement with the governor, Count Frontenac, shielded him from punishment. Theirs was probably the region's earliest graft system.

Chicago received its town charter in 1833, when it boasted 350 inhabitants. John Calhoun founded a weekly paper, *The Democrat*, which cost subscribers $2.50 a year and extolled the virtues of Jacksonism. *The Democrat*'s political features took second place to town scandal in 1834, when Chicago witnessed its first divorce suit and murder trial. In the second case, an Irish settler had killed his quarrelsome wife, but the legal proceedings did not result in his imprisonment or execution. The judge's instructions confused the jury, which acquitted the defendant. It was the first of many courtroom farces in Chicago.

The young town grew so quickly that by the 1850s, its first crime czar found fertile ground for business. Roger Plant was the grotesque overlord of a literal underworld. In 1855 the city's leading citizens, tired of floundering in the mud for which Chicago was notorious, had every building elevated ten feet and the entire city surface rebuilt with solid earth and stone. The project left miles of twisting, cavernous tunnels, niches, and torch-lit hideouts that sprawled beneath Chicago's streets like a secret cancer. Roger Plant ruled over the slouching, feral-eyed human creatures who scuttled like light-shy crabs through this labyrinth.

Plant, who had immigrated to the United States from his native England, was a five-foot, one-inch gnome who marched around his fiefdom bearing an arsenal that never consisted of fewer than two pistols, two knives, and one huge club. His diminutive size was overshadowed by his ferocity. When enraged, he not only used his weapons but also bit, gouged eyes, and kicked with his iron-tipped boots.

Roger's second in command (and only equal) was his wife, a 300-pound female Goliath who, when irked by her husband, would seize him by the collar, lift him in the air, and spank him vigorously. She managed the prostitution side of Roger's illegal enterprises. Under her direction, the second floor of Plant's headquarters was converted into a successful brothel.

Plant's home base was a sprawling clapboard structure at the corner of Wells and Monroe Streets, known locally as Roger's Barracks. Police officers on patrol gave it a wide berth. Frederick Francis Cooke, author of *Bygone Days In Chicago*, commented, "Plant's Emporium was one of the most talked-about if not one of the wickedest places on the continent . . . a refuge for the very nethermost strata of the underworld, the refuse of the Bridewell." It housed three cutthroat groggeries, countless gambling dens, and Mrs. Plant's second-floor bordello, where two hundred prostitutes entertained clients or enticed new ones inside by sitting at the windows, whose shades proclaimed WHY NOT? in gold lettering. Beneath this architectural monstrosity, which Roger dubbed "Under the Willow" after a nearby willow tree that he watered with his own urine, was a rabbit's warren of rooms inhabited by streetwalkers, homosexual hustlers, thieves, and killers.

Under the Willow was home to many of the era's most notorious scalawags. Speckled Jimmy Calwell, burglar and safecracker who put together the city's first homemade bomb, dropped by regularly. Calwell's innovative creation was intended to blow up a section of the Blue Island horse car line after a failed attempt to extort money from the owners, but the bomb was discovered in time. Mary Hodges, shoplifting queen, who boldly drove wagonloads of her stolen booty through the streets in broad daylight, and Mary Brennan, who ran a pickpocket school for girls, were also frequent recipients of Roger's hospitality.

Roger hated the police with a passion and insisted that he paid them off only to be spared the sight of their "dirty faces." Officers were only too happy to take his money and leave him alone. As one cop put it, "Trying to raid those barracks would be like trying to arrest an elephant."

Plant made millions during the Civil War by supplying the Union Army with unwary and unwilling enlistees. His agents lured young men into Under the Willow, plied them with drugged liquor, and tossed them on the next battlefield-bound train. The grateful army paid the tiny schemer three hundred to five hundred dollars for each new soldier. Roger further profited from the war by selling contraband and weapons to both the Union and Confederate armies, and robbing soldiers on leave in Chicago.

Much of his take went toward paying off the police and courts, but by the mid-1860s Plant had amassed enough of a personal fortune to retire. He closed Under the Willow in 1868, bought a mansion in the suburbs, and lived out the rest of his days in peaceful obscurity. His son, Roger Jr., and daughters Kitty and Daisy carried on the family tradition by becoming successful brothel keepers. When reformer W. T. Stead published his exposé *If Christ Came To Chicago* in 1894, he named all three as ringleaders of the city's flesh trade.

The public had been Plant's unwitting ally during his roaring days, their indifference shielding him and his cohorts from periodic attempts at citywide reform. It was only in the wake of a terrific scandal that reform found support; once the public furor died down, it was regarded as a restrictive nuisance. When Mayor Thomas Dyer included cartloads of hooting prostitutes in his inaugural parade, indignant voters tossed him out in the next election and brought in Long John Wentworth, a six-foot, six-inch giant with equally strong reform sentiments. The public applauded him when he cracked down on prostitution and raided two of the city's worst sinkholes,

The Sands on Lake Michigan and Conley's Patch (described by a contemporary writer as the "dirtiest, vilest, most rickety, one-sided, leaning-forward, propped-up, tumbled-down, sinking fast, low-roofed and most miserable shanties"), but when he decided that low-hanging shop signs and sidewalk displays were hazards and ordered the police to remove them, he fell out of favor. The Illinois legislature responded to outside pressure in 1861 and took the police force out of the mayor's control, curbing his power permanently.

The next King of Crime was Michael Cassius "Big Mike" MacDonald. Unlike Plant, who favored an escapee from a Dickens novel, MacDonald was a suave, well-groomed showman. He started out as a con artist, using crooked card games to fleece passengers on Midwestern railroad lines and Mississippi showboats. Like Plant, he used the Civil War to his advantage by organizing a gang of phony enlistees who joined up under different aliases to repeatedly collect the five-hundred-dollar bounties. After the war he and a partner opened a gambling house on Dearborn Street in Chicago, the first of many. He made the transition from gambling boss to Mr. Big when, thanks to generous backing from MacDonald, his friend Harvey D. Colvin was elected mayor in 1873.

Although he did have legitimate income sources, such as real-estate holdings and ownership of a newspaper, the *Chicago Globe*, MacDonald's wealth and power continued to be derived from his gambling enterprises. He opened a deluxe den at the corner of Clark and Monroe Streets and called it the Store, after the variety of gaming it offered. Its four floors were crammed wall to wall with dice tables, roulette wheels, and card players' alcoves. MacDonald's partner in the Store, Harry Lawrence, initially expressed concern that they would never get enough patrons to fill up a gaming house that large. MacDonald assured him, "Don't worry about that, Harry. There's a sucker born every minute." The quote later would be erroneously attributed to P. T. Barnum.

Like any governor, MacDonald levied taxes on his subjects. He dictated that all crooks operating in Chicago, no matter how small time, pay him 60 percent of their earnings. Of this tribute, he kept 40 percent for himself and dished out the remainder to the police on his payroll. He also deposited money into a slush fund used to buy off newly hired/elected city officials. If burglar or thief complained about MacDonald's collections, they rarely did it a second time.

"He never held office," historian Richard Little wrote of MacDonald, "but he ruled the city with an iron hand. He named the men who were to be candidates for election, he elected them, and after they were in office they were his puppets. He ran saloons and gambling houses, protected bunko steerers and confidence men and brace games without let or hindrance."

When reform mayor Monroe Heath was swept into office as part of a public backlash against the corrupt administration of Carter Harrison, MacDonald gave an outward impression of new respectability by passing control of his gambling interests to trusted partners and increasing his legal investments. He backed the supply of gravel and stone to the city and helped finance the construction of Chicago's first elevated railroad, the Lake Street Line.

A suspicious Mayor Heath continued to order raids on MacDonald's known gambling operations. On November 23, 1878, police raiders invaded MacDonald's apartment on the third floor of the Store. Big Mike was not there but his wife, Mary Noonan, an inveterate cop-hater, was. She snatched a pistol as the officers burst in, and shot one of them, inflicting a mortal wound. Mrs. MacDonald was arrested, but her husband's influence secured a quick release. A bribed judge later ruled the shooting a justifiable homicide.

In 1892 Carter Harrison was re-elected mayor, and once again all the stops were pulled. MacDonald emerged from his "retirement" and was often seen around town, an elegant figure in solid black suits with diamond-spattered shirts and ties. Precious stones also glittered and winked on his cuff links and stickpins. He drove about in carriages as elegant as any owned by the Palmers or McCormicks. MacDonald's flashy presence inspired writer Edna Ferber, who used him as the model for the gambler character in *Showboat.*

MacDonald supposedly gave Mayor Harrison permission to hold a World's Fair in Chicago in 1893. He made a tidy fortune from the affair when his agents circulated among the crowds, luring suckers into his gambling parlors. As the 1890s drew to a close, it became apparent that Big Mike had the Midas touch in everything.

Except love.

One evening in 1898, he attended a burlesque show and was instantly smitten by one of the showgirls, robust blonde Flora Barkley. His marriage to Mary Noonan had ended in 1889, after she left him and ran away to France with a defrocked priest. At twenty-three, Flora was thirty-five years his junior, and had even been one of his children's playmates. She was also married to ballplayer Sam Barkley. But MacDonald was determined to make the "18 kilowatt blonde" (as the press dubbed Flora) his wife, and he paid her husband thirty thousand dollars for an uncontested divorce. At her urging, MacDonald even renounced his lifelong Catholic faith and converted to Judaism.

After the wedding, MacDonald set Flora up in a palatial limestone mansion on Drexel Boulevard. He attended to business all day, dealing with politicians, cops, gamblers, thugs, and anyone else hungry for a piece of the Chicago pie, and at night submitted to Flora's lavish affections. She called him "Daddy" and pumped his heart and ego up so skillfully that he was completely oblivious to her hot-blooded affair with sixteen-year-old Webster Guerin, who lived down the street. Big Mike, the keeper of Chicago, did not learn of the tryst until the rest of the city did, on February 21, 1907.

That gray winter morning, Flora stormed to her young lover's commercial art studio at the corner of LaSalle and Van Buren Streets to confront him about a second affair he was having with a girl his own age. Witnesses heard the couple arguing violently in his closed office, followed by two gunshots. Workmen who had been doing repairs in the building smashed the door down and found Flora crouched over Guerin's bloodied body. She admitted her guilt, but insisted that Guerin had goaded her into shooting.

When MacDonald learned the whole sordid story, he was stunned. He had thought that Guerin's frequent visits to the mansion had stemmed from an interest in his daughter, not his wife. After learning that Flora had sneered to detectives, "The old man disgusts me!" he collapsed in his office and was carried home to bed. Both Flora and Mary Noonan, who had long since returned from France, knelt by his bedside and begged forgiveness, but his only response was to roll over and turn his face to the wall. He died on August 9, 1907, the biggest sucker of them all where love was concerned.

Flora MacDonald was acquitted of murder in early 1908, the jury deciding that she had been temporarily insane when she shot her lover. Before dying, MacDonald had placed a forty-thousand-dollar defense fund in the hands of her attorneys and instructed them to "get the little girl off any way you can." Guerin's friends and family grumbled that bribery and Big Mike's posthumous influence were responsible for the acquittal.

Big Mike MacDonald was the last crime boss to occupy a dictatorship over the entire city. Smaller operators ran their rackets during his tenure, but few without his knowledge and bought consent. His death left Chicago without a "Big Fellow." Instead, minor characters claimed certain areas and ruled like medieval barons in their own separate fiefdoms.

Big Jim O'Leary, whose mother's cow allegedly kicked over the lantern that started the Great Chicago Fire in 1871, ruled the South Side. O'Leary was a gambler who ran an assortment of betting parlors and poolrooms from his headquarters at 4183 South Halstead. He achieved a minor degree of celebrity when he became the first gambler in American history to rig out a ship as a floating casino. Each afternoon the City of Traverse cruised leisurely along the Lake Michigan shoreline, beyond police reach, while bettors waited for race results to be flashed by wire. The novel operation came to an end when police began arresting passengers as they disembarked and scrambling the wireless signals.

O'Leary's South Halstead headquarters were impressive by any standards. It contained a first-class restaurant, Turkish bath, bowling alleys, and poolrooms. The den in which race results were broadcast was furnished with plush leather couches where even the lowliest bettor could recline and be served refreshments by liveried servants. O'Leary was the most compulsive gambler of all—he once won ten thousand dollars on a bet that the month of May would witness at least eighteen days of rain.

Remarkably, O'Leary prospered without regular police payoffs. He sneered at crooked cops as lowlifes, and preferred to take his chances without their bought support. Ironbound oak doors that defied bombs and police sledgehammers fortified the entrance to his headquarters. Once in awhile the raiders made it through and collared O'Leary's staff and clientele, but such victories were rare. Once the police spent several frustrating minutes smashing past the doors, only to find the place empty except for an old man reading a prayer book. The cops attacked the walls with their axes, seeking hidden exits, only to get a faceful of the red pepper that O'Leary had secreted in the wall lining. Many of the unfortunate raiders required medical treatment for badly inflamed eyes.

Alderman Johnny Rogers, partner of North Side gambling boss Mont Tennes, controlled the West Side. Tennes was the closest claimant to Big Mike's vacant throne.

Like MacDonald before him, Tennes was a product of the showboat era. He got his start by fleecing passengers on Mississippi riverboat cruises. Upon moving to Chicago, he assumed controlling interest in a string of betting parlors and handbooks. Tennes's ascent began when he and Johnny Rogers pooled their resources and paid the Payne Telegraph Service of Cincinnati three hundred dollars a day to relay horse race results to Tennes–Rogers establishments. Their use of the service was exclusive, which allowed them to peddle it to other places at a subscription rate of one hundred dollars daily.

By 1904 Tennes had put together an efficient system that earned him uninterrupted millions. The Payne Telegraph Service sent race returns to a forty-five-wire switchboard in Tennes's Forest Park office. Bookmakers and poolroom owners not only paid fifty to one hundred dollars a day to receive the results but also kicked back 50 percent of their receipts in exchange for protection from police and gang raids. Each day his agents circulated to the various places, driving cars equipped with calliope whistles. Whenever they drew near a subscriber's establishment, they blasted the whistle. If danger were present, such as a token raid in progress, the Tennes men would be met outside and warned away.

The cops and, during some administrations, the mayor and chief of police, tolerated Tennes. He in turn allowed policemen to indulge in unlimited betting in his parlors. He even extended a certain generosity toward those who subscribed to his service, offering protection and picking up the bill for half of any losses they might incur.

Resistance from competitors was an occupational hazard. On the North Side, Tennes's biggest challenger was John O'Malley, a small-time but pugnacious gambler who controlled some action on the north edge of the Loop. O'Malley refused to swear allegiance or at least submission to Mont Tennes, and dented the skulls of some Tennes goons sent to put him out of business. In June 1907, O'Malley thugs slugged Tennes in front of his home while he and his wife were enjoying an evening stroll. It was intended as a back-off warning, but for the gambling king, it was an affront that meant war.

The infamous Bombing War of 1907 began in July of that year, when O'Malley men bombed the house of "Blind John" Condon, a Tennes ally. Tennes retaliated by planting a bomb in the basement of O'Malley's saloon at Clark and Kinzie Streets. Bombs exploded regularly afterward; no place was too sacred to be dynamited. Tennes's home was targeted twice, the second attempt blowing a hole a foot deep in his lawn and shattering his neighbors' windows. Those who did not realize by September 1907 that a mortal gamblers' war was being waged in Chicago were from out of town or dead.

First Ward Alderman Michael "Hinky Dink" Kenna took uneasy note of the way both property and business were being ruined by the conflict, and stepped in. His move was hardly altruistic; his coffers were regularly enriched by gambler payoffs. In 1908 he brought Tennes and O'Malley together and orchestrated a truce in which O'Malley was permitted to run his business as an independent and Tennes's power over the rest of the North Side was confirmed. Reformed gambler Harry Brolaski later said, "Little Mike [Kenna] got forty thousand out of it." Gamblers anxious to see the destruction end had raised much of that money.

In 1910 Tennes abandoned the Payne Telegraph Service and founded his own wire service, the General News Bureau. He went into competition with his old benefactor, selling race results not only in Chicago but also all over North America. He installed operatives in major cities who saw to it that places continuing to get their race results from Payne were harassed by police raids. Payne employees and subscribers protested so loudly that in 1911 a national investigation committee checked the legality of race wire services. The Interstate Commerce Commission finally ruled it legal, giving Mont Tennes free rein to continue destroying the competition.

A contemporary writer described him as "the boss of racetrack gambling all over the United States and Canada. He had corrupted the police of a score of cities, was enforcing his decrees with guns and dynamite, and was making profits of several million dollars a year."

He remained at the top of his profession for fourteen years, resisting the best attempts by law and underworld alike to dethrone him. He remained a low-profile figure throughout his career, shunning the limelight while he engineered front-page terror tactics. He was fifty-eight when former judge William Dever became mayor of

Chicago on a reform ticket in 1923. Dever ordered his chief of police, Morgan Collins, to crack down on the gambling rings. Within twelve months, more than 200 Tennes handbook joints were closed down, with a loss of $364,000. It was a minor setback in view of his nationwide holdings, but the gambling king, who had miraculously avoided arrest all those years in business, decided to retire. He was fifty-nine and a millionaire many times over.

He sold half his interest in the General News Bureau to newspaper publisher (and former strong-arm) Moses Annenberg, and faded from the public eye, reappearing only in 1925 and 1927 at the funerals of his brothers William and Edward. In 1929 he sold 40 percent of his remaining interest in the bureau to gambler Jack Lynch and divided the rest among his nephews. Mont Tennes died in 1941 at age 76, rich and unscathed, a rare end for a man of his profession.

Both Mike MacDonald and Mont Tennes scorned the one vice that rivaled theirs in profitability: prostitution. The pimp and the madam, for obvious reasons, did not enjoy the tolerant affection accorded the gambler. Ernest Bell, in his study *War on the White Slave Trade*, wrote, "In Chicago our politicians have set apart several districts for the traffickers in [white] slaves. The traders in girls are public, bold, defiant. They feel clean, almost virtuous, after city hall and a deluded preacher or two have given them an immunity bath—provided only the fiction of segregation is preserved."

Chicago's prostitution trade was "segregated" mainly in a region bordered on the north and south by Eighteenth and Twenty-second Streets and on the east and west by Clark and Wabash. Popularly referred to as the Levee, it hosted a nightly celebration of sin. Levee festivities ran around the clock, and were at their raunchiest after nightfall. The streets were ablaze with garish lights. Voices raised in drunken rage or laughter and riotous piano music spilled out of overcrowded saloons into the thoroughfares, which were crawling with freelance streetwalkers, homosexual hustlers, drug peddlers, and vulgar carousers of both sexes. In an effort to give a gay Paris elegance to the frenzied Dionysian antics, many Levee establishments favored European names, with *Paris* appearing frequently on windows and canopies.

The Chicago Vice Commission estimated that in 1910 the city's brothels numbered some 1,020, employing no fewer than five thousand madams, prostitutes, and their servants. The Levee, where most of the resorts were packed, saw a gross annual income of close to $60 million. It was an astonishing figure, and indicative of how much Chicago manhood craved wine, women, and song. One small-time madam with only one girl working in her house testified before the commission that her business took in an average of two hundred customers a week. When accused of endangering her female "boarder," she snapped, "When the girl is rushed, I help out!"

Some Levee bordellos were veritable Taj Mahals of pleasure. Foremost among these classier resorts was the Everleigh Club, the gilded brainchild of two regal sisters from Kentucky, Minna and Ada Everleigh. After successfully running bagnios in Boston, New York, New Orleans, and Washington, they came to Chicago in 1899 to cash in on the city's reputation as a red-blooded man's town. They bought madam Lizzie Allen's old place at 2131-3 South Dearborn Street, and spent two hundred thousand dollars preparing the three-story, fifty-room mansion for the carriage trade. The ornate doors of the Everleigh Club swung wide open on February 1, 1900, and offered the city's rich playboys amusement of a caliber never seen before.

Persian carpets covered the marble floors. The furnishings included easy chairs upholstered in silk damask, mahogany tables with marble inlays, rare paintings and statues, and even solid gold spittoons. Clients ate off of gold-rimmed china, used gold and silver cutlery, and drank from crystal glassware. Three orchestras played around the clock, with only the classics in their repertoire; the sisters were determined to rinse their operation of outward vulgarity.

The Everleigh courtesans were rare beauties, handpicked by Minna and Ada for their looks, good health, manners, and sexual finesse. In keeping with the club's courtly, regal atmosphere, they wore gowns and jewels befitting a duchess and were introduced to clients according to the strictest rules of etiquette. There were no lewd entreaties, no suggestive wriggling under filmy negligees, none of the rawness prevalent in most brothel transactions.

The bedroom was where the respectable charade was dropped. Twelve of the rooms were decorated by theme: Moorish, Copper, Gold, Silver, Blue, Rose, Green, Red, Oriental, Chinese, Japanese, and Egyptian. Ornamental incense burners and scented water fountains aided in seducing the senses. A bowl of firecrackers sat on each bedside table, ready to be set off by the girl at the crucial moment.

With meals and wine beginning at fifty dollars and the price of a girl ranging from ten dollars to fifty dollars, only the rich frequented the Everleigh Club. Regular visitors included Nathanial Ford Moore, son of railway magnate James Hobart Moore, Marshall Field Jr., and Clarence Clay, gentleman safecracker who, if he happened to run out of money during a visit, merely cracked a safe in the neighborhood and returned for a few more hours of Everleigh hospitality. So celebrated did the club become that Prince Henry of Prussia, brother of the Kaiser, asked to see it when he visited Chicago in 1902.

Minna and Ada Everleigh, who rarely saw less than two thousand dollars a night in profit, were Chicago's nightlife queens until 1911, when they dared to print a glossy brochure advertising the club. A furious Mayor Harrison ordered the place closed. The sisters took their millions and went to New York, where they lived in luxury to a ripe old age.

Other better-class brothels included French Emma's, where the bedrooms had wall-to-wall mirrors, Ed Weiss," the Sappho, and the Casino. On the lower end of the scale were the House of All Nations, which claimed to offer girls from every country, and Black May's, which supplied Negro girls to white clients exclusively and staged circuses renowned for their depravity. At rock bottom were the California, where the inmates cost a dollar a round, the Bucket of Blood, a vile whorehouse/saloon, and Bed Bug Row, a hideous collection of twenty-five-cent cubicles inhabited by black prostitutes and those whose looks had been destroyed by drink, drugs, and maltreatment.

Levee prostitutes rarely lasted more than five years in their profession. The liquor and opiates that most of them relied on to keep going sapped their vitality and aged them prematurely. New recruits proved easy to find; the early 1900s saw many young women leaving their rural homes for the big city only to end up starving on factory or shop wages. Most prostitutes had turned to the life voluntarily to escape destitution, but there were several documented cases of forceful recruitment, a practice that became known as "white slavery."

Male and female procurers lurked around Ellis Island seeking gullible immigrant girls, scouted train stations for unescorted prospects, or traveled from town to town in search of local girls who were especially attractive. Once they selected a victim, the pimp or madam offered her a job, promised assistance in locating friends and relatives in a distant city, or (in the case of male procurers) proposed marriage—whatever it took to get her into a closed carriage and on her way to a brothel. Once at the bordello, she was locked in a room, stripped, and raped. Constant supervision and loss of her street clothes ensured that she did not escape. Eventually despair and shame over her unwanted condition changed her imprisonment to self-imposed.

Chicago's leading panderers were James "Big Jim" Colosimo, a former street sweeper whose assets ran the gamut from the better-class Victoria to a handful of twenty-five-cent cribs, and Maurice Van Bever, a flashy dresser with a comfortable income from his Armour Avenue brothels. Colosimo and Van Bever jointly organized a white slave ring that imported girls from New York, St. Louis, and Milwaukee. The arrangement assured their customers a continuous influx of new faces. Problems arose when Congress passed the Mann Act in 1910, making it a criminal offense to transport a woman across state lines for immoral purposes. Although the prospect of a five-year prison term was daunting, the slavers did not halt their dealings to any appreciable degree; they merely went underground.

If prostitution was the lifeblood of the Levee, First Ward Aldermen Michael "Hinky Dink" Kenna and "Bathhouse" John Coughlin were its immune system. No brothel operated without paying them tribute. Their physical dissimilarities were comical: Hinky Dink stood about five-foot-one and was as fragile as a sparrow, while Bathhouse, who had once worked as a rubber in a Turkish bath, was six feet tall and built like a bull. He was as good-natured and loud as his diminutive partner was quiet and dour. Kenna dressed soberly in muted grays, blues, and blacks; Coughlin appeared at one ball wearing a jade green tailcoat, lavender trousers and cravat, mauve vest, pink kid gloves, and yellow pumps. Most people snickered at his outfits—one more charitable observer told him that he looked like an Evanston lawn kissed by the dew.

While Kenna was shrewdly calculating, Coughlin barely knew how to restrain himself. Once, a puzzled Mayor Carter Harrison II asked Kenna whether his partner was on drugs or just plain insane. The rueful reply was, "No, John isn't dotty and he ain't full of dope.

To tell you the God's truth, Mr. Mayor, they ain't found a name for it yet."

Prior to 1923, each Chicago ward had two aldermen on the city council. Coughlin was elected as First Ward representative in 1893, Kenna in 1897. Hinky Dink told his colleague, "Let's stick together and we'll rule the roost one day." By using their positions to extend protection, they amassed a following of saloonkeepers, pimps, and other Levee denizens whose votes kept them in office whether the incumbent mayor was a rascal or a reformer. Their protection game made them wealthy men. Minna Everleigh later estimated that in the eleven years the Everleigh Club remained in business, she paid them one hundred thousand dollars.

Chicago aldermen who granted favors and protection in exchange for handsome kickbacks were the rule rather than the exception. Nathan Brewer, one of the minority, commented once, "There are only three aldermen in the entire sixty-eight who are not willing and able to steal a red hot stove." William T. Stead agreed. "We shall probably not err on the side of charity if we admit that there are ten aldermen on the Council who have not sold their votes or received any corrupt consideration for voting away the patrimony of the people . . . but ten righteous aldermen out of sixty-eight are not sufficient to save city hall. . . ." The erring fifty-eight could count on pocketing an extra fifteen thousand to thirty thousand dollars per year, more if special matters such as zoning issues were put to a vote. Some city council members were both corrupt and stupid. When Alderman Mike Ryan was told that the city planned to purchase six gondolas for the Lincoln Park lagoon, he was puzzled. "Why waste the taxpayers' money?" he asked. "Get a pair of them and let nature take its course."

To further enhance their popularity among their constituents, Kenna and Coughlin sponsored an annual First Ward Ball. Initially held at the Armory, it was moved to the massive Coliseum on account of the huge crowds that attended. The Ball was a wild bacchanal where liquor flowed and blurred the distinctions between the criminal and non-criminal celebrants. At the stroke of midnight, clothes hit the floor and a wild orgy commenced. Kenna proudly observed, "Chicago ain't no sissy town!"

The First Ward Ball of 1908 was particularly depraved, provoking church and reform groups to rally and blast Mayor Fred Busse with righteous fury. Why, they demanded, was this event being allowed in the first place? Where were the police when such a vicious assortment of characters was congregating? A *Chicago Tribune* reporter noted, "If a great disaster had befallen the Coliseum, there would not have been a second story worker, a dip or plug ugly, porch climber, dope fiend, or scarlet woman remaining in Chicago."

Mayor Busse, a former saloonkeeper, was inclined to tolerate the Levee celebrations. But pressure from reformers forced him to ban the proposed 1909 ball. Encouraged, the reform element pushed for closure of the Levee itself. They hassled State's Attorney John E. W. Wayman out of inertia, and in 1912 he ordered the Levee brothels raided and padlocked.

Colosimo, Van Bever, and their associates called an emergency meeting, and devised an ingenious response to the closure threats. Under their direction, the Levee women swarmed into respectable neighborhoods, took seats in family-oriented restaurants, and turned up at decent lodging houses demanding rooms. The message was clear: Closing the Levee meant that a once concentrated evil would become widespread. Even the Vice Commission conceded that the problem was more tolerable if left in a segregated area. But the reformers were undaunted, so in November 1912, Chicago became the first American city to close its red-light zone.

The victory proved hollow, as the brothel keepers and their women merely relocated in other parts of the city and slowly crept back into the Levee after the heat died down. The only permanent result was that the district never regained its brazen blatancy, hiding its purpose instead under the guise of massage parlors, hotels, and cabarets.

Wayman next targeted the corrupt cops who had profited from brothel payoffs, launching an investigation that ended with Inspector Edward McCann being convicted of bribery and sent to Joliet, a superintendent being dismissed, and the suspension of several officers.

To add insult to an already injured force, Mayor Carter Harrison II established a morals squad to investigate and prosecute vice-related offenses independently. He bestowed on its head, retired army Major Metellius I. C. Funkhouser, the newly created post of Second Deputy Police Commissioner. Funkhouser had previously censored movies being considered for Chicago theaters, and tackled his new assignment with the same righteous zeal. In six months he and his men succeeded in arresting hundreds of gamblers, pimps, and prostitutes and permanently closing one vicious dive after another.

Funkhouser and his second in command, Inspector Dannenberg (whose past accomplishments included the jailing of Maurice Van Bever and his wife Julia) did not shut the city vice operations down completely, but they did disrupt enough business to warrant a death sentence from the Levee leaders. Miraculously, neither was ever injured, although in one bizarre episode Dannenberg and his men were caught in a three-way shootout with gangsters and two plain-clothes cops who had mistaken the Morals men for thugs. One policeman was killed and some of Dannenberg's men received crippling bullet wounds.

The morals squad proved so indefatigable that a disheartened Levee dweller commented, "I've seen reform come and reform go, but this is honestly the first time since the closing of the old Custom House Place and Federal Street Tenderloin that it looked as if it might stick."

He suffered from either pessimism or short-term memory. Reform in Chicago was never a long-lived phenomenon. The inhabitants had proven time and again that they resented having their indulgences curbed by those claiming to know best; former mayors Medill McCormick and Monroe Heath had tackled the vice problem only to be voted out in the next election. Chicagoans had always shown pro-vice leanings at the polls, and the politician desirous of a long career never forgot it.

Carter Harrison II, whose assassinated father had also been mayor, took office for another term in 1911, while the city was writhing with embarrassment over highly publicized white slave scandals. The morals squad had been a necessary political move at the time. But by the time the mayoral election rolled around in April 1915, Chicago had had enough of Harrison and reform.

His replacement was a brash bullhorn of a politician whose election opened a brand new chapter in the city's history of corruption. William Hale "Big Bill" Thompson advocated the open saloon, empty jail, and unchecked pursuit of happiness. Chicago had had its share of crooked mayors, but Thompson was unparalleled. He threw the town wide open, and it never closed again.

In 1900 the Municipal Voters' League, formed to combat political corruption, was looking for a candidate they could back for the post of Second Ward alderman. A Republican citizens group recommended Big Bill Thompson. "The worst thing you can say about Bill," one member offered, "is that he's stupid."

Thompson eagerly accepted the nomination, not because he had a burning desire to purify city hall, but to win a fifty-dollar bet. He won both the money and the office.

Thompson's success lay in his ability to morph himself into whatever each particular voting sector wanted to see. He won the backing of the silk-stocking element by reminding them of his own wealthy lineage; his father had owned one of Chicago's most prosperous real-estate companies. Levee dwellers recalled fondly the many times he and his companions had patronized the saloons and bought drinks for the house. Voters in the Black Belt warmed to him when he openly sympathized with them over the oppression they continued to face.

Thompson only held the position for one term. To oblige Aldermen Kenna and Coughlin, who had seen the Levee migrate slowly from its original location in the First Ward to settle within the geographical boundaries of the Second Ward, he voted for redrawing of ward boundaries. Under the new layout, the Levee was once more part of the First Ward and back under Kenna and Coughlin's control. His former district now absorbed, Thompson did not run for an aldermanic seat again. But his time in office was long enough for him to appreciate the lucrative rewards that came with political power. Someone was always willing to pay handsomely to have a revoked liquor license restored or get a zealous fire inspector to ease up on a firetrap brothel. Greed and ambition pierced his rather dull intellect. In 1902 he ran for Cook County Commissioner on the Republican ticket, using the chameleon-like tactics that had served him well in the aldermanic race, and won the election hands down.

It was a greater success than anyone, even his own family, would have forecast for Big Bill Thompson. Born in Boston and bred in Chicago, William Hale Thompson Jr. came from a distinguished old New England family. His forefathers had been military and naval officers, and his own father headed a prosperous real estate business. Billy, as his friends called him, envisioned a different future for himself. The senior Thompson wanted his son to have a genteel education and one day take over the family business, but the only books Billy chose to learn from were Wild West pulp novels. He wanted to be a cowboy.

He struck a deal with his reluctant father. He would spend each winter at school in Chicago, and pass the spring, summer, and fall months roaming the ranges of Wyoming, Utah, and Nebraska. Rustling cattle, cooking over a campfire, and sleeping under the stars undid any refinement acquired at school, making Bill Thompson fit into his elegant family like a rawhide patch on a silk suit. He favored ten-gallon hats, spoke in bullhorn tones, and stampeded on horseback through the Chicago streets with little regard for public safety or sensitivity.

It was after one such wild ride that he saw firsthand how clout worked in Chicago. When he was fourteen, he and some friends stampeded merrily across one of many ramshackle bridges that spanned the Chicago River. An irate bridge tender seized Thompson's horse by the bridle and told him to seek his wild fun elsewhere. The beefy teenager thumped him solidly and ended up in jail. The elder Thompson, whose influence in city hall was considerable, sprang his son and had to be cajoled by the mayor, chief of police, and captain of the station where Billy had been taken into not seeking the dismissal of every cop associated with his son's arrest.

Young Thompson was impressed but still had no ambition to play politics, and he might have been a cowpuncher indefinitely were it not for his father's death in 1891. Twenty-four-year-old Billy came home at his grieving mother's request to manage the family business, but as soon as he could toss all responsibility onto the shoulders of his father's longtime partner, he joined the Chicago Athletic Club and became a football player and coach. At night he frequented the Levee dives with his boyhood cronies. One of them, Gene Pike, with whom he shared a bachelor suite at the Hotel Metropole, dared him to run for Second Ward alderman in 1900.

Thompson's time in office was spent racing yachts along Lake Michigan instead of chairing neighborhood beautification committees, but Republican Party seniors figured that they might have a candidate for mayor in him. Congressman Fred Lundin commented, "He may not be big in brains, but he gets through to people."

Thompson agreed to run for mayor in the April 1915 election on the Republican ticket. His opponent, Robert M. Sweitzer, was a

German Catholic. With help from Fred Lundin, who used to peddle quack medicines to a gullible public, Thompson put on a show that made his run for Cook County commissioner seem a mild spectacle by comparison.

When addressing Polish audiences, he blared anti-German slogans and gleefully reminded them of Sweitzer's heritage. In the German districts, he came across as so sympathetic to their war-created scapegoat status that his detractors nicknamed him "Kaiser Bill." His fiery denunciation of the British enthused Irish voters so much that they paid scant attention to the anti-Catholic speeches he made to Protestant audiences. He assured the silk-stocking voters that he would "clean up this city and drive out the crooks! I'll make Chicago the cleanest city in the world!" He promised reformers that he would stamp out gambling and force saloons to close on Sunday. To women he proclaimed, "I'll appoint a mother to the board of education! Who knows better than a mother what is good for children?" He cajoled black voters with, "If you want to shoot craps, go ahead and do it. When I'm mayor, the police will have something better to do than break up a friendly little crap game." He assured the saloonkeepers that the Sunday closing law would be a farce and signed a pledge to that effect, saying, "I see no harm in a friendly little drink in a friendly little saloon."

He won all-around support by attacking the gas trust, a popular enemy. Jumping on the fact that Sweitzer was a protégé of Roger Sullivan, the Democratic boss who figured in the 1890s furor over ridiculously high gas prices, he boomed, "It [the gas trust] gets its profits by gouging unfair profits from the little fellow. Do the people want to turn the government over to Roger Sullivan and the utilities?" A week before the polls opened, he filed a petition with the utilities commission to reduce natural gas prices by 30 percent. He made sure everyone knew it, too.

Robert Sweitzer, recalling how "constructively" Thompson had spent his term as alderman, dismissed him with, "Who has ever heard of him doing anything? I find he is the man who plays with sailboats."

The voters, however, reacted with predicted enthusiasm, electing Big Bill Thompson, whom a contemporary described as having the "carcass of a rhinoceros and the brains of a baboon," mayor of Chicago by the greatest majority ever accorded a Republican candidate.

In his 1971 work *Capone*, author John Kobler described the aftermath of the Thompson victory:

> Within six months, he had violated every campaign promise but one. He did keep Chicago wide open. After a flurry of token arrests in the Levee and elsewhere, a live and let live policy prevailed anew. Slot machines manufactured by Chicago's Mills Novelty Company clicked and clattered away all over the city, with the bigwigs of city hall getting a cut of the profits. The Sportsmen's Club, a Republican organization, was used as a collection agency for the graft. Not only gamblers, but also saloon and brothel keepers received solicitations for one-hundred-dollar "Life Memberships" on club letterheads bearing the mayor's name. The members included Thompson's chief of police, Charles C. Healey, Herbert S. Mills, president of the slot machine company, Mont Tennes, the gambling magnate, Jim Colosimo, whose liquor license the mayor restored . . .

If Chicago crooks said any prayers at all, Thompson was the answer to them. One of his first duties as mayor was to cut off appropriation to the morals squad, forcing it to disband. During a 1917 raid on a vice resort, State's Attorney Maclay Hoyne confiscated from a crooked cop a notebook with the names of shady hotels and graft rates. It revealed how comfortably the law and the lawless had settled in together in the wake of Thompson's election. The book listed some resorts as "Chief's Places," meaning that the payoffs went directly to Chief of Police Healy. Other places were marked "3 ways," indicating that graft was split between Captain Thomas Costello, underworld bail bondsman Billy Skidmore, and panderer Mike Heitler. One page listed saloons allowed to violate the Sunday closing laws and 1 A.M. curfew. Another page designated places as "can be raided" or "can't be raided," depending on who was kicking back graft on schedule. Despite such glaring evidence of corruption, Chief Healey was not dismissed from his post or censured in any way. At his trial, famed criminal lawyers Clarence Darrow and Charles Erbstein presented a colorful and brilliant defense, and he was acquitted.

Thompson bristled at the suggestion that Chicago was becoming the Barbary Coast of the Midwest. "It's all newspaper talk!" the cowboy mayor scoffed.

Attracted by the fertile grounds for profit, gangsters from less tolerant locations poured into Chicago. Big Bill's first eight months in office produced a flood of lawlessness that made the roaring years under Fred Busse look like an era of virtue. Reform alderman Charles Merriam commented bitterly, "Chicago is unique. It is the only completely corrupt city in America."

During Big Bill Thompson's first term as mayor, Dean O'Banion was still a small-time hoodlum. He was not important enough to share the wealth; on the contrary, he and other unconnected gangsters were natural prey for cops who weren't allowed to touch the bigger criminals.

Power and greatness were still years away for O'Banion in 1915. But when a controversial new law settled over the land in 1920, he acquired a greater appreciation of Thompson's impact on underworld fortunes. For without the rollicking, rowdy cowboy mayor, O'Banion and the other Chicago gangsters who made the Twenties roar could never have existed.

5

Perfect Landlord, Unwelcome Guest

THE RESIDENTS OF THE SMALL APARTMENT building at 1704 Otto Street agreed that they were fortunate to have Frederick Schoeps as a landlord. Soon after he purchased the property in 1917, they pegged him as an easygoing, understanding type. He sympathized when hard times hit and allowed cash-strapped tenants to retain their apartments on credit until things improved. They observed that his second wife, Madeleine, adored him, and that he was a caring father to their children, Verna and Kenneth. What they didn't know was that his first wife had died years previously of what a coroner's jury ruled accidental asphyxiation. Nor were they aware of the rumor that he had beaten her to death after she threatened to turn him in to the police.

The benign Otto Street landlord had a past and present that would have shocked his tenants had they known. Frederick Schoeps, alias Charles "the Ox" Reiser, was reckoned by the police to be the most brutal and prolific "peterman" (safecracker) of his day, drawing comparisons with safe-blowing legend Eddie Fay.

Dubbed "the Ox" because of a supposedly Herculean strength, he was an opportunistic, ruthless criminal with several murders on what little conscience he had.

Born in Elgin, Illinois, in 1882 to immigrants from the German province of Alsace Lorraine, Reiser's reputation in Chicago began on September 15, 1903, when he was arrested for burglary and safe-cracking. He scorned bribery in favor of killing the witnesses against him while he was out on bond, and walked out of the courtroom a free man. The same savage tactics worked for him when he faced another burglary charge in September 1905 and an arrest for robbery in January 1907.

By 1908 it became a running joke that finding an honest thief in Chicago would be far easier than persuading someone to testify against Reiser. Therefore, it came as a huge surprise to everyone, especially the Ox, when he committed an assault with a deadly weapon on March 30, 1907, and the victim pressed charges. Police protection frustrated any attempt to silence his accuser, and he received a thirty-day jail sentence.

He would never serve time in prison again. In 1909 he left Chicago for Seattle, to attend the Alaska Yukon Pacific Exposition, which drew thousands of visitors during its June 1–October 16 run. While there, he broke into a local business to steal the safe's contents, and shot the night watchman who stumbled upon him in mid-deed. He fled the city when news of the crime became public, but Seattle authorities tracked him down in November and worked with the Chicago Police Department to secure his extradition. Reiser had no intention of going back to jail, and one by one the state witnesses died under mysterious circumstances. The judge presiding over the case was forced to dismiss it for lack of evidence, and Reiser returned to Chicago to resume building his legend in the safe-blowing craft.

The peterman had long been embroiled in a battle of wits with safe manufacturers. The earliest tool of the trade was the "drag," a screw-like instrument that crushed the area around the box's combination lock and allowed it to be pulled off. The manufacturers strengthened the safe walls, forcing the crackers to devise the "jackscrew," a gadget that forced steel wedges into the door crack until the door popped off its hinges. The manufacturers reconstructed the doors so that they were bolted from all four sides, and built dovetailed formations into the jamb that made insertion of a jackscrew impossible.

Reiser was one of the first of his brethren to tackle this new obstacle with nitroglycerine. He used an air pump to scatter a wispy line of gunpowder around the door crack, placed the pump at the bottom and a funnel of powder at the top, and sealed the rest of the crack with putty. When applied, the pump sucked air from the safe's interior, creating a vacuum that drew the powder inside. After being set off by a cap, the powder exploded, shaking the steel box open with a whoosh of acrid, eye-burning smoke.

In 1915 the Maurice Tourneur film *Alias Jimmy Valentine* hit the American cinema circuit and turned the safecracker into a nationwide *cause celébre*. Based on a 1911 short story by O. Henry, the movie portrayed the peterman as a redeemable character capable of using his talents for the purpose of good (in this case, opening a safe to rescue a little girl who had been locked inside). Such skillful manipulation of public sentiment by the Hollywood moguls made one forget that for every Jimmy Valentine with a conscience, there were hundreds of opportunists like the Ox who robbed payrolls and shot down watchmen who interrupted them in mid-deed.

Reiser, although impulsively violent, usually exercised patience and precision when planning a safecracking job. He spread the word that anyone who tipped him off about a safe loaded with payroll or deposit money would receive a generous sum if he succeeded in stealing its contents. Once he'd chosen a target, he would find an excuse to visit the offices in question and familiarize himself with the layout so that entry and exit points could be determined in advance. He would even shell out cash to acquire a set of floor plans, explaining once to O'Banion, "I'll pay a hundred dollars any time to score a thousand." In the days prior to the planned robbery, he would work for hours in his basement, extracting nitroglycerine from sticks of dynamite.

Reiser reasoned that for bigger jobs, like stealing union and company payrolls, a small gang was necessary. Some environments called for lookouts, and armed watchmen were always a concern for the lone operator. Like a twentieth-century Fagin, Reiser recruited a bevy of young hoodlums to form the city's greatest safecracking gang. Dean O'Banion, whom he had known casually for years, was one of his first pupils.

After finishing his second jail term, O'Banion went back to work for Bob McGovern as a bartender. He served customers who joined him after hours in robbing warehouses, shops, and other depots storing valuable merchandise. O'Banion was a risky accomplice, being shrewd and streetwise but totally bereft of caution. It was not unusual for him to burglarize an establishment, and then spend an hour sitting outside, drinking and singing. Some McGovern habitués saw working with O'Banion as a sure ticket to jail, but others recognized a diamond in the rough, an intelligent, charismatic youth who needed guidance to temper his compulsive bravado. Charles Reiser was one of the latter.

Organized crime as defined today was, in the mid-1910s, nonexistent. It was still the era of the "hard yegg," the beetle-browed thug who glared at the civilized world from beneath the brim of a skullcap, ate and drank with the delicacy of a starved wolf, and cherished brass knuckles as the weapon of a man. Such characters had little opportunity to make the type of money needed to give them the superficial respectability of a Mike MacDonald or Mont Tennes. The vice and gambling fields were rigidly controlled by bosses who thought little of interlopers and even less of crushing them. O'Banion, with his aimless burglaries and stickups, was part of that lower strata of underworld life in 1917, but differed from his fellows in one crucial respect. He did not steal to survive or acquire luxuries; he did it for the thrill alone.

Psychologically speaking, he was a born safecracker. The risks involved in handling explosives thrilled the man who, as a boy, would walk on only the tallest stilts. But he lacked the patience to become a master at it, rendering nitroglycerine deadlier than usual in his hands. Unless supervised, he used too much explosive and burned the safe contents to a worthless crisp, in the process raising a stink that a patrolman could smell a mile away. Time and practice did little to improve his technique and once, in what was a coup de grace of ineptitude, he blew out the side of an office building but left the safe intact.

Reiser's teachings were better absorbed by nineteen-year-old Earl J. Wojciechowski, alias Hymie Weiss, a Polish youth and longtime friend of O'Banion. Weiss's record included arrests for auto theft and burglary. More recently he had been offering his services as a labor slugger to both unions and employers. He was wiry and sharp featured, and possessed a hair-trigger temper and powerful fists. But beneath the violent exterior lurked a sharp, calculating brain. Unless riled, he had a coolness and deliberation requisite to becoming not just a top-notch safecracker but also a criminal mastermind.

Weiss was born in Chicago in 1898. His father, Walente Wojciechowski, ran a saloon at 768 Austin Avenue (telephone Ogden 1135 in the 1903 city directory, Humboldt 6833 in 1906). The young Earl was impressed by the rough trade that crowded into the place nightly. His mother, Mary, separated from her husband while the five children (Earl, Violet, Bernard, Frederick, and Joe, who died at age thirteen) were still young. She changed their surname to the more pronounceable "Weiss," and sent Earl to St. Malachy's Catholic school in a probable attempt to repair any damage caused by the saloon environment.

Like O'Banion, Weiss adored his mother and got on well with his brother Bernard and sister Violet, but between himself and Frederick there was a bitter hatred. In 1926, when Frederick Weiss was called to testify about his brother's past, he said scathingly, "The last time I saw him was at Christmas 1923. I do not know where he lived, or where my parents live, for all that. They live on the West Side somewhere." He told a reporter, "I only saw him once in the last twenty years. That was when he shot me."

Chicago resident Bob Koznecki, whose grandfather Frank was Hymie Weiss's first cousin, related a family story about the gangster's violent temper. At a family get-together in the early 1920s, Hymie, Frank, and others were in the basement, enjoying drinks and conversation. Weiss, said Koznecki, "was as nice, as friendly, as can be." But an argument suddenly erupted between Hymie and Frank, which ended in Hymie shoving his cousin. Frank, a skilled fighter, struck back and knocked him to the floor. The gangster got slowly to his feet, eyes blazing, and hissed, "I know you're my cousin, but if you ever hit me again I swear I'll kill you."

"No one doubted that he meant every word," Koznecki said.

His career in crime began at age ten, when he joined neighborhood boys in looting West Side warehouses and shops. His was a playground only slightly different from O'Banion's stomping grounds in Little Hell. Train tracks, canals, docks, factories, breweries, and lumberyards were everywhere, leaving little space for parks or playgrounds. Weiss's neighborhood, estimated in 1927 to contain fifty thousand inhabitants per square mile, was known locally as "Bucktown" and had the reputation of being the toughest area northwest of Little Hell. Gangs from Bucktown fought regular, pitched battles with the juvenile terrorists of "Pojay Town," another Polish colony further south. Their battles were as ferocious as any adult gang war.

Another friend of O'Banion who became a Reiser protégé was George "Bugs" Moran. A stout character with a permanently somber expression, Moran had little to say and gave the impression of being slow-witted. One thing guaranteed to light his fuse was to call him Bugs, a slang term for crazy. He hated it, and no one lacking a death wish used the nickname in his presence.

He was born George Clarence Moran on August 21, 1893, to Julius and Diana Moran in St. Paul, Minnesota. Even in those frontier days, St. Paul was a protective haven for desperadoes on the run. Young Moran observed and admired the freewheeling ways of the professional criminal. In his autobiography, *Public Enemy Number One*, kidnapper and bank robber Alvin Karpis described St. Paul in the 1930s, which had changed very little since Moran's boyhood:

> It was a crook's haven. Every criminal of any importance in the 1930s made his home in St. Paul. If you were looking for a guy you hadn't seen in a few months, you usually thought of two places: prison or St. Paul. If he wasn't locked up in one, he was probably hanging out in the other. . . . You could relax in (St. Paul) joints and speakeasies without any fear of arrest, and when you were planning a score, you could have your pick of all the top men at all the top crimes.

When Julius Moran moved his family to Chicago, young George put into practice many of the lessons he'd learned back home. His first criminal enterprise was the unhitching of horses from delivery wagons so that he might hold them for ransom. It was an oddball, marginally profitable scheme that he abandoned in favor of burglary.

Bad luck plagued his porch-climbing career from the start. By 1917, he had collected the following notations on his record:

September 17, 1910—sent to the penitentiary for robbery under the name George Miller: paroled June 18, 1912.
October 3, 1913—sent to the penitentiary from MacLean County for burglary and larceny. Served minor sentence.
December 19, 1917—forfeited bonds in a robbery case; case subsequently stricken off by the court.

The Reiser Gang expanded to include Tom Sweeney, a former cop; Johnny Mahoney, an ambitious fledgling safecracker; Clarence White, a burglar; Johnny Sheehy, a barroom brawler with a knack for explosives; and a handful of lesser thugs who did not participate regularly.

O'Banion's hazardous enthusiasm aside, the Reiser Gang became the boldest and most prolific safecracking crew in the city. In 1918 the following jobs were credited to them:

January 29—The safe at the Western Dairy Company was blown open and $2,000 was stolen.
September 2—The night watchman at the Standard Oil Company was slugged and relieved of his keys. The paymaster's safe was found open and emptied of $2,060.
September 3—The offices of Schaeffer Brothers were entered through a coal chute and $1,400 was stolen.
November 5—The Prudential Life Insurance Company was entered via a fire escape and $3,865 was stolen.
December 2—The safe at the Borden Farm Products Company was robbed of $594.61.

Reiser's skill and vigilance saved them from detection each time, something George Moran did not appreciate until it was too late. On May 24, 1918, he did a freelance robbery of a department store. The night watchman caught him red-handed and turned him in to the police. The judge presiding over his case handed him a five-year sentence in Joliet Penitentiary, which he promptly evaded by assuming the name of Morrissey and hiding out. His battle to stay free would not end until 1923, when he was re-arrested on the robbery charge. By that point his wartime associates were big names in

Chicago gangland, and after they appealed to Governor Len Small, Moran was paroled the same day that he was convicted for the last time.

As the 1910s drew to a close, Dean O'Banion and Earl Weiss not only became close friends, they also showed the makings of a formidable team. O'Banion was the extroverted, energetic doer, Weiss the normally cautious, reserved thinker. O'Banion put Weiss's ideas into action, using his charisma to attract the supporters needed to make them possible. Chicago history was full of successful pairings: Hinky Dink Kenna and Bathhouse John Coughlin ruled the Levee; James Colosimo and Maurice Van Bever organized the white slavery ring that infused their brothels with enticing new faces on a regular basis; and Big Bill Thompson and Fred Lundin planned the theatrical campaigns that snared Chicago's majority vote. O'Banion and Weiss discovered their ideas and ambitions to be in equally strong sync.

They grudgingly acknowledged that they owed Charles Reiser for lifting them out of the underworld cesspool and giving them a reputation that garnered respect among their peers, but they disliked him personally; he was boorish and made it clear that he was the boss and not running any democracies. O'Banion and Weiss hungered to run their own show, and possibly one day have a piece of the city like Kenna and Coughlin or Mont Tennes or Big Mike MacDonald.

They had the necessary ambition; what they needed was an opportunity.

6

Circulation Soldier

It was the type of assignment that every reporter simultaneously craves and dreads. In the sweltering July of 1919 a race riot devastated Chicago's black ghetto, and the *Herald and Examiner* gave Edward Dean Sullivan the dubious honor of reporting conditions in the battle zone.

Hostilities commenced on Sunday, July 27, when a fourteen-year-old black youth, Eugene Williams, and his friends made the mistake of steering their raft from an all-black bathing area at Twenty-fifth Street to a section of Twenty-ninth Street beach reserved for whites. An irate white bather threw rocks at the raft, one of which struck Williams on the head, causing him to topple overboard and drown. His friends made it back to the safety of the black swimming area, where they reported the attack to a black policeman. The officer went to a white colleague and demanded that the man who'd struck Williams be arrested. The white policeman paid lip service to the request but did nothing, which prompted angry blacks to storm the Twenty-ninth Street beach to attack the assailant, one George Stauber. Another group chased the white officer down Twenty-ninth.

When police reinforcements and indignant white citizens fought back, the battle was on. Black rioters torched buildings and assaulted whites. Black war veterans loaded their service weapons, and bullets whanged and whined through previously quiet streets.

Getting a cab to enter the ravaged area was impossible, so the *Examiner* obtained motorcycles to shuttle reporters past the police barricades. Fortified by encouragement from Editor Walter Howey, Sullivan jumped into the sidecar of a motorcycle idling outside the paper's offices. The driver was a short, husky individual with windblown blond hair and boyish features. They exchanged brief greetings before driving to the police lines on South State Street. What Sullivan saw beyond the barricade lessened his nerve and journalistic zeal.

Rubble and debris littered the street. Negro faces twisted with hate pressed against the windows on both sides of State. Policemen huddled in doorways, clutching weapons and nervously eyeing those faces. The time-bomb atmosphere made Sullivan uneasy.

He turned to his driver. "How about it? Shall we go in there?"

"Sure." The other man gestured toward a banner bearing the paper's name in bold lettering, which had been attached to the motorcycle. "This will get us by. The paper's been giving the jigaboos all the best of it. They won't pop off at us."

Reassured by his confidence, Sullivan agreed. They drove alone down State Street, in his later words "a one-motorcycle procession." As they passed one window full of glaring onlookers after another, the reporter began to lose his faith in their supposed immunity. The blacks were seething from a sense of injustice. The *Examiner*'s editorials had supported their cause, but Sullivan reminded himself that many of the gun-toting Negroes glaring at them now could not even read.

His fears materialized at the corner of State and Thirty-first Streets, where they came upon a wounded policeman who died before their eyes. Sullivan was still transfixed by the sight when the driver yanked out a pistol and fired at something on a nearby roof. With his other hand, he steered the vehicle into an alley to take cover.

The move nearly cost both of them their lives. They found themselves face to face with a group of drunken blacks who were cursing and firing shotguns into the sky. The driver effected a speedy retreat before any slugs could start flying their way.

Sullivan, heart hammering, held on tight as the motorcycle flew up State Street at breakneck speed. He looked back toward the roof where the driver had aimed his shot, and saw a disheveled Negro trying to train his rifle on them. A gigantic black woman dressed in white was trying to wrest his rifle away. Her intervention allowed the two men to get out of shooting range, but the district was suddenly alive with gunfire again. Pistol and rifle shots cracked the smoky air, and someone hurled a metal shovel down at the cycle.

The driver remained vigilant but cool. He steered the vehicle along the curb, pistol cocked as he eyed the buildings opposite. "One side's enough to worry about!" he yelled.

They managed to get back to the police lines in one piece. An hour after their escape, the militia arrived, and a fire broke out that damaged over a million dollars worth of property. By the time the rioting was over, thirty-eight people were dead and five hundred seriously injured.

Sullivan did not breathe normally until the motorcycle growled to a halt in front of the Examiner Building. After climbing out of the sidecar, he faced the driver, whom he now acknowledged as his savior.

"What's your name?" he asked.

The young man dismounted the cycle. Sullivan noticed that he walked with a limp. "Dean O'Banion," he said, introducing himself.

O'Banion had been working for the *Herald and Examiner* for over a year. He had easily escaped the World War I draft; the registrar for his ward, after interviewing him, noted in her report, "Left leg one inch short. Limps. Leg was broken in two places." He walked away from the U.S. Army and promptly enlisted in a fighting force whose battleground was not the fields of Europe but the streets of Chicago.

The circulation wars, as they were later called, had started in 1910—over a penny. Two prominent dailies, William Randolph Hearst's *American* and Medill McCormick's *Tribune*, were vying for a monopoly on the city's morning readership. While the publishers plotted marketing strategies, thugs they had hired took to the streets and beat up newsboys, burned down newsstands, and killed one another. These battles were initially confined to those with a direct interest in the conflict, but when McCormick gained an edge by cutting the single-copy price of the *Tribune* to one cent, all hell broke loose. Now even newspaper *readers* were fair game.

O'Banion had left his job at McGovern's after reformers pushed the police into a series of harassing raids. (The saloon was padlocked soon after by an injunction from the righteous Committee of Fifteen.)

He decided to join the circulation wars and employ the strong-arm skills he'd acquired at McGovern's. He was a *Tribune* slugger initially but switched allegiance within a matter of months because many of his friends were fighting for Hearst. They had pitched him enthusiastically to the hardboiled publisher, Andrew M. "Long Green Andy" Lawrence, and O'Banion had the job before he even applied.

To illustrate what it took to be a Hearst employee, biographer Ferdinand Lundberg described what transpired when a young man, fresh out of college, applied for a reporter's job at the *Chicago American*:

> The editor eyed the eager applicant coldly and demanded, "Do you smoke?"
>
> "No, sir," the youth replied.
>
> "Do you drink?"
>
> "No, sir."
>
> "Would you seduce a luscious young girl if she was left alone in your company?"
>
> The young man's eyes widened and red crept into his cheeks, but he managed to reply, "No, sir."
>
> "Do you beat your mother?"
>
> "No."
>
> "Do you use drugs?"
>
> "No."
>
> "Would you steal to get ahead in the world?"
>
> "No."
>
> The editor's nostrils flared. "Well, then, you don't want to work for Hearst, you virtuous son of a bitch! Get out of here!!"

Newsmen and editors alike on the Hearst payroll earned their salaries not by reporting the news but by warping it. They were hard-drinking, rip-roaring daredevils who were equal parts scribe and scoundrel. When the news was insufficiently lurid, they did such a literary airbrush job on it that no one who knew the facts would recognize them in print.

Failure to come across worthwhile stories motivated the Hearst boys to create their own. Once, after the accidental death of a Negro, the *American* city editor and a reporter telephoned every black undertaker in the city and told them that the deceased's family had requested their services. Careful timing of each call ensured that the undertakers would all arrive at the family home at the same time. To ensure that something "interesting" would ensue, the Hearst men told the undertakers that the family wanted them to bar others of their profession from attempting to get the body. "Then there'll be something doing," the editor predicted, "or I'm a poor guesser." He wasn't. A mini-riot ensued, with the *American* scooping the competition in reporting details.

Gangsters got on well with these innovative charlatans, and assisted them in bringing in news from the field—literally. William Salisbury, a reporter employed at the *American*, once observed a burly specimen hanging around the editorial department, chatting with the night staff. Salisbury, new to the job, was surprised that such a character would be admitted to the building, much less be allowed to sit alone at a desk. The man left, and when he returned at 2 A.M., Salisbury saw why he was so welcome. Racing into the room from a back stairway, breathing hard, the man reached into his coat and pulled out copies of the other Chicago morning papers, still warm from the presses.

"Gee, I had a fierce tussle makin' a getaway dis time!" he explained, wiping sweat from his brow. "Dey're getting' on to me. It was hard work gettin' dese first editions from de delivery wagons. I guess I'll make Mr. Hoist raise me salary, or else buy me an armor soot."

"The rest of us were given clippings from the papers he brought in," Salisbury recalled, "and told to rewrite the news from them as quickly as possible." It was a popular plagiarism scam known as "cribbing." The *American* employed hoods to steal rival papers' morning editions and give them to the night staff to redo. Everyone at the paper benefited. The gangsters made good money doing what they did best, and the reporters, spared the necessity of having to find their own news, got to spend more time hanging out in their favorite saloons.

O'Banion worked in the circulation department, intimidating news dealers and paperboys into carrying Hearst's papers exclusively. Fighting alongside him were such lethal characters as Frank McErlane, a glassy-eyed, murderous thug whom the *Illinois Crime Survey* dubbed "the most brutal gunman who ever pulled a trigger in Chicago"; Edward Barrett, a knife-wielding maniac; and the vicious Gentleman brothers, Gus, Dutch, and Pete.

O'Banion spent his working hours hunting down newsstands that carried the *Tribune* and suggesting to the dealer that it would be wiser—not to mention healthier—to sell only the *American* (after 1918 he used the same tactics to push the *Examiner*). He was always friendly when outlining the proposal, but if the answer he got was not to his liking, his stare turned cold, his smile tightened, and his large hands hammered the stubborn dealer senseless. Repeat offenders had their stands burned down.

Both papers supplied their sluggers with guns. The *Tribune* terrorists initiated the practice of ambushing thugs working for rival papers at designated points and cutting them down with a fusillade of lead. The Hearst men fought back with counter-ambushes, using delivery trucks to lure the hidden McCormick gunners within shooting range. Stray bullets sometimes struck newsboys and passersby.

The Chicago *Inter-Ocean*, which kept out of the battle, carried a sarcastic editorial in its June 11, 1911 edition explaining to a terrified public why the carnage was going on unchecked.

"Why should not Mr. Wayman [State's Attorney Charles Wayman] ascertain, or at least hold up to public reprobation, the men whose money nourished and sustained these bravos trained to swagger through the streets with automatic guns, in five-thousand-dollar automobiles, wounding or killing whoever their employers dislike?" it demanded. "But Mr. Wayman will not. He dares not. Everybody knows that."

It was common knowledge that the *Tribune* dominated first Wayman and then his successor, Maclay Hoyne. Hearst controlled Chief of Police John McWeeny. With such powerful obligations tying its agents' hands, the law proved powerless to stop the fighting.

Newsboys were innocent victims. Some were crippled and unable to flee when stalked by gangsters or caught in a crossfire. On August 22, 1911, Charles Gallantry, a newsboy who hawked his wares at the corner of Chicago Avenue and Robey Street, was confronted by *Tribune* thug Bob Holbrook. When ordered to take thirty additional copies of the *Tribune*, the boy protested that he would not be able to sell them. Holbrook punched him in the face, knocking him to the sidewalk, and proceeded to beat him to a bloody pulp while a horrified crowd, held at bay by Holbrook's cronies, looked on. The big gangster dragged his victim toward an alley, but Gallantry caught hold of a weighing machine and held fast.

Holbrook, enraged, slugged him unconscious and left him lying in a thick pool of blood on the pavement.

The public was also fair game. One evening in 1912, three Hearst sluggers—Edward and Charles Barrett and seventeen-year-old Louis "the Farmer" Friedman—boarded a streetcar in the vicinity of Fifth Avenue (now Wells Street) and Washington Street. Without warning they started shooting up the car, which was packed with men, women, and children. Two male passengers and the conductor, Frank Witt, were mortally wounded and died later in a hospital. Charles Barrett was struck in the left side by a police bullet while resisting arrest but survived. He and his accomplices beat the murder charges. When the grieving families threatened to sue Hearst for the damage his minions had done, shadowy emissaries from the *American* visited them and advised them that silence was the best insurance against the "accidents" that were so prevalent these days.

It later came to light that the shootings had been specifically ordered by the *American* bosses to discredit (and lay the blame on) striking union pressmen who had been locked out of their jobs and were protesting noisily as a result. But the Hearst gunmen had no qualms about shooting citizens caught reading a rival paper. People lost life and limb for preferring the more dignified style of the *Tribune.*

Prior to the 1910 price cut, the chief bone of contention between the Hearst and McCormick camps had been an 1895 agreement between the board of education and the *Tribune* and *The Chicago Daily News.* The newspaper publishers had succeeded in leasing a large tract of downtown school property at a startlingly low rate for a ninety-nine-year term, and built their printing plants there. Critics of the deal pointed out the coincidence that the head of the board of education, A. S. Trude, was also a *Tribune* lawyer. The lease originally contained a clause that called for the lease to be renegotiated each year, but McCormick, aware of rising land values, asked the board to eliminate that troublesome stipulation. The Hearst papers latched onto the story and exposed it, gleefully reminding its readers that the cancellation of the renewal clause meant an enormous loss of revenue to the school system.

Edward F. Dunne, a Hearst man, was elected mayor in 1905. He initiated a series of unsuccessful but harassing suits to cancel the 1895 lease. The *Tribune* struck back in 1907 when a Republican mayor whom it backed, Fred Busse, was elected. The McCormick forces also lured onto its payroll Moses and Max Annenberg, Hearst's prize sluggers. The *American* sued Max Annenberg for breach of contract, but a court ruled that the gangster's agreement with his former employer was invalid because it was a *contract to commit illegal acts.*

Long Green Andy Lawrence hastily strengthened his goon squad to compensate for the loss of his key fighters. His first wave of recruits included the Gentleman brothers, Jack Nolan, "Chicago Jack" Daly, Edward Barrett, and Frank McErlane.

Fierce as they were, the *American*'s new sluggers were hard put to match the Annenbergs. Both in person and through issuing orders, the Jewish killers murdered dozens of Hearst men during the twenty years that the circulation wars raged.

An early casualty was Dutch Gentleman, who was standing at the bar of a State Street saloon, boasting of his shooting prowess, when *Tribune* killer Maurice "Mossy" Enright walked in. Enright approached Dutch from behind, whirled him about, and pumped six .44-caliber slugs into his abdomen. Gentleman staggered backward, face blank with shock, and, as Lundberg gruesomely described it, "his entrails, which until then had been enjoying food and drink at the expense of William Randolph Hearst, came spilling out onto the sawdust floor." Enright brazenly admitted his guilt to the police, but the *Tribune* came to his rescue and managed to get the murder charge dropped. When an unforgiving William Gentleman burst into Pat O'Malley's saloon in May 1911 looking for Enright, Mossy drew his gun faster and pumped ten slugs into Gentleman, whose dying words were, "I had to get him before he got me."

Dutch and William Gentleman had been preceded to the grave by ace *American* slugger Vincent Altman, who, in the presence of off-duty detectives, was relaxing in the bar of the Briggs House one evening in March 1911 and chatting with none other than Mossy Enright. Without warning, Enright grabbed him, fired two bullets into his abdomen, and ran upstairs. The detectives claimed they had never seen the killer before, but witnesses insisted that they had exchanged winks with him. When a doctor attempted to treat the dying gangster, Altman warned him to back off or get killed himself. True to the code of the underworld, Altman died without fingering Enright. Some witnesses did talk, and after his trial Enright, bane of the Hearst gangsters, received a life sentence. He never served a day of it. On February 3, 1920, Enright's past caught up with him, and he was shotgunned in front of his home at 1110 Garfield Boulevard in the presence of his nine-year-old son.

On the humid night of July 13, 1912, Max Annenberg fought a gun duel with a rebellious subordinate, Harold Whipple, in no less public a place than the heart of the Loop. Uniformed officers stood among the onlookers, watching the combatants blast away at each other. While Whipple's attention was fixed on Max, Moe Annenberg attacked his blind side, pushed a Colt into his groin, and warned him to drop his gun or become a eunuch. Stunned, Whipple complied, and the policemen came forward to take him into custody. When they went so far as to salute Moe for his bravery, the gangster grinned and waved them away.

The *American* thugs, lacking the bloody leadership that the Annenbergs supplied their men, roamed the streets and indulged in random acts of terrorism. One shot up a Madison Street trolley when he saw that none of the papers being read were Hearst's. A gang ravaged the el station at Wellington Avenue when a woman news dealer there refused to carry the *American*.

Perhaps the lack of structure attracted O'Banion and kept him from deserting Hearst for McCormick as the Annenbergs had done. He had always rebelled at excessive direction; he was a compliant, observant pupil only until he figured he had learned all he needed to. Then he had to strike out and go his own way. Much would be made of his independent streak later in his career, but in truth O'Banion only followed the cherished Chicago tradition of making other people's ideas work for you, instead of vice versa.

The circulation wars, which reached their zenith in 1913, received next to no press coverage save in the independent *Inter-Ocean* and *Daily Socialist*. The *Tribune* and *American* dutifully reported individual acts of violence lest they lose credibility, but not in the context of a war. Ferdinand Lundberg explained, "The news stories falsified events to make it seem as if union labor was causing the trouble. But even at the later stage, no news of the happenings went over the Associated Press wires, which were controlled by the Chicago publishers. Nor did the New York newspapers and magazines carry an account of the Chicago terror."

Enough deaths were registered in the county clerk's ledgers and enough injuries treated in city hospitals to assure future cynics that the circulation wars did occur, and that subsequent accounts of them were not embellished. Another reminder lay in their aftermath, as many of the combatants used skills and contacts they had acquired to expand into other fields, such as unions, gambling, and vice. Like O'Banion, they would be heard from again when Prohibition made a joke out of law and order and handed the country over to organized crime.

The men who wrote and sometimes created the news at the *American* were as ruthless in their own way as any gangster. They were also colorful, larger-than-life characters whose doings could have made excellent vaudeville.

Topping the list was the man at the top, Editor Walter Howey. Howey had a meek, unassuming appearance. His blondish hair was neatly combed at all times, he wore polka-dot ties, and his wire-rimmed glasses gave him an owlish countenance. His only physical feature that might be termed unsettling was his glass eye, whose immobility posed an eerie contrast to the quick glances of his good one. Playwright and one-time Chicago reporter Ben Hecht credited this mild-looking man with an ability to "plot like Cesare Borgia and strike like Genghis Khan."

Howey had considerable influence and wielded it like a weapon. Reporters from other papers would enter state offices for information about upcoming murder trials only to learn that the staff would only talk to journalists from the *American.* Howey had a high-ranking state official's resignation in his desk drawer and was ready to publish it if refused a favor. He had caught the politician in question with his hands in some dirty business and blackmailed the resignation out of him, thereby acquiring a useful pawn. Rumor had it that Walter Howey had several such letters tucked away someplace safe.

Howey's influence even launched the career of one of Hollywood's greatest silent-film stars. In 1917 he persuaded movie mogul D. W. Griffith to give his niece Kathleen Morrison a six-month contract in exchange for help in getting Griffith's controversial epic *Birth of a Nation* past the Chicago censors. At Howey's suggestion, Miss Morrison changed her name to Colleen Moore and went on to become one of the film industry's most beloved actresses.

Foremost among the *Examiner*'s daredevil reporting team was Charles MacArthur, a tall, lanky character with more talent for hellraising than reporting. He had worked for the *Tribune* before World War I but, after a brief spell in the artillery, took a job with Hearst. He found a kindred spirit in *Daily News* scribe Ben Hecht, and between the two of them, they turned Chicago journalism into a chapter from vaudeville. When Carl Wanderer, who had murdered his pregnant wife, was sent to the gallows in 1921, MacArthur and Hecht persuaded him to read a letter denouncing their editors while he stood on the scaffold. The plan went awry when Wanderer's arms were strapped to his sides, making it impossible for him to read the pages they had given him—but it was the thought that counted, and MacArthur and Hecht had many such thoughts.

MacArthur's wildness was a forging element in his friendship with Dean O'Banion. O'Banion got along well with reporters, a trait he displayed even when rolling in his bootlegging millions, but in MacArthur he saw a rabble-rouser after his own heart. One of their favorite pastimes was their midnight "bullfight." After a few hours of saloon-hopping, they would climb into O'Banion's car, and the gangster would drive to the corner of Michigan Avenue and Randolph Street. There O'Banion would press the gas pedal to the floor and speed down the sidewalk all the way to Twelfth Street, yelling and cheering like a high-spirited college boy. Beat cops and pedestrians had to get out of the way quickly, and it was probably more due to their vigilance than O'Banion's that no one was ever injured.

The young hoodlum, impressed and likely encouraged by his reporter cronies, decided to try his hand at writing. He did a few literary pieces and in the 1920 Illinois census gave his occupation as "newspaper reporter." The enthusiasm soon faded, as his slugger activities left him with little time or inclination to pursue a journalism career.

It was during those roaring years that O'Banion perfected the art of hijacking. Whenever a *Tribune* truck drove within striking range, he would jump onto the running board, coldcock the driver, and take possession of the vehicle, which he would then drive down to the river to dispose of its freshly printed contents. Sometimes he and his cronies would come across *Tribune* thugs desecrating the *Examiner* in like manner, and a gun battle would erupt. Bloody newspapers and bodies were a gruesome but not uncommon sight in the Chicago River.

The worst of the circulation wars were over by 1920, when Prohibition gave the sluggers something more lucrative to fight over than Hearst or McCormick paychecks. Some of the key players went into bootlegging, while others went on to have semi-respectable careers in journalism.

Max Annenberg left the *Tribune* and went to New York to manage the circulation department for the *Daily News.* His brother, Moe, migrated to Milwaukee and founded a news bureau that specialized in sporting events. Eventually he took possession of several racing publications and became a major news mogul. He suffered a minor embarrassment when one of his few non-sports holdings, *Baltimore Brevities,* earned him an indictment for sending obscene material through the mail, but his solid position in the industry remained unshaken. His son, Walter Annenberg, became publisher of the *Miami Daily Tribune* and later served as Ronald Reagan's ambassador to Great Britain.

Charles MacArthur married actress Helen Hayes in 1926. (His ex-wife, reporter Caryl Frink, sued her glamorous replacement for "alienation of affection.") He and Ben Hecht put their pens together the following year and wrote a play called *The Front Page,* a spoof of the newspaper industry. It was not their last creative collaboration, and they are still remembered in film and theater circles as masters of black satire. MacArthur prepared for his death in 1956 by writing with his typical cynicism, "I don't think God is interested in us after puberty. He is only interested in our births, for this requires His magic. Our dying requires only His indifference."

Edward Dean Sullivan became sporting editor of the *Examiner* and later authored at least two books. He wrote extensively of his friendship with O'Banion. In *Rattling The Cup on Chicago Crime,* he related the now legendary anecdote about O'Banion stopping him and asking where he could find a box of the best cigars. He explained that he had been going across the Madison Street Bridge that morning, lost in thought, when a car behind him backfired. He had been suspicious that someone was following him, and mistaking the noise for assassin gunfire, drew his own weapon and shot the only man he saw. He showed Sullivan a news clipping describing the shooting of one Arthur Vadis by an unseen assailant. O'Banion, remorseful, wanted to send Vadis some cigars in apology.

Whether this incident really took place or not is a matter of debate, as a search of Chicago dailies for that period failed to turn up an account of Vadis's wounding. Sullivan put forth this story and others to present himself to the public as a gang authority. No matter that the gangsters who were supposedly his closest friends were all dead at the time of publication. Sullivan had, if nothing else, a shrewd sense of timing.

O'Banion retired from the circulation wars with a keener sense of ambition. After working for a big shot like Hearst, he wanted to be one. Between his salary at the paper and the proceeds from his safe-cracking and robberies, he earned more in a night than most men of that era took home each week. But it wasn't money that obsessed O'Banion so much as power.

He had learned to appreciate the value of clout from his earliest days in Chicago, when he had seen the harried police defer to the vicious but politically insulated Market Streeters. As a Hearst hooligan, he saw firsthand not only how the graft system worked, but also who was on the take and for how much. Once for sale, always for sale.

The groundwork for Dean O'Banion's ascent into power was already in place. He had charisma and intelligence, a reputation acquired through his association with Reiser and the Hearst forces, and a good understanding of how Chicago worked. Now he awaited his chance.

7

NOBLE EXPERIMENT

December 30, 1919

IT WAS BUT ONE DAY AWAY from what promised to be the most memorable New Year's Eve Chicago had ever witnessed. Balsam Christmas wreaths and red ribbons still adorned the telephone poles along the major thoroughfares, and stores windows retained their holiday lighting and adornments. The air was electric with more festive anticipation than usual, for not only a New Year but also a much-publicized New Era was on the horizon.

The American people had a short time left in which to drink legally. On January 17, 1920, thanks to passage of the Volstead Act, Prohibition would become the law of the land. Liquor wholesalers who had once despaired of ever clearing out their back stock did a brisk trade selling to businesses and citizens alike. Even the lowest saloons suddenly found themselves crowded with customers who might otherwise have passed them with a shudder. Hotels and restaurants had been stocking their bars and wine cellars for weeks in anticipation of the December 31 parties. As memorable as New Year's Eve 1919 promised to be, judging from the unprecedented liquor sales, no one planned on being able to remember it.

O'Banion was walking south on Wells Street that morning, hands jammed into his coat pockets and collar turned up against the freezing wind. After crossing Randolph, he found his path blocked by a flatbed truck that had backed into an alley beside the Bismarck Hotel (the hotel's name had officially been changed to the Randolph after anti-German sentiments gripped the city during World War I, but it was still popularly known as the Bismarck). Stamping his feet to stay warm, O'Banion waited for the truck to retreat farther into the alley. He had little choice; snow piled along both sides of Wells Street meant an awkward climb to get around the nose of the vehicle and pass it. Other pedestrians joined him in his predicament until a small crowd was standing around, shivering and cursing. The truck driver watched them with visible amusement, for some reason making no effort to move and free up the sidewalk.

O'Banion became curious about the tarpaulin-covered cargo and lifted the canvas to take a peek. He saw stacked cases of Grommes and Ulrich whiskey, and recognized an opportunity immediately.

He approached the cab of the truck and signaled to the driver, who leaned out the window in response. With a speed that belied his bulk, O'Banion sprang onto the running board, got the driver in a headlock, and pounded him unconscious with his other fist, in which he clenched a roll of nickels to intensify the blows. No one interfered, as such sights were not uncommon in Chicago, and besides which, the driver had done little to arouse onlooker sympathy. O'Banion jumped down, pulled the truck door open, and propped his dazed target against the frosty brick wall of the hotel. He got behind the wheel, guided the vehicle the rest of the way into the street, and drove off.

As the scene of the crime faded into the distance, O'Banion asked himself where he was going to take his liquid bonanza. After driving about aimlessly for several minutes, he decided to head for the Maxwell Street garage of his friend Nails Morton, who used the place as a depot to strip and resell stolen cars. Morton, a Jewish gang leader with dozens of West Side saloonkeepers on his contacts list, agreed to help O'Banion find buyers for the stolen booze in exchange for a percentage of the take. Within twenty minutes, all of the stolen cases were sold. Even the truck was purchased, by a brewery in Peoria. O'Banion came home that night several thousand dollars richer. He now knew what his latest business venture would be.

At midnight on January 16, 1920, Prohibition became law. The teetotalers were jubilant. Longtime crusaders such as the Anti-Saloon League and the Women's Christian Temperance Union congratulated themselves and on another for finally bringing about the birth of a new nation, one whose citizens would have sweet breath and white, sinless hearts brimming with Christian love. Demon rum, they had always preached, was responsible for the poverty and violence that shamed any town evil or misguided enough to harbor saloons. The Prohibitionists knew that their methods in getting the new law passed had been underhanded at times, but they responded to any criticism with the insistence that the end justified the means.

The Prohibition movement had been an American political force since the early 1800s, when the Methodist Church, embarrassed by the epidemic of dipsomaniacal ministers, began a crusade against the manufacture and sale of liquor. It found support among teetotalers and citizens who, although not opposed to the occasional glass of wine or beer, were repulsed by the filthy dram shops, gin mills, and saloons where men and women ruined themselves mentally and physically. The Anti-Saloon League, Women's Christian Temperance Union, Methodist Board of Temperance, Prohibition, and Public Morals, and other groups campaigned politically for a dry America.

They did not limit themselves to verbal haranguing. One of their most effective champions was the fiery, white-haired Carry Nation, who spent ten years tearing through American saloons and smashing beer kegs, liquor bottles, and everything else with her trademark hatchet. Her presence inspired as much fear as any gangster. Another dry hero, Dr. Charles Foster Kent, professor of biblical history at Yale, "fixed" the Bible as shamelessly as hoodlums fixed elections and sports results. After he was through, Judges 9:13, which originally read, "And the vine said unto them, 'shall I leave my wine, which cheereth God and man?'" now appeared as ". . . 'shall I leave my juice that gladdens God and men?'" Also, 2 Samuel 6:3, which had formerly read, "And he dealt among all the people, even among the whole multitude of Israel, as well to the women as to men, to everyone, a cake of bread, and a good piece of flesh, and a flagon of wine" now appeared as, "And he distributed to the whole assembled multitude a roll of bread, a portion of meat, and a cake of raisins."

Unethical or not, it worked. In 1907 Georgia was the first state to proclaim itself dry, followed soon afterward by Tennessee, Oklahoma, West Virginia, North Carolina, and Mississippi. A constitutional amendment was presented in 1914 before the House of Representatives, but lacked the two-thirds majority needed to carry it through. It was a close enough call to suggest that a teetotal victory was only a matter of time. The Anti-Saloon League and Women's Christian Temperance Union proclaimed their hopes for a "saloonless nation in 1920," celebrating the three-hundredth anniversary of the landing of the Pilgrims.

For the Prohibitionists, the First World War was a prize opportunity to drive their philosophy into the law books. They charged that liquor adversely affected the war effort, and made soldiers and factory hands less competent. The grain used to make whiskey, they said, was better used for bread in this time of rationing. Seen in a wartime light, their arguments made perfect sense. The dry forces also skillfully played on the rampant prejudice against the Germans by hinting that most beer and liquor being produced had German investment or craft involved.

When the Eighteenth Amendment, drawn up by Texas Senator Morris Sheppard, returned to the Senate in 1917, it was rapidly approved. It was ratified by the House of Representatives, and in January 1919 the requisite thirty-six states voted in favor of nationwide Prohibition. Senator. Andrew Volstead of Minnesota drew up legislation for its enforcement, claiming, "Law does regulate morality, has regulated morality since the Ten Commandments."

President Woodrow Wilson had last-minute doubts about the feasibility of the Eighteenth Amendment and vetoed it, but the Senate overrode him. The Volstead Act, national Prohibition, went into effect on January 17, 1920.

In Norfolk, Virginia, religion met vaudeville in a memorable dry celebration. Ten thousand spectators in a tightly packed tabernacle watched as flamboyant evangelist Billy Sunday staged a mock funeral for John Barleycorn. A horsedrawn hearse carrying an effigy of Barleycorn paraded through the streets, escorted by twenty pallbearers and followed by a sorrow-wracked figure in a devil's costume. After the bizarre procession arrived at the tabernacle, Sunday preached his sermon while the devil and some designated drunks languished on a mourner's bench.

"Goodbye, John," the preacher said grandly. "You were God's worst enemy; you were hell's best friend. I hate you with a perfect hatred. I love to hate you. . . . The reign of tears is over. The slums will soon be only a memory. We will turn our prisons into factories, and our jails into storehouses and corn crib. Men will walk upright now, women will smile, and children will laugh. Hell will be forever for rent."

Former President William Howard Taft was less optimistic. He commented, "The business of manufacturing alcohol, liquor, and beer will go out of the hands of the law-abiding members of the community and will be transferred to the quasi-criminal class."

The "quasi-criminal class" could count on making a fortune. In 1788 a congressman, Fisher Ames, had said, "If any man supposes that a mere law can turn the taste of a people from ardent spirits to malt liquors, he has a most romantic notion of legislative power." He was commenting on a period of Prohibition in Georgia's history. When the British Parliament forbade the importation of rum and brandy into the state, the colonists suddenly lost all interest in building up Georgia and devoted their energies to getting liquor on the sly. Rumrunners shipped boatloads of booze to them. Speakeasies, called "nurseries of villainy" by contemporary writers, sprang up throughout the colony. Officials earned fortunes in bribes, and no bootlegger was ever convicted because few jurors saw the trade as criminal. The ban was finally scrapped and, coincidentally, public drunkenness plummeted.

With ratification of the Volstead Act, history was set to repeat itself on a much larger scale. The country's more ambitious, forward-thinking criminals realized they had been presented with an opportunity that would easily bring in as much money as gambling and prostitution, possibly more. Those with the means bought shares in breweries and distilleries, eager to get an edge on what looked like the most profitable forbidden market of all time.

The drys had hoped to staunch the flow of criminality by drying up the country. What they had seriously underestimated was the rebellious spirit of the American people. In 1776 they had defied British rule; in 1920 they would react to curtailed drinking with equal spite. Those who might never have abused alcohol otherwise began to get drunk at the wild parties that always pop up in defiance of a strict regime, and the underworld was all too happy to help out.

Bootlegging would give gangsters the wherewithal to buy police protection and defy the law like never before.

The first recorded violation of the new law took place just fifty-nine minutes after it went into effect. A gang of masked men broke into two freight cars in a Chicago railroad yard, tied up the night watchman, and stole one hundred thousand dollars' worth of whiskey stamped for medicinal use. Later that night, barrels of alcohol disappeared from a Chicago warehouse and a whiskey-laden truck was hijacked. Eleven days later, Prohibition agents raided a North Side drinking hole, the Red Lantern, and made forty arrests, distinguishing the city as the site of the first federal speakeasy raid. By June 1920 almost five hundred indictments for illegal boozing had been posted on Chicago trial calendars. The federal Prohibition administrator for Illinois estimated that during the first six months under the new law, Chicago doctors had issued three hundred thousand dubious prescriptions for medicinal liquor.

Prohibition was off to a bad start.

The number of agents assigned to enforce the Volstead Act numbered at any given time between fifteen hundred and twenty-three hundred. Chicago was policed by a microscopic force of 134 agents who were also responsible for all of Illinois, Iowa, and part of Wisconsin. Anyone caught on a liquor violation was eligible for a maximum one-thousand-dollar fine and a year in jail, but so few judges handed down these harsh sentences that those agents who were not corrupt must have wondered what they were getting paid for.

Prohibition agents did not become civil servants until January 1, 1927, when the Federal Bureau of Prohibition was reorganized. The early defenders of public sobriety were appointed through a political patronage system that did not demand honesty as a prerequisite. The pay was so low—twelve hundred to two thousand dollars a year—and the law itself such a flagrantly disregarded joke that only the very pure of heart resisted bribes from bootleggers to keep their eyes averted.

Instead of purifying the nation, Prohibition corrupted it. One only had to follow a shipment of liquor from Ontario, Canada, to its Chicago destination to see how those entrusted with enforcing the law could be just as intent on exploiting it as any gangster. The moment that the valuable cargo crossed the border, a crooked railway employee at its first stopover would get it through, and then call an equally crooked fellow worker in Chicago, advising him to expect it. If the Prohibitionists had hoped that U.S. Customs and railway officials would join the crusade to keep the demon drink out, they were soon disillusioned. Sometimes, if a booze cargo were especially valuable, the railroad worker would tip off a greedy Prohibition agent and initiate an intricate double-cross.

The ambitious agent would intercept the liquor, hold it, and notify the waiting bootlegger that release could be bought at a hefty price. The gangster always paid, not willing to risk losing the shipment, and the ransom would be split between the agent and the railroad employee. This extortion scheme was regularly practiced until the bootlegging gangs began uniting into syndicates. They had decided early in the game that federal agents would be risky kills, but turncoat rail workers were easier revenge targets, especially since falling in front of oncoming trains was one of their occupational hazards.

Dean O'Banion was forced by necessity to pay off these opportunists and be civil to them, but deep inside he despised them. His thoughts on the matter blistered the ears of a cop listening in one night on a wiretap placed on his flower shop phone. A trucker for Johnny Torrio called O'Banion in desperation. Two cops had intercepted his beer truck on a West Side street and shaken down him and his companions for $250. They told the trucker that he could "buy" the beer from their custody for another $300.

"A couple of cops just hijacked us," he complained to O'Banion. "They took $250 off us but they say that they won't give us the beer unless we come through with $300 more. How about it."

"Three hundred dollars?" O'Banion bellowed. "Three hundred dollars to them bums? Why, say, I can get 'em knocked off for half that much."

He was angry enough to do it, too, and both trucker and eavesdropping cop knew it. The officer notified police headquarters, and squads of riflemen were dispatched to search the West Side streets in order to prevent a slaughter. The trucker, not wanted to be party to a cop-killing, called Johnny Torrio. After a brief conversation, he called O'Banion back.

"Say, Deanie," he said, "I just been talking to Johnny, and he says to let the cops have the three hundred. He says he don't want no trouble."

Al Capone, who later typified the Prohibition-era gangster not only in Chicago but also throughout the world, could have appreciated O'Banion's feelings. He also had a hatred for the greedy cops, politicians, and dry agents that he had to pay off in order to survive. He complained once, "A crook is a crook, and there's something healthy about his frankness in the matter. But a guy who pretends he is enforcing the law and steals on his authority is a swell snake. The worst type of these punks is the big politician, who gives about half his time to covering up so that no one will know he's a thief. A hard-working crook will—and can—buy these birds by the dozen, but right down in his heart he hates the sight of them."

The Volstead Act offered a set of strict but easily manipulated rules for the future preparation and use of beer and alcohol. Brewers had the option of keeping their places open to produce "near beer," a weak concoction with less than 0.5 percent alcohol, which they made by brewing beer via the usual method and then siphoning off the alcohol to the permitted level. The brewers realized a handsome profit by selling the excess alcohol to bootleggers, who later reintroduced it into the near beer via hypodermic needles. The rejuvenated brew, called "needle beer," was considered inferior to the real stuff.

Physicians could prescribe hard liquor for medicinal purposes, opening for the medical community a new opportunity for profit. Permits to handle industrial alcohol were granted to anyone who wanted to supply it to cosmetic firms, toilet water manufacturers, and other legitimate users, but little of the product ever found legal use. A dangerous percentage was mixed with flavor and colorants, bottled, and sold as whiskey, rye, bourbon, or whatever the bootlegger decided to label it. Anyone unfortunate enough to get one of these bad bottles could suffer a range of alcohol-poisoning effects, most notably blindness, paralysis, impotency, and death.

Hazards like these did not deter people from buying anything bottled as liquor, especially in Chicago, where the citizenry had voiced loud opposition to being dry from day one. They had rejected an earlier referendum calling for closure of the vile Levee saloons and had no intention of giving up their booze. Even Chief of Police Charles Fitzsimmons admitted that the case was hopeless. "Sixty percent of my police are in the bootleg business," he said.

Nails Morton, who had assisted O'Banion in disposing of his heisted liquor, was a rare breed of gangster in that he was also a war hero. Born Samuel J. Markovitz in Chicago's Jewish ghetto on Maxwell Street, Morton had fought in France during the Great War as part of the 131st Illinois Infantry and had won the Croix de Guerre and a battlefield commission for leading his squad over the top despite severe shrapnel wounds. Back in Chicago, he resumed his business as a gambler and specialist in stolen merchandise.

The Jewish community revered Morton because he defended it from "Jew baiters" who derived malicious delight from breaking temple windows, smashing vendors' carts, and assaulting Jews in the streets. His loyalty to those of his religious background allowed him to retain their respect despite his well-publicized crimes. Outwardly, he was a refined gentleman, dressing well and adopting genteel mannerisms.

It was Morton who gave O'Banion the ambition and means to become a bootlegging boss. The Jewish gangster already had contacts in port cities such as Detroit, thanks to his longtime fencing of stolen automobiles, and these contacts were having liquor run in from Windsor, Amherstberg, and other Canadian points of exit. Morton, being primarily a fence, suggested to O'Banion that the two of them throw in together and use each other's talents (Morton's contacts and O'Banion's organized gang), pointing out that a controlling interest in the liquor traffic would generate far greater profits than warehouse looting or hijacking alone. O'Banion agreed; up to that point, thievery had been his only means of obtaining product for his growing list of customers.

He recognized in Prohibition an opportunity not only for wealth but for power. Since the turn of the century, the king of high-rolling crime in his North Side home turf had been Mont Tennes, the racing-wire czar. Tennes was not absolute in his rule; he only wanted to be top dog in the race-results business and did not care who chose to control bootlegging, as long as they left his operation alone. Supremacy over booze distribution on the North Side was therefore open to anyone strong and resourceful enough to seize it.

O'Banion knew that he had little to fear from the police, who took money from gamblers, pimps, and news sluggers, and were equally accommodating to bootleggers. Even cops who might have refused money from a lowlife pimp would be more receptive to bribes from bootleggers, who were popularly regarded as public benefactors. Some officers, if Chief Fitzmorris was accurate, were handling liquor themselves. The biggest boodler of all was Big Bill Thompson, the mayor. There was a surplus in the city treasury when Thompson won a second term in office in 1919, but already there was a $4.5 million deficit. Payoffs were more than tolerated—they were welcome.

Chicago city government at this time was as farcical as the new law. Charles Fitzmorris, a former city editor on Hearst's *American*, was the third chief of police appointed by Big Bill, the previous two having been caught in crooked deals and dismissed after intense public outcry. He was, at age thirty-six, the youngest ever to hold the position. When Thompson publicly gave him the order to drive out the crooks—those who were not paying, at least—and restore Chicago's good name, Fitzmorris obediently smashed up a few pool halls and busted some floating crap games. Nobody important was ever inconvenienced. After filling the city jails with vagabonds, drunks, and hoodlums without cash or connections, Fitzmorris slacked off. He had gone as far as he was going to but exulted to the press that the crooks had been driven out and the city cleaned up.

One of the only members of the Thompson administration who was not corrupt to the point of absurdity was Robert E. Crowe, the state's attorney for Cook County. Born in Peoria in 1879, Crowe had graduated from Yale and entered politics as an assistant state's attorney to John E. W. Wayman, the reluctant crusader who had clamped down on the Levee in 1912. He became an assistant city corporation counsel under the Democratic administration of Carter Harrison II, served a year as Cook County Circuit Court judge, and in 1919 was appointed the youngest-ever chief justice of the Criminal Court. Heavily built, with a wide forehead, strong jaw, and tiny, close-set eyes that shrank even more behind his thick glasses, Crowe presented an imposing courtroom figure both on and off the bench. He married Candida Cuneo, the daughter of a wealthy Italian merchant who had founded the city's oldest wholesale produce firm.

When he became state's attorney, he upped the standards of recruitment to his team, hiring law school graduates with a bright future. Through appeals to administrative and civic communities, he changed the quota of judges available to the state attorney's office from six to twenty. He asked for, and got, an additional yearly appropriation of one hundred thousand dollars to hire special investigators, and through his efforts, a thousand more policemen were added to the city force. He never hesitated to try the hardest and most politically explosive cases himself, even when the potential risk to his career was huge.

For all his legal acumen and fine record as a lawyer, Crowe was a failure when it came to making a dent in the Chicago underworld's reign. He tried more than a few cases involving high-profile gangsters during his tenure as state's attorney, but did not secure a single conviction. Almost all charges were nol-prossed. This oddity in an otherwise successful courtroom record was attributed to the fact that Crowe, like most of his political cronies, employed gang help at the polls when running for office.

Hymie Weiss appeared before Crowe on a larceny charge in January 1920, while the latter was still a judge. Keeping his expression and voice severe, Crowe told the gangster, "There is not enough evidence here to convict, I am sorry to say. I have heard of you, young man. The police tell me you are in all kinds of mischief and just laugh at the law. I warn you to straighten up. Society will not stand for this sort of thing. If you ever come before me again, and there is enough evidence to convict, I'll give you the limit. I hope it never happens. Now think of your mother and try to do better."

He neglected to mention that the night before, he had received both O'Banion and Weiss at his home to secure their backing in his run for state's attorney. Robert Crowe had no real love for the gangster element, but he recognized its support as a necessary ingredient for political success in Chicago.

O'Banion dismissed the thought of interference from Crowe or Fitzmorris and went on with his plans. Under the guidance of Nails Morton, he invested money in North Side breweries and distilleries operating under the guise of producing legal near beer and industrial alcohol. He came to an agreement with the owners/operators: They would see to the day-to-day operations and keep the product flowing, and he would pay off the police, deal with interlopers and hijackers, and "take the rap" in the event of a liquor raid. Many brewers and distillers were willing to go along with the deal rather than close up or produce within Prohibition guidelines.

Members of Reiser's gang and acquaintances he had known since adolescence drifted toward him as he became more organized.

Like him, they were enthused by the prospect of earning big money, but needed a leader. The North Side Gang accumulated members slowly but surely; however, the core group around O'Banion never changed.

His best friend and second in command was the shrewd Pole Hymie Weiss. Weiss was a natural strategist with enough business sense to compensate for the laissez-faire attitude of his cohorts. Some sources credit him with steering the Reiser Gang into bootlegging. O'Banion actually initiated the venture, but Weiss steered it onto firmer ground, cementing deals that O'Banion might have mishandled and seeing to the fine details that his wilder friend would have found tedious. The same formula of contrasts that created their friendship made them click as a business team. O'Banion's easy sociability made him a natural negotiator, and Weiss saw to the business side of things after the ice had been broken.

The rest of the core group were as individual; Vincent "the Schemer" Drucci (real name Victor di Ambrosia and known as "Schemer" because of his tirelessly wild imagination) was a burglar and jewel thief who, like Nails Morton, had fought honorably during the War. Drucci had made his criminal debut by smashing up public telephones and looting the coins inside. Born in Chicago to John and Rose di Ambrosia, both Italian immigrants, he had been friends with O'Banion since adolescence. Drucci's effectiveness as a businessman was minimized by his rampaging temper, making his enforcing and intimidating abilities his primary asset to the gang.

"Drucci could be a crazy bastard when set off, but he also had the wildest sense of humor," a former truck driver for the North Side Gang recalled. "Once he got ahold of a priest's outfit, put it on, and stood in front of a café on Rush Street. Every time a couple would walk by, he'd say, 'Nice ass, honey,' and shock the hell out of them. When the girl turned around, he'd say, 'Not you, lady, your fellow.' Then they'd be shocked again. Once Dean joined in on the fun by pretending to kick the shit out of him. People were going nuts, thinking that some priest was being beaten up."

Drucci's position in the gang disputes the claim that O'Banion hated Italians. Writers and students of the Capone era have put it forth that an inherent spite toward Italians caused O'Banion's later problems with Johnny Torrio and Al Capone. Those who knew O'Banion personally dispute this.

"Deanie had nothing whatsoever against Italians, I don't know how that story ever got around," the former truck driver reminisced further. "Not too many people knew, but he understood the language really well and could even speak it some. I heard him myself, talking on the phone with someone, a customer, I think, because he was taking notes. I don't think he spoke it like a native, because after a few minutes he switched to English, but he knew enough. He told me that where he grew up on the near North Side, you either learned a little Italian or you moved. It's been said that he was killed because he said 'To hell with the Sicilians' or something like that. Bullshit. I heard him say 'To hell with those damn Irish' once when an Irish truck driver kept showing up late. It didn't mean he hated the Irish, did it? It had nothing to do with hating any type of people in general, it was just something people said back then when they were pissed at one guy or gang in particular."

The upper echelon also included Dan McCarthy, dubbed "Dapper Dan" by the press because of his unusual good looks and fashion smarts. McCarthy was a labor racketeer, serving as a business agent for the Journeyman Plumbers Union. Vicious when cornered, he shot a cop who had come to arrest him for desertion from the army in 1918. McCarthy proved to be as adept at liquor hijacking as he was at infiltrating unions. He joined O'Banion, Weiss, and Drucci on many a nighttime foray into Chicago's side streets, where they'd lie in wait for likely targets or a specific vehicle, if they'd been tipped off in advance.

Maxie Eisen, while not an active member of O'Banion's Gang, was on intimate terms with them. He was first and foremost an extortionist, targeting unions such as the Jewish Chicken Killers and threatening independent entrepreneurs into paying to avoid property damage. For all his parasitic actions, Eisen was esteemed in the underworld as an arbitrator. He had a cool head, a sharp mind, and Solomon-like wisdom. He, O'Banion, Weiss, Alterie, McCarthy, and West Side Jewish gangster Jacob Epstein backed ex-policeman Warren Levin in the purchase of the Cragin Products Company, which denatured alcohol. Eisen gave Levin a private office over his restaurant at Roosevelt Road and Blue Island Avenue, and through the ex-cop the North Siders sold a greater percentage of the Cragin output to bootleggers specializing in moonshine and strengthening the alcohol level of near beer.

O'Banion began hiring freelance truck drivers to meet his Canadian shipments and transport them from Detroit and other U.S. entry points to Chicago. One of them was twenty-two-year-old E. Barnett, who went on to work for the North Side Gang until 1924.

"It was April 1921," Barnett recalled in a 1988 interview. "I hadn't been able to get much work back home, and my brother, who'd gone to Chicago the previous fall, wrote to say that the construction company he was working for was looking to hire men for the spring and summer. I decided I might as well go.

"I got a job, and stayed in a rooming house on North Clark with my brother. But I got laid off in the fall, and was looking for work when I ran into one of the guys from the construction site one day. He asked me if I'd found a job yet. I hadn't. He says, "Can you drive a truck?" I said yeah. He says, "You aren't teetotal, are you?" I said, "Not at all." He said, "I know a guy who wants to hire truckers to haul in booze long distance. But I got to let you know now, it's Dean O'Banion.'

"I knew who O'Banion was. So did everybody in Chicago. He'd been mentioned a lot in the newspapers, and anyone who took a drink on the North Side knew that they were buying his stuff. My friend wasn't warning me about him as such, he was just trying to let me know that this could be dangerous work. It wasn't milk I'd be hauling for miles and miles, it was liquor. You heard about hijackings all the time. This was before the gangs started warring with each other, but there were still the independents who wanted to earn cash by stealing stuff and peddling it door to door. The big gangs cleaned up a lot of those little bastards, but there was always someone wanting to try his luck."

The following weekend his friend took him to a Surf Street address. "It was a house that O'Banion owned, and where he sometimes met people. I'd made up my mind to take the job if the money was good. With all that booze at stake, I figured that I'd have an escort on the run or be given a gun myself, and that didn't bother me. I'd used one before, shooting deer when I was a kid in Kansas, and if I was ever in a spot where it was me or some bastard pointing a pistol at me, I wouldn't be the one going down. But mind you, I wasn't going to do it for nothing."

Barnett's first impression of O'Banion left him surprised. "I can still remember O'Banion opening the door to us before we'd even gone up the steps. The first thing I thought was, *My God, he's short.* I'm five-foot-seven, and I could look down at him. The next thought was, *He doesn't look tough at all!* Of course, he was tough! You didn't get to where he was in Chicago by being Creampuff Charlie. But he didn't look it.

"He was very well dressed, smiling, and had a tight handshake. He really looked like a banker or a lawyer, some high profession like that. The first thing he said to me was, 'Jimmy says you can drive a truck and that you're all right.' I said, 'Yeah, Jimmy's been known to tell the truth sometimes, Mr. O'Banion.' He liked that. He laughed and said, 'Come in then and let's talk about it. And call me Dean.'"

Over whiskey and coffee, O'Banion outlined the details of the proposed trucking job. While the three men sat at a dining room table, a fourth man stood out in the hallway and observed them with his hands crossed in front and gaze placid but alert. Barnett assumed him to be a bodyguard. Footsteps and voices could also be heard behind a closed door down the hall.

"He told me that he needed me to go to Detroit at least once a week to pick up a load of Canadian hard liquor. Whiskey, rum, brandy, that sort of stuff. He said he got all the beer he needed locally. I would pick up a truck at some place in advance, then drive to Detroit. I'd have someone with me riding shotgun and taking over the driving if need be. He'd give me thirty-five dollars a week. I said yes on the spot. Who wouldn't? I didn't know anyone else making that much just for driving. I gave him my number at the rooming house and he said he'd call the next day."

Barnett walked away from the meeting with a sincere admiration for his new employer. "He did like to boast about himself a bit, but Dean really had a way of talking to people. He didn't swear much and he was always respectful."

True to his word, O'Banion called the following afternoon. "He told me to be in front of the old Liberty Inn at eight o'clock sharp. I showed up, and pretty soon a truck pulled up with a Jew guy named Myers driving. He asked if I was Barnett, I said I was. He says, 'I'm your shotgun man,' and introduced himself. It took us around six hours to get to Detroit. We drove out of Illinois, down around through Indiana, and made it to Detroit at around two in the morning. We went to a blind pig, [a camouflaged, illegal saloon] on Third Street, in the railway yards. Myers told me to wait in the truck. The guys who met us seemed to know him, so he did all the talking. He was the one who paid them. He told me later that they were a gang called the Jew Navy, and that Dean dealt with them to bring whiskey in from Canada. I stayed in the truck until Myers called me to come help carry the whiskey crates up from the cellar, as one of their guys was sick and they were short a hand.

"That was it. We got some beer and sandwiches from the guys at the blind pig and then drove back. Nothing exciting happened. In fact, I was never hijacked once in all the years I worked for Dean. I never heard of his trucks being hijacked all that often, maybe because of the way he had his booze hauled in. He never sent a whole fleet of trucks out, like some guys did. He'd send one, maybe two at a time. Nobody pays much attention to one or two trucks, but a whole fleet would be noticed for sure.

"I liked running booze in for Dean. He paid well; he never stiffed his drivers like some of the other gangs did. I figured out why when he took me and my shotgun guy out for coffee after we hauled in two hundred crates from Detroit during a bad storm. We saw the shop owner yell at this poor waitress who had too many customers and not enough help. Dean couldn't keep his mouth shut. He hollered back at the owner, 'Why don't you treat her better, pal?' The guy didn't dare answer back; he knew who Dean was. He did stop yelling at her, though, and when she came over to give us refills, O'Banion slipped her ten bucks and said, 'You're too good for this, honey.'

"Dean told us that he thought the owner was a fool bastard to treat his help like dirt, because how's the girl going to do a good job when she's treated like a dog? He meant it, too. He really believed in treating his people well. His problem was that he didn't think quite so much of anyone he had to partner with, like the guys on the South Side. Sometimes he used to go on about how he thought that they were holding out on him, or not backing him up."

Barnett's recollections of Hymie Weiss were not as favorable.

"Weiss was different from O'Banion, not as friendly. I didn't really take to him as well, although he was always all right with me, because I did my job. I remember that he used to get these terrible headaches, and they even moved a little sofa into Dean's office so that he could lie down if he had to. One of the other drivers told me that once Weiss actually had a fit on the floor of the upstairs smoking room because the pain was so bad. He used to go into the hospital all the time for stuff like headaches and fainting, and I believe he once went to Hot Springs for treatment. But all told, Weiss was all right.

"Vince Drucci was another one I liked. He was a Sicilian, I think, a really snappy dresser and good-looking young guy. He was like Dean: If you crossed him, watch out, but if you were one of his people, he was great to you. He used to play practical jokes. He even got me once. When I parked my car in the delivery alley behind the flower shop, which I used to do whenever I had an overnight run, he came into the office where I was talking to Dean and my shotgun rider and asked me for my car keys. He said he needed to move my car so that he and a couple of the shop employees could clear the snow away from the delivery door. There was a blizzard that night, and the city used to miss the back streets all the time when snow was cleared. So I handed the keys over and listened to Dean's instructions until Drucci came back. He just gave me the keys, said thanks, and left there a little too quickly, now that I think of it.

"When I finished my smoke and went downstairs, I saw that he'd been busy with the snow all right—shoveling the shit into my goddamn car! I'm serious; the goddamn windows were white. Well, mister, I began cursing because I'd just bought the damn thing in the fall and the melting snow would ruin it now. Dean heard me yelling and came downstairs. When he saw it, he started laughing. I said, 'I don't find this goddamn funny.' He said, 'I guess I can laugh because it isn't my car.' One of the guys came in from the shop and says that my truck was out front. Dean said, 'Give me the keys and just go. I'll have it cleaned up for you.' He did, too. I can laugh about it now, but I didn't then. And I never did get Drucci back."

Barnett asserted that O'Banion never produced or sold the poisonous home brew that a lot of gangs specialized in because of its low production cost. In fact, he later had problems with the Genna Gang when they tried to push their rotgut on the sly on the North Side, targeting slum dwellers unable to afford the superior O'Banion product.

Alky-cooking, or producing booze at home in small stills, was the worst method in terms of hygiene and safety. It predominated in immigrant colonies where gangs were in control. Immigrants were given stills and told how to use them to extract alcohol from corn sugar, which was also supplied. In Chicago's Little Italy, which was ruled by the Gennas, stills were operated in apartments, houses, and shop backrooms, sending the reek of fermenting mash into the already fetid air.

Cooking in slum conditions guaranteed an unhealthy product. Rats, attracted by the smell of bubbling mash, would fall in the vats, drown, and become an unexpected ingredient in the final beverage. One raid on a West Side alky-making operation revealed that a cat had pursued its prey right into the vat, and neither succeeded in getting out. Next to this nauseating sight was an assortment of bottles bearing the labels of America's finest whiskies, all ready to be filled. Hosiery, gloves, and other unappealing ingredients were regularly found in home stills, and for every unsanitary barrel seized, hundreds more made their way to unsuspecting customers.

A less repugnant but still dangerous bootlegging practice was "cutting" bottles of legitimate liquor into several bottles of possibly deadly brew. Booze imported from abroad or pilfered from government warehouses was diluted with water to increase product volume and bring in many times what was paid for it. To add strength to the weakened product, the cutter put in fusil oil, creosote, and ethyl, the latter used to power automobiles. Coal tar dyes were mixed in to supply the rich dark coloring of good whiskey, rum, whatever. The resulting product looked and tasted like the genuine article, but could knock out an elephant. If too much fusil oil was added, a comatose stupor followed within hours of consumption, and if the drinker had a weak constitution, death sometimes followed. Scarcely a day went by without scores of alcohol poisoning deaths being reported in the papers.

No poisonous substances were ever used in the cutting-down process in O'Banion's operations, and his prices reflected the more expensive ingredients used to cut the liquor safely. O'Banion bottles were diluted with water and darkened with caramel, and contained more of the original liquor. He did charge more for his wares; six to nine dollars a bottle, whereas the going rate for the home-cooked stuff was three dollars. He relied on his breweries, distilleries, Canadian connections, and hijacked wares to maintain the supply of liquor, and did not at any time cultivate a home brew industry. He soon acquired a reputation for selling good, safe liquor, and his list of customers included the finest restaurants and nightclubs on the North Side.

As his business grew and fortunes increased, O'Banion began to dress and act the part of a successful businessman. He wore well-cut, expensive but conservative suits, all of which were specially tailored with three extra pockets—one under the left armpit, another in the right coat front, and the third behind the trouser zipper. These hidden niches were meant to carry firearms. Being ambidextrous, he could whip out any two guns at the same time. He tidied up his manners and vocabulary when out in public and ordered his men to do the same. Whenever he and his friends went on a social outing to the theater or a first-class restaurant, they wore tuxedos, spoke in civil tones, and behaved as if born to an elevated station in life. O'Banion, it was said, was a great civilizing influence on those around him. "We're big business without high hats," he often said to his men, to both impress and remind them.

He never did lose his potential for violence, though, and dealt viciously with hijackers and other encroachers. Judge John H. Lyle, in his memoirs, *The Dry and Lawless Years,* described how a hulking bootlegger of Polish extraction, Big Steve Wisniewski, hijacked a truckload of O'Banion liquor in July 1921. Lyle claimed that on O'Banion's orders, Hymie Weiss and some followers tracked Wisniewski to a Valley saloon, dragged him into a car waiting outside, and after driving north to Libertyville, shot him in the head and dumped the corpse. Wisniewski was the first recognized victim of the now legendary one-way ride, that method of motorized murder that allowed a victim to be transported into a more convenient killing spot, and Hymie Weiss has been a macabre celebrity as the first executioner.

Whether or not he actually did it is not known for sure, as Big Steve had also angered the Druggan–Lake Gang on the West Side by looting a liquor warehouse before they could get to it and then punching out Terry Druggan when confronted. Big Steve could have been the victim of either gang, and at any rate, there would be more Big Steves found during O'Banion's four-year reign, some of them having less ambiguous circumstances behind their deaths.

"I don't know anything about any killings," Barnett insisted, "but I do know that all that money and success in the booze business did not make Dean soft. Not at all. One night a group of us were at a chop suey joint on North Clark, not too far from the Liberty Inn where he used to work. This drunken idiot and his girl sat at a table close to ours, and the man started going at it with the name-calling while the woman sat there and cried. You couldn't help but stare at a scene like that. Suddenly the guy looks right at Dean, who was sitting on the outside of our booth.

"'What the hell are you looking at?' he says.

"'Not a hell of a lot,' Dean says back. 'What about you?'

"The guy gets up and comes right over. I was nervous as hell. He was big, and I felt sure that Dean or someone else would say to hell with it and just shoot him. But Dean just waited till he got close enough, then swung out his foot and kicked the guy in the kneecap. Hard. The guy fell down with his leg at a funny angle. Dean jumped out of his chair, got on top of him, and got him in a tight headlock. He pinned the guy's wrists with his other hand, and kept choking him until he begged for mercy. Good thing he did beg, because no one was helping him. Even the Chinese people who ran the place stood there and looked fascinated."

After listening to a few more minutes of pleading, O'Banion released his prisoner, got up, and rejoined his comrades with a pleased expression on his face. "I could tell that he was really proud of himself," Barnett said. "Some of the gang leaders were only big men because their guns made them big; without weapons they were nothing. Not O'Banion. Stick him in any situation and he'd have faced it with courage. Men like him were different from the Italian gangs, who had others do their fighting for them and were only as dangerous as the weapon they carried. And looking back now, I think that was one of the reasons why they hated him so much."

In 1920, Chicago's illustrious Blackstone Hotel hosted a historic political meeting. Republican party leaders chose Warren G. Harding as their presidential candidate after he swore under oath that there was no reason, moral or otherwise, why he would not do honor to his office.

It wasn't until after he was elected the twenty-eighth president of the United States that unsavory personal details came out. The married Harding had an illegitimate child by a much younger woman and at the same time kept a mistress, who also happened to be the wife of an old friend. His administration was rocked by one scandal after another. The chief of the Veteran Bureau sold contraband drugs to dealers, helped himself to some of the proceeds from war surplus sales, and accepted bribes from purchasing agents; the Alien

Property custodian was caught taking bribes and using the attorney general's personal aide as collector. The biggest embarrassment of all was the Teapot Dome scandal, which erupted when the secretary of the interior took a hundred-thousand-dollar bribe to allow an oil company to tap into the navy oil reserve at Teapot Dome, Wyoming.

Between the election of an opportunistic president and the commencement of Prohibition, the decade began with a roar. It was a lusty, free-spirited, and rowdy sound that set the tone of the nation for the next thirteen years.

8

TORRIO—THE LITTLE BIG FELLOW

JOHNNY TORRIO HAD BEEN WAITING for Prohibition—or something like it—to happen for a long time. A natural organizer who made it his business to understand human vices, he saw that the dry forces had handed American gangsters a gold mine on a platter, and was sure that he knew how to derive the maximum benefit from this disguised boon. Torrio, who had been overseeing a thriving prostitution and gambling empire in Chicago and its environs since 1909, tasked himself with making the city gangs see that "every man for himself" was not as beneficial a motto as "one for all and all for one."

Torrio was a genius. He had to be, in order to have survived his criminal apprenticeship in the slums of New York. At a time when the ideal gang leader was a brawny, solid-fisted fighter who earned his position by trouncing all his subordinates. Torrio was a short, pleasantly featured, almost daintily built figure. What he lacked in muscle power he more than compensated for with his brilliant mind and iron will. He had no need to be tough himself—by carefully and skillfully cultivating loyalty, he had more than enough leg breakers eager to enforce his dictates. Torrio never even carried a gun.

Born in 1882 in Orsara di Puglia, about sixty miles east of Naples, Torrio had been brought to the United States at the age of two by his widowed mother. Mrs. Torrio remarried around 1886, and her husband, Salvatore Caputo, ran a blind pig at 86 James Street on New York's Lower East Side. From age seven until well into his teens, Johnny worked for his stepfather as a porter. It was his entry into the world that existed outside the law. At nineteen, he became a boxing promoter under the pseudonym J. T. McCarthy (anyone seeking success in the sporting scene adopted an Irish name) and soon mastered the art of rigging matches. With the proceeds from his scams, Torrio bought a bar of his own on James Street. Determined to provide his clients with any nature of amusement they might want, he leased a nearby boarding house and store and opened a brothel and pool hall. Even at an early age, Torrio had dreams of becoming a public benefactor.

His sharp mind and criminal genius attracted followers, and by 1905 he headed his own gang, the James Street Boys. Under Torrio's direction the gang affiliated itself with the Five Pointers, a crew of fifteen hundred rough and tumble fighters that, at the time of the alliance, was embroiled in a fierce gang war with a mob led by the ape-like Monk Eastman. Torrio's choice of who to side with was influenced by his worship of the Five Pointer leader, Paul Kelly.

Kelly, whose real name was Paolo Antonini Vaccarelli, was an odd type to lead such a free-fisted gang. A short, elfin figure, he dressed with impeccable taste and spoke in soft, modulated tones. Only when angered did he let fly with the punch that had once made him a formidable boxer. His ability to command was unquestioned, and under his leadership the Five Pointers enjoyed riches stemming from gambling, prostitution, and extortion rackets practiced in the large area between Broadway and Bowery, and City Hall Park and Fourteenth Street.

Kelly aroused Torrio's instinctive desire to be a gentleman. A businessman at heart, the younger Italian assumed the appearance of one. He dressed more respectably, shucking his yegg cap and patched-up clothes in favor of a black derby and three-piece suits. He became conversational in topics such as politics, music, and literature, and repeated exposure to the opera soon transformed him into an ardent fan.

Broken-nosed brawlers like Monk Eastman sneered at Paul Kelly and John Torrio for what they perceived as weakness, but the day of the bruiser was almost at its end. The politicians were more inclined to deal with gangsters who eschewed gratuitous violence in favor of more subtle means of achieving their ends. Tammany Hall, New York's grafting political machine, got rid of Eastman in 1904 to prevent a war between his gang and the Five Pointers. When he was jailed for assault during a holdup, his patrons did nothing to secure his release and he received a ten-year jail sentence. Upon his release, Eastman fought in the Great War, and returned to New York to find that his old turf had been taken over by younger gangsters who had no intention of cutting him in on the action. He was shot to death on December 26, 1920, a forgotten shadow of what he had once been.

Johnny Torrio operated his business first in Manhattan and then Brooklyn. His followers nicknamed him "Little John" or "Terrible John," which could not have been a reflection of his fairness. On the contrary, he was scrupulously fair in the division of spoils, giving his men a bigger share than most gang leaders would have doled out. He believed there was plenty for everyone.

In 1909 Torrio received an urgent call for help from Chicago. He had a cousin there, Victoria Moresco, who was the wife of Big Jim Colosimo, the flashy Lord of the Levee. Black Hand gangs demanding money had plagued Colosimo since his ascent to wealth. He had dealt with some of the extortionists himself, killing at least one with his bear-paw hands. But they kept after him, and their anonymity made them a difficult target to fight. The latest demand had been for twenty-five thousand dollars and gradually increased to fifty thousand, when Colosimo refused to pay. Something must have happened to convince the vice king that he needed outside help, as a worried Victoria Colosimo contacted her cousin Johnny, who had a reputation in New York as a man capable to taking care of trouble.

Torrio agreed to come to Chicago to deal with Colosimo's Black Hand problems. The gang war situation in New York, even with Monk Eastman's removal, was getting worse. In Torrio's Brooklyn borough, Irish gangsters were clashing with Italians for domination over waterfront racketeering. Battles over the Brooklyn docks made life unsafe for anyone involved. It was a time of senseless slaughter that Torrio deplored. He could only hope that by the time he finished with

Colosimo's pursuers, the situation in Brooklyn would have sorted itself out somehow.

Once in Chicago, his first move was to notify the extortionists that Colosimo had agreed to pay up. When three men showed up at a railroad underpass to collect the money in a prearranged drop-off spot, Torrio was waiting. He nodded to two gunmen hiding with him in a parked carriage, and the three Black Handers were mowed down by shotgun fire. Two died instantly, the third lived long enough to summon Colosimo to his bedside and curse him as a traitor. The triple killing halted the flood of extortion commands. A grateful Big Jim rewarded Torrio with a job in his thriving brothel business.

Colosimo believed that starting out small and working your way up was the best way of rising in life. Brought to the United States at the age of ten, he had worked as a newsboy, bootblack, and waterboy for a railroad section gang, supplementing his income by stealing and picking pockets. At eighteen, the suave, dashing Colosimo became a pimp but was forced to abandon the trade when the law closed in on him. Realizing that he needed clout, he took a street-sweeping job and organized his fellow sweepers into a social and athletic club that voted en masse for First Ward Aldermen Kenna and Coughlin. The two returned the favor by making Colosimo a precinct captain and smoothing his way into a new position as saloonkeeper and poolroom manager. He also became brothel bagman for the two aldermen, collecting protection money from bordellos and punishing those who balked at paying.

In 1902 Colosimo married Victoria Moresco, a fat, homely madam of a low-class Armour Avenue brothel. He renamed the establishment the Victoria in his new bride's honor. As the years passed, he added more brothels and cheap cribs to his business. His management skills and backing from Kenna and Coughlin proved the right combination to take Big Jim to the top. At the time of Torrio's arrival, he owned a string of scarlet houses ranging in class from the fancy Victoria to twenty-five-cent cribs on Bed Bug Row.

To show his gratitude to the ruthless New Yorker, Colosimo made him manager of the Saratoga, one of the classier resorts. Torrio soon moved on to supervise all of Colosimo's vice holdings. He solidified the business, oversaw police and politician payoffs, and even arranged for the prostitutes to modify their attire to make them more attractive.

One of the more profitable Torrio inventions was the roadhouse. The little Italian had noticed that reformer attacks on the Levee were worsening and that it might be best to expand their interests. He was also aware that the six-year period between 1908 and 1913 had seen the number of motor vehicle owners in the United States increase almost tenfold, to 1,192, 262. Taking these two factors into consideration, Torrio established roadhouses in rural areas. The first was set up in Burnham, a tiny town on the Illinois-Indiana border. It was a prime location because, if officials from either state led a raid, the girls and their customers only had to scurry a few feet across the border to sanctuary. The rural officials were as receptive to bribe money as their city counterparts, making Torrio's expansion a wild success.

Big Jim Colosimo had such faith in his partner that he gave Torrio free rein to act as he saw fit and began to pursue other pastimes. In 1910 he opened a restaurant, Colosimo's Café, at 2126 South Wabash Avenue. It was a gilded palace designed to amuse the city's rich and visiting celebrities who could not leave Chicago without visiting the notorious Levee. A major part of the appeal was its location in the heart of the vice zone. Its tuxedoed and mink-swaddled patrons bemoaned with a secret thrill how they had to plunge into the wickedness to get to the restaurant.

Once inside its doors, patrons were confronted by a splendorous display of green velvet-coated walls, gold and crystal chandeliers hanging from a ceiling decorated by a breathtaking sky mural, a mahogany and glass bar, richly embroidered tapestries, and most unusual of all, a dance floor that could be raised or lowered by hydraulic lift. Cordon bleu chefs prepared the meals, and the most beautiful singers and chorus girls supplied the entertainment.

At the center of all the dazzle and fantasy was Big Jim. With his zesty Italian grace, he was the perfect host, slapping men on the back and charming the women with compliments as he circled among his guests. Colosimo played host to such celebrities as Enrico Caruso, Sophie Tucker, Al Jolson, and John Barrymore, and subsequently became friends with many of them. He acquired a degree of celebrity of his own as a diamond fanatic, covering his suspender and garter buckles, tie pins, shirt front, and cuffs with the glittering stones, and carrying chamois bags of unset diamonds in his pockets. The fetish earned him the nickname "Diamond Jim." Colosimo's other moniker was "Bank," because of the huge roll of cash he carried around to advance stakes to losing gamblers.

Torrio remained in the background, a colorless yet omnipotent presence directing the daily operations of the Colosimo empire. When the news came that Prohibition was on its way, Torrio made the necessary arrangements to buy into breweries and distilleries. A legend that continues to circulate is that Colosimo tried to stop the expansion into bootlegging. He had fallen in love with Dale Winter, a personable young singer who performed at the café, and actively sought refinement to make himself a fitting escort for her. Hours spent clarifying his speech with an English tutor, riding on horseback with Dale through Lincoln Park, and socializing with people not of his original world were smoothing away Colosimo's rough edges, and the story is that he had not the energy or daring left to expand into another illegal enterprise. Prohibition's enforcement by the federal government was another supposed deterrent for Colosimo, who had been paying off city cops but worried that the federal boys were incorruptible. He balked at risking jail because he did not want to leave Dale, whom he wanted to marry.

Most of this theory is nonsense. Colosimo did not prohibit Torrio from bootlegging; as long as he got his share, he was complacent about it. Nor was he afraid of the federal authorities; he had been risking their wrath ever since the Mann Act, which prohibited moving women across state lines for immoral purposes, was passed in 1911. What is true is that Colosimo was so in love with Dale Winter that he did not lead the venture into bootlegging with his usual force and fire. This frustrated Torrio, who knew that Big Jim's aggressive leadership was necessary to forge alliances with other gangs and to cow insurgents. He tried repeatedly to arouse Colosimo from the love-struck complacency he had lapsed into. And when Big Jim told Torrio that he was divorcing Victoria to marry Dale, he lost even more esteem in Torrio's eyes.

Big Jim and Dale eloped and were married in French Lick, Indiana, in May 1920, after he had given the portly and plain Victoria fifty thousand dollars not to contest a divorce action. She later commented bitterly, "I raised one husband for another woman, and there's nothing to it."

Torrio reached a difficult decision. Big Jim had grown so refined that he had become a danger to the organization. Where he had once fought off the Black Handers, he was now caving in to their demands, because they were threatening Dale, too. He neglected his political and underworld contacts in favor of the artists and wealthy who were part of his new wife's social circle. There were murmurings in the underworld that Jim was getting soft.

Johnny Torrio, like most Italians, cherished family loyalty above most things, but he was first and foremost a businessman. Something had to be done about Colosimo; he had lost much of his bluster and fire, and was simply not competent to lead the gang into the massive new booze market. Torrio had to move fast, before the more ambitious of Colosimo's minions revolted, and assume control in name as well as fact.

On May 11, 1920, not long after the newly wedded Big Jim and Dale had returned from their honeymoon, Torrio called Colosimo to say that gambler Jim O'Leary wanted to meet with him at the café to discuss delivery of two truckloads of prewar whiskey. O'Leary would be by around 4 P.M. to smooth out the details.

While driving to the café, Colosimo's chauffeur noticed that his boss was behaving strangely. The gang leader was muttering to himself in Italian and seemed unusually agitated. After being dropped off in front of his restaurant, Colosimo went through a small entrance vestibule, walked across the silent dining room, and entered a small office where his bookkeeper, Frank Camilla, was working. He asked Camilla if anyone had called for him, and received her negative response with visible unease. After calling his lawyer, Rocco de Stefano, for a brief chat, Colosimo went to the front of the café, heading for the doors, stopping only once to talk to some employees he encountered. Then he walked on toward one of the two entrances, which opened into a small foyer.

Both Frank Camilla and chef Antonio Caesarino heard two noises that sounded like tire blowouts. The chef checked the back alley, and Camilla looked out front, into the street. As he stepped onto the sidewalk, the spring lock on the door he had used closed behind him, forcing him to walk up the street and use the alternate entrance to get back in. As he pushed the swinging doors open, he saw Colosimo lying facedown on the vestibule floor, blood oozing from head wounds.

Police later concluded that the killer had hidden in a nearby cloakroom and shot Big Jim as he was preparing to leave the building.

One bullet had missed and cracked the plaster behind the cashier's booth twenty feet away. Big Jim's own gun was tucked in his hip pocket, but death overtook him before he could use it.

When Dale was notified of the murder, she fainted. Torrio wept openly, exclaiming to detectives, "Me kill Jim? Jim and me were like brothers!" Alphonse Capone, a hulking young Torrio protégé from New York, was also questioned, but he provided an unshakable alibi. Both were released.

Colosimo's murder was marked unsolved, although the killer had at one point been in police custody. A porter at the café had seen a man waiting briefly by the door leading into the vestibule where Colosimo died, and said that the stranger had been around five-foot-eight, round-faced, dark complexioned, and wearing a black derby. On the off chance that the killer had been imported, the Chicago police sent the description to New York. It fit Francesco Ioele, alias Frankie Yale, one of the city's most prominent and well-connected gangsters. When a mug shot was sent to Chicago, the porter, Joseph Gabrela, exclaimed, "That's the man!" But by the time he was sent to New York to face Yale in a police lineup, he had changed his mind. He was unable to make a positive identification, and Yale was released.

Frankie Yale, like Torrio and Capone, had been affiliated with the bloodthirsty Five Points Gang. He had mentored Capone, employing the younger man as a bartender in one of his dives. When Capone beat up an Irish gangster in response to a crass insult, Yale sent him to Chicago to evade the victim's friends.

Torrio needed more than an ordinary gunsel for the Colosimo hit. Big Jim had had many friends, and anyone who was hired to perform the hit had to be careful, fast, and ideally not from Chicago. Torrio consulted Capone, who recommended Yale and made the arrangements. The Brooklyn gangster was paid ten thousand dollars for the assassination.

No one voiced any opposition to Torrio assuming control of Colosimo's empire. Aldermen Kenna and Coughlin supported him because it was understood that all previous arrangements made with Colosimo would continue to stand. No one in the Levee voiced any objection either.

With Colosimo dead and buried, Torrio turned his attention to the expansion of his bootlegging business. He knew that Prohibition was the Chicago underworld's biggest gift since Big Bill Thompson, and he meant to maximize its profitability to him. That meant reaching understandings with Chicago's other reigning gangs, any one of which could cost him dearly in both money and lives if its members became greedy. His ideal scenario was to unify these individual mobs and form an unofficial corporation that dealt in booze. He reasoned that banding together in this fashion would offer more immunity from the law and more financial rewards than going it alone.

He resolved to meet with the primary leaders and present his plan to them.

In Little Italy, an immigrant colony on the South Side, the overlords were the Genna brothers: Sam, Pete, Vincenzo ("Jim"), Antonio ("Tony"), Angelo ("Bloody Angelo"), and Mike, who was also known as "Il Diabolo" or "Mike the Devil." They controlled Chicago's largest alky-cooking operation, having installed home stills in thousands of tenement apartments, shop backrooms, and basements. They paid Italian immigrants fifteen dollars per day to monitor the simmering brew, keep the fire beneath the vat burning, and skim off the distillate. It was a cushy job compared to the rigorous work most tenement dwellers were used to, but there were dangers involved. Carelessly attended stills sometimes exploded, scarring or killing those nearby. When gas was used for fuel, the people tapped mains to avoid raising the meter readings suspiciously high, and many a careless gas robber was accidentally asphyxiated.

The Gennas collected about 350 gallons of raw alcohol from each home per week. Each gallon cost fifty to seventy-five cents to make, and the brothers sold it to speakeasy proprietors for three to six dollars a gallon. Their monthly gross totaled roughly $350,000, with the net after payoffs being $150,000.

It was an excellent income for a family that had started out in life dirt poor. The Gennas had emigrated from Marsala, Sicily, in the early 1900s and put down roots in Little Italy, which stood in the heart of Chicago's "Bloody Nineteenth" Ward (later the Twenty-fifth Ward after a 1920 rezoning). Each brother assumed a specific role in the family business. Sam, the eldest and a Black Hander, was the chief, the one who made the business arrangements and evaluated new prospects. Jim and Pete worked as saloonkeepers and saw to the day-to-day business operations. Angelo and Mike were the enforcers.

Only the dapper, bespectacled Tony Genna shunned the rough trades, putting his keen mind to work as family advisor, turning Sam's ideas and decisions into successful ventures. An art connoisseur and intellectual, he differed greatly from his coarser brothers. He studied music and architecture, built low-rent housing for poor Sicilians, and lived in a luxury suite at the Congress Hotel with his mistress. Incurably vain, he prepared for a minor surgical procedure by getting a pedicure, not wishing to be seen with unattractive feet.

Violence by the brothers themselves was unnecessary—they had amassed a crew of fearsome killers. Their ace gunners were tall, thin John Scalise and short, squat Albert Anselmi. Both originally came from Marsala, the Genna birthplace, which resulted in the brothers welcoming them into the organization with open arms. They killed without mercy or hesitation and initiated the practice of rubbing their bullets with garlic in the belief that any resulting wounds would develop gangrene and finish off a victim if death was not immediate. It was a useless trick that gangland denizens imitated for years. Scalise in particular was a frightening individual to behold; a slight cast to his right eye gave him a lopsided and sinister stare.

The Genna army included Samuzzo "Samoots" Amatuna, who, like Tony Genna, was a stylish dresser and music lover. A professional fiddler and singer, he took pride in his membership in the musician's union. Amatuna had a collection of two hundred monogrammed silk shirts that he cherished. Once, when a Chinese laundry sent back one of them with a faint scorch mark, a berserk Amatuna chased the delivery wagon through the streets, initially intent on shooting the delivery man. When he caught up with it, he changed his mind and killed the horse instead. For all his dandified appearance and flaky habits, he was an effective killer of people as well as horses.

Another Genna gunman was the terror of Little Italy, swarthy, hawk-nosed Orazio "the Scourge" Tropea, who superstitious Italians believed possessed *il malocchio,* the "evil eye." His glare could produce results faster than a hard pair of fists, leading Tropea to believe that he was a sorcerer gifted with hypnotic powers that could bend his scared, sheeplike victims to his will.

Rounding out the Genna murder squad were Guiseppe Nerone, known as "Il Cavaliere" because of his genteel manners, a former mathematics professor and University of Palermo graduate whom the Gennas valued chiefly as a torpedo; Ecola "the Eagle" Baldelli; Vito Bascone; and Felipe Gnolfo.

The Gennas played an active role in the aldermanic wars of 1921, in which the Democratic incumbent John Powers and challenger Anthony D'Andrea fought for the Nineteenth Ward aldermanic seat. More than thirty men died in the power struggle. A gnarled old tree on Loomis Street was universally referred to as "Dead Man's Tree" because intended victims found their names tacked to its trunk days before their demise. The Gennas made extensive use of it in 1921.

They threw their support behind D'Andrea, a lawyer who was also a defrocked priest and former bank robber and counterfeiter with a prison record. D'Andrea, a nonpartisan candidate, had already made two unsuccessful runs for office; once in 1914, when he ran for county commissioner, and again in 1916, when he ran against Powers protégé James Bowler for Democratic alderman nominee. When Frank Raimondi, a Powers ward heeler, was shot to death in a saloon, the murder was laid at the door of the Gennas.

The 1921 conflict proved deadlier on both sides. Bombs exploded at the homes of both candidates, at a D'Andrea rally, and at D'Andrea's headquarters, leaving five people badly injured. Gunmen ran wild in the streets. Both candidates required round-the-clock protection. "It is worse than the Middle Ages," Alderman James Bowler lamented. D'Andrea lost the election, but the bloodshed continued. The Gennas were particularly vindictive. Angelo Genna and three henchmen—Samoots Amatuna, Frank "Don Chick" Gambino, and Johnny "Two-Gun" Guardino—waylaid Paul Labriola, a municipal court bailiff and Powers supporter, at the corner of Halstead and Congress Streets. After Labriola fell with several bullets in him, Genna stood over the bailiff and fired three more shots for good measure before escaping with his companions in a waiting automobile. Later the same day, ex-D'Andrea supporter Harry Raimondi was shot down in his Taylor Street cigar store.

When Powers man Nicolo Adamo was murdered, his wife identified Jim Genna as the killer. Another, Paul Notte, lived long enough to name Angelo as his assailant. Both accusations were dismissed on flimsy pretexts. Only one murder resulted in arrest and a trial: Angelo Genna was charged with Labriola's killing. He went free after prosecution witnesses disappeared or suffered memory loss.

No one questioned the Genna rule over Little Italy. Only the church made a valiant but ineffective effort to see justice done. D'Andrea was killed by two shotgun blasts to the chest on May 11, 1921, as he climbed the steps to his apartment. His bodyguard Joe Laspisa swore to avenge him. Laspisa never had the chance; he was gunned down a month later as his car approached the Church of San Filippo Benzi. The distressed parish priest posted a sign on the church doors pleading with his parishioners to fight the evil that was blackening the name of the community. During his sermons he urged anyone with information of benefit to the police to come forward at once. No one was brave or suicidal enough to do so.

By 1920 the Gennas had leased a three-story warehouse at 1022 Taylor Street. Through political connections, they obtained a government license to handle industrial alcohol and used the warehouse as a storage depot and headquarters. They did distribute some of the product to legitimate users, such as cosmetic or perfume manufacturers, but a greater percentage was fortified with flavoring and coal tar (for coloring), then bottled and sold as genuine liquor. The warehouse was only four blocks from the Maxwell Street police station, but in the words of criminal lawyer Patrick H. O'Donnell, it was "as public as the greatest department store on State Street."

Policemen and state's attorney representatives converged on 1022 Taylor Street regularly to collect their graft. Neighbors nicknamed the building "the police station," after the uniformed cops who would waltz in and emerge minutes later to count their graft money on the sidewalk. A government investigation of the Genna operation produced a confession from their former office manager, who wrote:

> Each month said warehouse was visited by 400 uniformed police and by squads—sometimes four per month—out of the central bureau. It was visited, moreover, by representatives with stars but not in uniform, commonly known around the warehouse as representatives of the state's attorney's office of Cook County.
>
> That police might not impose upon the Gennas by falsely representing themselves as assigned to the Maxwell Street Station, each month there came by letter or messenger a list for all stars worn by officers and men

> at the Maxwell Street Station. These were on short slips of paper, and were taken by this affiant.
>
> The entire list of stars was run off on the adding machine and the papers sent from the station were destroyed.
>
> As each man came in for his pay, his star was observed. If his star was on the list sent in, he was paid. . . .
>
> On occasions when truckloads of alcohol would be going to different parts of the city and they would be intercepted by strange policemen, complaint was lodged by the Gennas. It was arranged then between the Gennas and the squads in the central detail as follows:
>
> When a long haul was to be made through strange territory, the Gennas on the preceding night would call certain numbers and say, "Tomorrow at seven." On the next morning at 7 A.M. a uniformed squad of police would remain in the offing until a truckload of alcohol would start from the Genna warehouse. This squad would convey them through the zones of danger.

The Genna brothers, with the exception of the dapper Tony, were a crude lot, a collection of bloody scrappers who probably offended Torrio's more refined and restrained nature. But their clout with the cops and widely feared stable of killers, not to mention the fact that their territory might have to be crossed during liquor shipments, made their cooperation in Torrio's master plan vital.

Next to the Genna territory, on the West Side between Little Italy and the township of Cicero, the old Valley Gang ruled. One of the longest-standing gangs in Chicago, having been formed in the 1880s, all of its leaders had earned their place in local legend. Prior to Prohibition there had been "Big Heinie" Miller, a brawler with matchless shooting ability, and the recently deceased "Paddy the Bear" Ryan. Now, at the dawn of the Noble Experiment, Terry Druggan and Frankie Lake were at the helm.

Druggan was a small man with thick-rimmed spectacles and a toothy smile that made him look like a comic-strip character. The son of a garbage collector, he had worked on his father's truck long enough to be disgusted with honest living and decide to seek his fortune as a member of the Valley Gang. Frankie Lake, a bear of a man, had worked first as a railroad switchman and then as a firefighter. When he wore glasses on the odd occasion, he looked like a taller, meatier version of his diminutive partner.

Like Torrio, the duo saw bootlegging as the gang's future. Lake already had some experience, having sold illegal hooch to local saloons when wartime Prohibition was in effect. They assured themselves of success when they went into partnership with beer scion Joseph Stensen in five breweries: Gambrinus, Standard, George Hoffman, Pfeiffer, and Stege. With a steady income now guaranteed, they saw no need to go beyond the Valley in search of business. The territory was a workingman's area, a rough collection of red brick tenements and rowdy saloons that soaked up beer like a sponge.

Like the Genna brothers, Druggan and Lake were devout churchgoers, but Druggan in particular gloried in his Catholicism. Once, when hijacking a beer truck parked in front of a church, Druggan recognized the drivers as Jewish gangsters. He yelled, "Hats off, you Jews, when you're passing the House of God, or I'll shoot 'em off!"

The gray assortment of slaughterhouses, industrial buildings, and train tracks that snaked across the terrain like iron stitchwork was known as "Back o' the Yards." This wasteland on the Southwest Side was the bailiwick of Joe Saltis.

Saltis, a six-foot-tall, 200-pound hulk of Hungarian descent, had been a saloonkeeper before Prohibition. He presented an imposing figure, but in reality his cowardice had long been a source of derision among his gangster colleagues. Only when dealing with someone weaker would he display any ferocity; he once beat an elderly woman to death after she refused to let him turn her ice cream parlor into a speakeasy. Only his close ties to influential underworld and political figures such as John O'Berta prevented rivals from eating him alive and taking over his business.

A labor racketeer and Thirteenth Ward politician who was also of Slavic descent, O'Berta's Irish surname was a fudging of his real name of Oberta. He had changed it to court the favor of the Thirteenth Ward's thousands of Irish voters. Childhood comrades had nicknamed him "Dingbat" after a popular comic strip of the day, but the shrewd and ruthless O'Berta was far from laughable and his ambition stopped at nothing. When rivals gunned down prominent labor racketeer "Big Tim" Murphy, O'Berta stepped further up the ladder of underworld prominence by marrying Murphy's widow, Florence.

Saltis ran beer in from Wisconsin until he amassed a fortune large enough to buy one brewery and invest in three others. They were staffed mostly by Mexican workers whose willingness to work long hours for low wages saved Saltis a bundle. To show his gratitude, Saltis determined to buy them a Mexican pony when a gangster friend told him that a North Side riding stable had one. The stable owner initially refused to sell, insisting that the pony was a pet. Saltis refused to back down.

"If you think five hundred dollars isn't enough," he said, "just name your price."

After the stable owner awoke from a deep swoon, the pony was sold, and the Mexicans at Saltis's Wisconsin brewery had a thunderous fiesta.

Joe Saltis retained a connection to Wisconsin. The greater percentage of his brewery holdings was there, and in his later prosperity, he bought a summer home in Eagle River Country, a favorite retreat for millionaires in the northern tip of the state.

In 1922 he joined forces with homicidal gangster Frank McErlane. At five-foot-eight and 190 pounds, McErlane was portly like Saltis, but hard muscle lurked beneath the fat. Alcohol made him crazy. When drunk, his eyes glazed, a fierce red flush tinged his face, and the impulse to kill seized him. He had fought alongside Dean O'Banion for the Hearst interests.

He was not choosy about who he shot at, or why. One night, after he had drunk himself into a flat-eyed rage at a saloon in Crown Point, Indiana, one of his cronies teased him about his shooting ability. McErlane picked out a stranger in the crowd and shot him through the head. He fled the state just before the Indiana police closed in, and managed to fight off extradition for a year. During that time, the state's star witness was found with his skull laid open by an ax. When McErlane finally surrendered to authorities and went to trial, he was acquitted.

McErlane gave Joe Saltis the menacing element previously missing from the latter's operations. It didn't take long for the word to get around that crossing Saltis would arouse the mad wrath of the man whom the *Illinois Crime Survey* dubbed "the most brutal gunman who ever pulled a trigger in Chicago."

Southeast of Joe Saltis's domain and sandwiched between Forty-second and Sixty-third Streets was Ralph Sheldon's territory. Sheldon, a small figure made frail by tuberculosis, headed a gang that had evolved from the old Ragen's Colts mob.

The Colts dated back to the 1890s, when a group of young Irishmen started a baseball team called the Morgan Athletic Club. By 1902 the club numbered 160 members and expanded from baseball alone into soccer, wrestling, football, and other rowdy sports. Frank Ragen, a fight-loving pitcher, captured the presidency in 1908, following a fight over who should head the club that broke out during an annual outing at Santa Fe Park. Hundreds of dollars' worth of damage later, Ragen was the official president and the club's name was changed to Ragen's Colts. At the height of its notoriety, the gang's roster was so huge that its members' slogan was "Hit me and you hit one thousand."

Many a Colt went on to hold political office. Ragen himself joined the Democratic Party and was elected city commissioner. His followers backed him with unparalleled ferocity. "When we dropped into a polling place," one remarked, "everyone else dropped out." Voting locations that they didn't demolish were rigidly supervised to ensure that the balloting went in Ragen's favor. During their more than twenty years of existence, the Colts gave Chicago many aldermen, county sheriffs, policemen, ballplayers, and even one mayor, Richard J. Daley, who allegedly had been a Colt.

The Colts were notorious for their racism. They saw the Negro as a subhuman threat to Chicago whites. It was alleged that George Stauber, the white bystander whose rock throwing initiated the July 1919 race riots, was either a member of or in sympathy with the Colts.

Ralph Sheldon's crew was a smaller offshoot. Sheldon himself was only eighteen in 1920, yet his gang consisted of such hardened killers as slugger and labor racketeer Danny Stanton, compulsive murderer William "Gunner" McPadden, and gambling gunman Hugh "Stubby" McGovern. Like Torrio, Sheldon maintained his leadership by using his keen mind to bring prosperity to his followers. He had mastered the political fix as early as his sixteenth year, when he escaped a conviction for highway robbery. The fix was so obvious that the trial judge made a bitter comment about miscarriages of justice.

Sheldon also was a devout Catholic, and the Colts once planned to assemble a strike force to go to Oklahoma and thrash the Ku Klux Klan for anti-Catholic activity going on there. He scorned prostitution as immoral, opting to make himself and his gang rich through bootlegging.

The territory claimed by the West Side O'Donnells was wedged between Halstead and Austin Avenue on the West Side and extended south to Cicero, a township bordering Chicago's southwestern limits. The gang was referred to as the Klondike O'Donnell mob, although three brothers led it; the other two simply paled in comparison to the more aggressive frontman.

William "Klondike" O'Donnell was a husky, ruddy-complexioned gangster who acted as unofficial mayor of Cicero. Joseph Z. Klenha, who actually held the post, deferred to him in every respect. He operated alongside two other Cicero big names: Eddie Vogel, who ran a slot machine operation, and Eddie Tancl, a pugnacious saloonkeeper who was a throwback to the publican/political "boss" days.

Despite the political corruption, Cicero was a relatively crime-free town. Most of its 60,000 inhabitants enjoyed a mug or two of O'Donnell beer after work, and played Eddie Vogel's slot machines whenever they felt daring.

These five forces (six, including O'Banion's North Siders) were the only gangs that had enough clout and connections in their respective territories to warrant consideration in Torrio's master plan.

There was a seventh group, but in one of his rare lapses of good judgment, Torrio ignored it. This mob's leaders also were named O'Donnell, but because their home base was on the Far South Side of Chicago, they were known as the South Side O'Donnells to distinguish them from Klondike's West Side Gang. Steve, Walter, and Tommy O'Donnell were colorless and without ambition, but the eldest brother, Edward, aka "Spike," had enough flash, force, and intelligence to compensate. A raffish, outwardly cheerful character who wore plaid suits and outlandish bow ties, Spike was a dedicated killer who had already been tried twice for homicide. He was the brains and major-general of his gang, his brothers functioning merely as muscle. "When arguments fail, use a blackjack," he was fond of saying to his followers.

When Prohibition became law, Spike was doing a five-year sentence for the daylight robbery of twelve thousand dollars from the Stockyards Savings and Trust Bank. Torrio reckoned correctly that without Spike's leadership, his three brothers were an inconsequential skeleton crew. Instead of counting them in on his plan, Torrio hired them as general help for the Four Deuces nightspot, where Al Capone was doorman and bouncer for a time. The little Italian underestimated Spike O'Donnell's political connections—Governor Len Small had received pardon requests on his behalf from six senators, five state representatives, and a criminal court judge. In early 1920 Torrio had no way of knowing that Spike O'Donnell would be home . . . and soon. He had three relatively idyllic years to look forward to.

Louise Gentle

Nine-year-old Dean O'Banion (front row, fifth from right) joins students in Maroa, Illinois, for this class portrait taken in 1901.

Maroa Ill
Feb. 4, 1900

Dear Mamma.
I love you awful well
at school I have only
got a lock box and two
tablets and a book and a
book to write things in
that Miss Hill puts
on the board and a box
of pins and a pen and
a pencil and a ruler
and bell that ~~says~~
Dr Bells pine tar honey
on it.
I have only used five
pages in my tablet.
Tomorrow it will be
colder weather. I will
draw a picture now.

a little girl

Dean O Banion
Banion

Eddie Holtsclaw and Bob Gentle

O'Banion sent this letter to his mother in 1901 while she was recuperating in a TB hospital.

Author's Collection

Emma O'Banion's grave in Maroa is marked by this stone purchased by Dean. The birth and death dates are incorrect.

AUTHOR'S COLLECTION

Dean and Viola O'Banion on their wedding day, February 5, 1921.

AUTHOR'S COLLECTION

William Hale Thompson, the man who wanted to be a cowboy, served three colorful terms as Chicago's mayor. "Big Bill" threw the city wide open, and it never closed again.

AUTHOR'S COLLECTION

O'Banion made powerful enemies during his criminal career, including three who ultimately ordered his demise (clockwise from right): Johnny Torrio, "Bloody Angelo" Genna, and Alphonse Capone. In May 1920, the dapper Torrio had engineered the killing of Lord of the Levee "Big Jim" Colisimo in the vestibule of the latter's popular restaurant (above).

GODDARD COLLECTION

AUTHOR'S COLLECTION

GODDARD COLLECTION

AUTHOR'S COLLECTION

The seemingly benign countenance of Dean Charles O'Banion, the most powerful gang boss in early 1920s Chicago, is captured in this rare photograph. Few images exist of O'Banion and other gangsters of the pre-Capone era, as most studiously avoided photographers in order to reduce their chances of being identified by crime victims or witnesses.

AUTHOR'S COLLECTION

GODDARD COLLECTION

AUTHOR'S COLLECTION

Among notable O'Banion associates were (clockwise from above left) bodyguard Louis Alterie; vice monger Jack Zuta; Samuel J. "Nails" Morton, whose connections helped O'Banion's bootlegging business get off the ground; and newsman and playwright Charles MacArthur, who accompanied O'Banion on many a nocturnal prank.

AUTHOR'S COLLECTION

GODDARD COLLECTION

Earl "Hymie" Weiss (left), O'Banion's best friend and the only man Al Capone ever really feared, assumed command of the North Side Gang after O'Banion's murder. He was succeeded by Vincent "the Schemer" Drucci (below left, with wife Cecelia), O'Banion's "faithful Italian," who in turn was succeeded by George "Bugs" Moran (below right).

GODDARD COLLECTION

GODDARD COLLECTION

AUTHOR'S COLLECTION

Author's Collection

John Stewart

In February 1924, O'Banion (above left) was questioned in connection with John Duffy's murder, and in March, he and Hymie Weiss (above right, face covered by hat) were in court to answer charges stemming from the January assault on Dave Miller. This rare image is the only known photograph of O'Banion and Weiss together. In October, O'Banion and Viola (below, third and fourth from left in front row) and Louis Alterie (front row with arms crossed) and his wife (third from left atop fence) made a sojourn to Colorado. "Kiss of Death" girl Margaret Collins (right) was the darling of Chicago's underworld. She and O'Banion were suspected lovers.

Author's Collection

Author's Collection

AUTHOR'S COLLECTION

A large crowd gathers outside the William F. Schofield flower shop (above) just minutes after the noontime murder of Dean O'Banion. The North Sider's murder sparked the bloody gang war that gave Chicago its reputation for violence, and his funeral (below) was the most lavish gangster sendoff the city had witnessed up until that time.

AUTHOR'S COLLECTION

Daily - - - 614,669
Sunday - - 969,556

Chicago Daily Tribune

THE WORLD'S GREATEST NEWSPAPER

VOLUME LXXXIII—NO. 271 TUESDAY, NOVEMBER 11, 1924.—38 PAGES PRICE TWO CENTS

KILL O'BANION, GANG LEADER

CONGRESS MAY PROMPTLY STOP TAX PUBLICITY

Treasury Thinks It Reduces Revenue.

NEWS SUMMARY

ARMISTICE DAY FINDS THE WORLD, INCLUDING THE BALKANS AND MEXICO, PRETTY MUCH AT PEACE

BEGIN HILL SUIT TO LEARN WHAT IS INTOXICATNG

Some of It Had 11%, U.S. Chemist Says.

Shut 4 Up in Bank Vault in $15,000 Raid

MRS. HARDING NOT IMPROVED, DOCTOR REPORTS

FOUND STARVING GERMANS TOO PROUD TO WORK

He Fishes for Ducks, but Trout Steal His Bait

3-GUN FLORIST SLAIN IN SHOP NEAR CHURCH

Police Predict War of Revenge.

KILLERS' GETAWAY PERFECT

Dog Leads to Suspect in Girl Murder

THE WEATHER

Divorces Gain Faster Than Marriages

Banner headlines like the one above trumpeted the slaying of O'Banion, Chicago's most important Big Shot to go down since Big Jim Colosimo. The artist's rendering at right gave readers the vicarious thrill of witnessing the ultimate moment of the so-called "handshake murder."

AUTHOR'S COLLECTION

AUTHOR'S COLLECTION

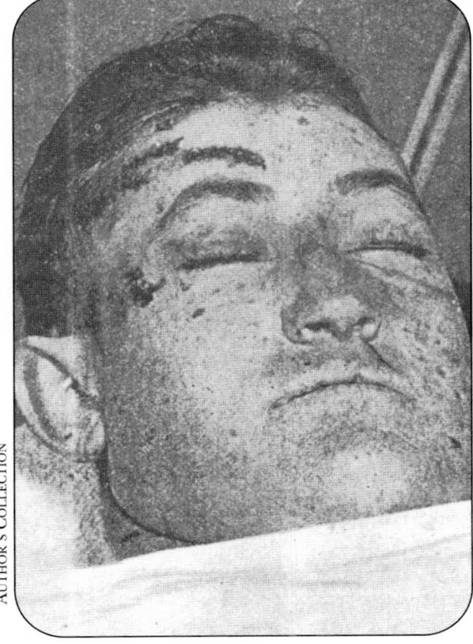

AUTHOR'S COLLECTION

GODDARD COLLECTION

Dean O'Banion's killers included (clockwise from above left) John Scalise, Albert Anselmi, and Frankie Yale, who gave O'Banion (left, in morgue) the fatal handshake.

Goddard Collection

Gangland warfare that erupted after Dean O'Banion's slaying took a heavy toll on all sides. After months of escalating body counts, North Sider chief Hymie Weiss and Vincent Drucci were attacked in front of the Standard Oil Building in Chicago by South Side gunmen (as depicted in the artist's rendering above) but escaped unharmed. Some two months later, Capone henchmen ambushed Weiss and four associates as they approached Schofield's flower shop, killing Weiss and bodyguard Patrick "Paddy" Murray and wounding the three others, including Sam Pellar (below, on stretcher).

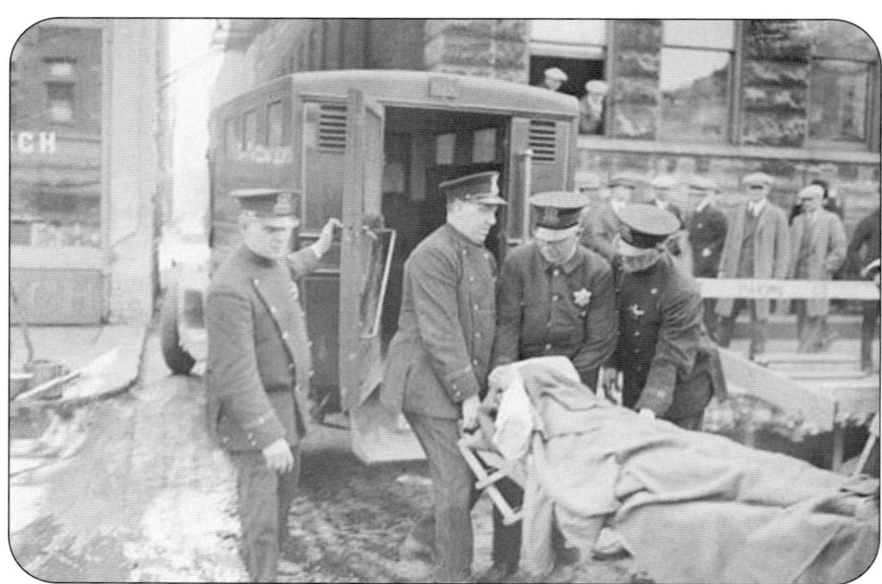

Sarah Simard

SARAH SIMARD

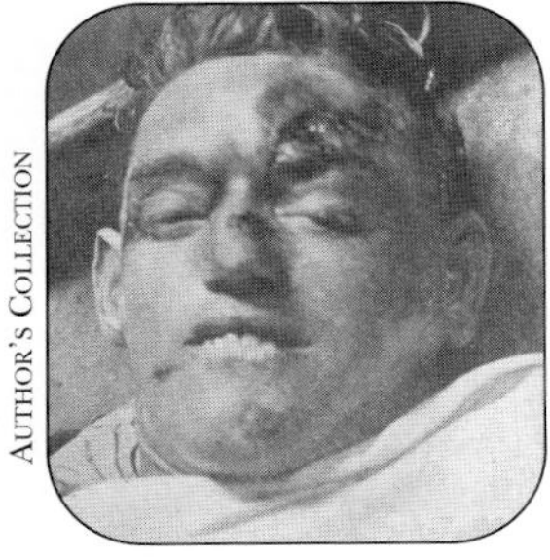

AUTHOR'S COLLECTION

Police attempt to keep curious citizens away from the lifeless body of Paddy Murray (above). Capone's gunners waited for their quarry in an upstairs room (below) of a boarding house at 740 North State Street that provided a clear view of the flower shop's entrance. At left: Hymie Weiss in the morgue.

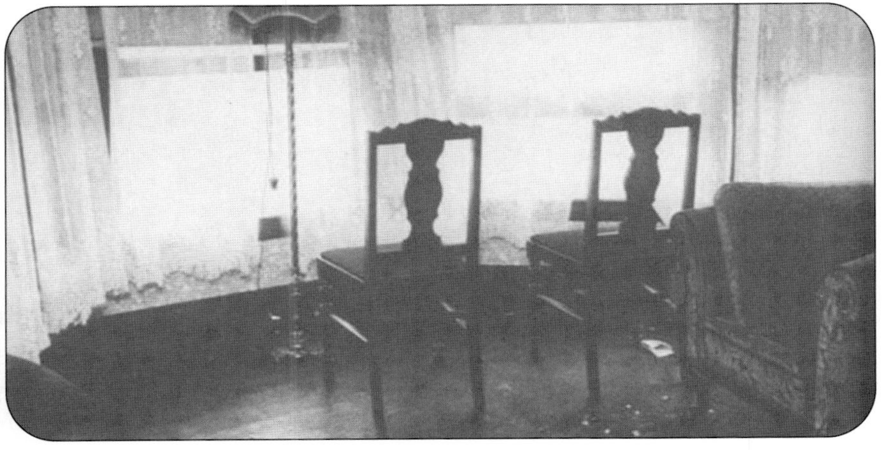

SARAH SIMARD

Josephine Simard (right) claimed to be legally married to Hymie Weiss at the time of his death. Weiss's youngest brother, Frederick (at right below), testifies during the inquest into his notorious sibling's murder.

SARAH SIMARD

SARAH SIMARD

AUTHOR'S COLLECTION

When Vincent Drucci was killed while in police custody in April 1927, Bugs Moran (above, with wife Lucy, aka Alice Roberts) took over the North Side Gang. After several North Siders were cut down in the infamous St. Valentine's Day Massacre, Moran's power ebbed and he eventually left Chicago, teaming with Virgil Summers (below left) in the Bookie Gang activities of the late 1930s and bank robberies in the '40s. The last of the North Side generals was nabbed by the FBI in 1946 (below right) and died behind bars in 1957 of lung cancer.

AUTHOR'S COLLECTION

AUTHOR'S COLLECTION

Author's Collection

Author's Collection

The remains of Vincent "the Schemer" Drucci, born Victor di Ambrosia, were laid to rest with full military honors in the family mausoleum (above) in Chicago's Mount Carmel Cemetery. Hymie Weiss was interred in the Weiss family mausoleum (right), also at Mount Carmel Cemetery.

AUTHOR'S COLLECTION

AUTHOR'S COLLECTION

Another resident of Mount Carmel is Dean O'Banion himself, whose grave, marked by a large obelisk (above) and a footstone (left), is not far from the tomb of his longtime pal Hymie Weiss.

On February 14, 1929, seven men awaiting a shipment of hijacked booze were gunned down in a garage on Chicago's North Clark Street (below). The St. Valentine's Day Massacre was orchestrated by Al Capone and had as its primary target North Side Gang leader Bugs Moran, who avoided the hit but never again seriously threatened Capone's control of the city's underworld. The slain included (clockwise from top left) North Siders Frank and Pete Gusenberg, Adam Heyer, Al Weinshank, James Clark, and mechanic Johnny May. Also killed was Reinhardt Schwimmer, whose fascination with gangsters proved fatal on that snowy morning. (Goddard Collection photos.)

9

A City Divided

O'Banion initially was receptive when Johnny Torrio approached him. He anticipated the unity plan as a chance to strengthen his growing operation unmolested. Torrio assured him that under the proposed intra-city alliance, the North Side was his; no one else could move in without retribution coming fast and hard, and no watering hole of any kind would buy its wares from anyone but O'Banion. The North Sider would have been quick to punish transgressors himself, but as part of a combine that agreed to respect one another's boundaries, he could rest assured that none of the larger gangs would encroach on him.

Torrio settled the question of who ruled where merely by confirming the existing boundaries and affiliations. To O'Banion went the chunk of land bordered on the north by the Chicago city limits and the south by Madison Street, on the east by Lake Michigan, and the west by the North branch of the Chicago River. West of the river, adjoining O'Banion, was the future jurisdiction of Roger "the Terrible" Touhy, a Des Plaines-based bootlegger who generally kept to himself unless provoked. A wedge of land between the river and the West Side O'Donnell Gang was later split between two molecular gangs led by Martin Guilfoyle and Claude "Screwy" Maddox. Klondike O'Donnell and his brothers retained their Cicero beer route and usual West Side territory. The Gennas, Joseph Saltis, Druggan and Lake, and Ralph Sheldon also kept their existing districts. Torrio absorbed the South Side O'Donnell turf and also took everything south of Madison Street down to the Indiana state line.

Torrio decreed that each gang could supply its customers with beer and liquor from any source they chose, but he offered beer wholesale at fifty dollars a barrel to those who might not have their own ready connections. His liquor-running operations were less secure, so he reached an agreement with O'Banion, whose mainstay was the hard liquors run in from Canada. He would supply beer to O'Banion, whose brewery holdings at the time were minimal, and O'Banion would provide him with the hard stuff.

In the younger, sometimes refined but more often impetuous O'Banion, Torrio recognized an unpolished leader with all the necessary qualities for greatness. O'Banion was charismatic; like Torrio, he could sway people to act as he chose, but where Torrio opened his wallet to achieve a certain end, O'Banion could often perform the same feat through sheer force of personality. "He could do with a smile and a handshake what the other bosses had to shell out big money for," Barnett said. The North Sider bound his men to him with fraternal affection, not money or fear. He was intelligent and cunning. He could be too impulsive and careless for Torrio's comfort, but these were traits and habits that structure and discipline could get out of his system.

The other gang leaders acquiesced to Torrio's plan. They agreed that he should be the arbitrary figure who settled disputes and interpreted how the rules applied to various situations.

The plan ratified and his role in it properly defined, O'Banion went on with business as usual, relying on the counsel of Hymie Weiss and Nails Morton. The advice of the latter was steadier because Weiss, for all his intelligence, was only twenty-two and had a temper that sometimes interfered with his judgment. Morton was calmer, more conscious of protocol and diplomacy, but even he could be quick on the trigger.

On the night of August 23, 1920, Morton and Hirschie Miller, chief of a small Jewish gang based on the West Side, entered the Pekin Inn shortly after the 1 A.M. closing hour. They walked through the darkened establishment and went upstairs to the Beaux Arts Café, a black and tan cabaret that opened as soon as the place downstairs closed.

Detective Sergeants James "Pluck" Mulcahey and William "Spike" Hennessy joined Morton and Miller at 3 A.M. After a brief exchange of greetings, Morton and Sergeant Mulcahey repaired to a private alcove to discuss a liquor deal. Sometime during the discussion, things went awry, for reasons never determined. A shouting match escalated into a fistfight. The two men stumbled into the public seating area, pummeling each other. The chunky Morton struck his opponent in the mouth and knocked him to the floor. Before the Jewish gangster could attack again, Hirschie Miller seized him and pushed him away, pleading with him to calm down.

Sgt. Hennessy arrived with his gun drawn, having missed the fight while chatting to an acquaintance. Mulcahey drew his pistol as well, and staggered painfully to his feet. Morton, knowing when enough was enough, backed away, but got his legs tangled in a chair and fell over backwards. The vengeful officer lunged forward and kicked him in the head, splitting the scalp.

Hirschie Miller yanked out his gun and killed both cops, Hennessy with four shots and Mulcahey with one. He and Morton were arrested and charged with murder, but claimed self-defense and were acquitted at their trial. Ironically, the site of the Pekin Inn and Beaux Arts Café later housed a police station and courtroom.

Dean O'Banion's North Side was, in 1920, an unreal world where the rich and poor co-existed within blocks of each other, the bohemian and the aristocrat found their perfect niches, and the impertinent young and the dignified old found equally compelling reasons to call the area home.

It was divided into east and west by State Street, which also marked the border between the Gold Coast, Chicago's most exclusive residential area, and the slum. East of State was where the wealthy lived in their palatial mansions overlooking Lake Michigan, worked (when necessary) in high-rise offices, and dropped hundreds of dollars on Michigan Avenue shopping sprees. Going west, one encountered signs of the less affluent; rooming houses, tenement buildings, hole-in-the-wall cafes, pawnshops, and second-hand stores. North Clark Street boasted a few banks and office buildings, but the majority of businesses that lined it were cheap movie houses, cigar stores, news and taxi stands, and hockshops. At night, North Clark came alive with electric lights that beckoned people into its saloons, cabarets, and sleazy hotels; a 1918 survey of North Clark between North Avenue and the river revealed a total of fifty-seven saloons and twenty cabarets. This particular stretch was popularly known as the "Wilds of North Clark Street."

O'Banion's North Side hosted a new breed of humanity as the Twenties progressed. Poets and artists of all persuasions moved into the slums and set up a bohemian community in the vicinity of the old water tower at Michigan and Chicago Avenues. These long-haired boys and barefaced girls made their presence known by setting up tea shops, art stores, bookstalls selling obscure poetry and anarchistic literature, and studio apartments decorated with window boxes. The Bohemians were probably the nation's first real youth power movement, a knee-jerk reaction to the strict moral standards of the not-so-distant Victorian and Edwardian eras.

Kenneth Rexroth, a young writer who was later integral to the emergence of the Beat poet movement, was one of the flamboyant crowd who thronged the district during the Twenties. He recalled attending the Goethe Street house of Jake Loeb, an insurance broker related to the wealthy Loeb family, who loved to host gatherings of the poets and artists. "Every few days the neighboring florist sent a boy over with flowers to decorate the house and a suitcase full of the best cognac and the best whiskey," he wrote in his memoirs. "The florist's name was Dion O'Banion."

Many of them were overtly homosexual. "Sometimes you'd see them in the streets, holding hands, around Chestnut, East Chicago Avenue, that area," E. Barnett remembered. "A lot of their bars and cafes used to buy booze from Dean. Mostly wine and sherry, as I recall. Some of the boys refused to deliver to them, they couldn't stand fairies. A few times Dean had to do the deliveries himself. He'd complain to me about the boys' attitudes. "I don't know what their goddamn problem is," he'd say. "I'm asking them to deliver a case of sherry, not date one of the bastards!'"

Barnett and the other truckers soon learned that one of the shotgun men accompanying them on their long-distance hauls was from the Bohemian district, and gay.

"His name was O'Connor; he was a young fellow who was just a little too fussy about his hair and his looks, so we suspected for a long time before we actually knew. I didn't care myself, as long as he didn't try it on with me. But the other boys did. They complained to Dean and Weiss, but Dean just said, "You don't know that for a fact, now go out and drive and shut up."

"Well, one day one of the drivers actually caught O'Connor with an envelope full of naked male pictures. They weren't real photos, you couldn't get something like that too easily in those days; they were sketches and photos cut out of medical books. The envelope dropped out of O'Connor's coat when he got out of the truck to piss during a stopover, and the driver snatched it. He figured he had enough proof to make Dean fire him then.

"I was there when Sammy [the driver] brought his evidence into this smoking room that Dean kept over the flower shop. "Look at this," he says, all flustered. He shows all of us the pictures and tells us how he got them. Dean said, "I haven't got time, I'll ask him about it and deal with it later." He picked up the envelope, stuffed it in his inside pocket, grabbed his coat, and left. We all figured that O'Connor would be history after this. I actually felt sorry for the poor bastard.

"Well, the next day I hear this unbelievable story from Myers, the guy who rode shotgun with me on my first run. He stopped me in the street and says, "Remember those pictures that Sammy got off of the fairy?" I said, "Yeah, did Dean fire him?" He says, "I got to tell you this. Remember how Dean took them with him when he went out? He went to meet that cop Hughes to give him his money, and guess which envelope he gives Hughes by accident?" I says, "Jesus H. Christ, I hope you're kidding." He said he wasn't. He said, "I hear Deanie got a phone call at the shop an hour later and had a helluva lot of explaining to do." Then he laughed so hard that he started bawling. I did, too. How the hell O'Banion ever lived that one down I never figured out. He never did fire O'Connor, just told the drivers that the poor bastard couldn't help the way he was and to find another job if they were that scared of him. I don't think anyone did.'"

This incident illustrates the genuine pity he had for the disadvantaged, well as the poor. Now wealthy, O'Banion no longer worried about starvation, rent dodging, or finding a job, but he never forgot his years of difficulty. He sympathized with those who lived hard, and as soon as he had acquired a large enough fortune to do so, did his share to alleviate suffering on the North Side. He loaded his car with food, clothing, and blankets and drove to areas where the need was the most rampant. Parking his car at one end of the street, he and his assistants went from building to building distributing the goods. O'Banion's charity extended to the point of paying rent and medical bills for those down on their luck. He supposedly sent a crippled boy to the Mayo clinic for treatment; although it has been impossible to prove that this actually happened, it is without a doubt something he would have done had such a plight been brought to his attention.

These altruistic gestures were genuine and not an attempt to gain popular support. Years later, Al Capone would open soup kitchens for those staggered by the Great Depression and cheerfully encourage newsmen to witness and proclaim his self-claimed position as a public benefactor. O'Banion was not interested in public applause; he made a point of avoiding organized charities, suspicious that most donations went into the pockets of the wrong people. "No high salaried organization to distribute my doles," he commented once. "My money goes straight to those who need it."

This sympathetic side to his personality, hidden all too often behind his impulsiveness, was what drew Helen Viola Kaniff to him in December 1920.

By Christmas 1920, it looked as if Chicago gangland had sailed through the first year of Prohibition successfully. Thanks to Torrio, everyone was aware of his territorial limitations and respected them. The police and dry agents were posing no serious difficulties.

For O'Banion in particular, life was good. He was still working for Hearst, to give the impression of receiving legal income, and lived with his father and stepmother at 822 Oakdale Avenue. Charles had married a Wisconsin woman, Margaret, a few years earlier. Instead of resenting her for taking his beloved mother's place, Dean welcomed her enthusiastically and called her "Mother."

Just before Christmas, O'Banion attended a dance held at a North Side café. A tall, solidly built girl with dark blonde hair and a mischievous smile caught his eye. She was home from her Iowa boarding school for the holidays, and, being a vivacious and slightly rebellious type, attended the boozy dance in the company of a few girlfriends. Her brassy style appealing to him, O'Banion introduced himself and invited her and her companions to join him at his table.

Her name was Helen Viola Kaniff. Born March 27, 1901, in Chicago to Thomas and Bridget (Dee) Kaniff, she and her twin sister, Catherine Vivian, were nineteen and the youngest of four children. When Dean boasted to her that everyone present at the dance was drinking liquor he had supplied, she was impressed. He may even have told her that he was a newspaper reporter as well, having indicated that occupation in the 1920 census.

They were a steady couple from that night onward, and after a courtship that lasted a month and a half, were married on February 5, 1921, at Our Lady of Sorrows Basilica on Jackson Boulevard. The bride's sister Vivian and O'Banion family friend Ralph E. Moss stood as witnesses. The couple moved to 6081 Ridge Avenue after the wedding. It was obvious to everyone who knew them that they lived together very happily and that their marriage was not tarnished by the numerous infidelities that wracked underworld unions. O'Banion never took a mistress like many of his friends opted to do; he and Viola remained devoted to each other. She accompanied him to restaurants and the theater, and they were frequently observed riding together on the Lincoln Park bridle paths.

Such devotion was typical of O'Banion. Kenneth Allsop, author of *The Bootleggers*, wrote of him, "He divided humanity into "right guys" and "wrong guys." To those whom he considered friends, he was unfailingly supportive. He lent money freely to associates; at one point he had fifty thousand dollars in IOUs out. He never bothered collecting. The warmth and generosity that bound his men to him left an equally favorable impression on his young wife.

The generous nature was selective, however. The basic rule was that if you were *with* O'Banion, you were all right—he never turned on one of his own. If he had reason to be wary of someone, he could be as dangerous as one's worst enemy. Nails Morton, Hymie Weiss, and even the grafting cop who had completely sold out to O'Banion's dollars were varying degrees of "right guys." Johnny

Torrio, who was neither friend nor lackey, was a type of "wrong guy." O'Banion would participate in Torrio's plan as long as it reaped more benefits for him than he might have earned independently. But as far as he was concerned, he owed Torrio nothing, and if the day should come that the partnership hindered him, he could forget that it had ever been agreed to.

Despite the guaranteed inflow of liquor and beer, the North Sider continued to hijack booze trucks and lift alcohol from legitimate storage depots. On March 14, 1921, he heisted twenty barrels of alcohol, valued at fifty-five hundred dollars, from the Price Flavoring Extract Company. When O'Banion learned that the police were seeking him, he went into hiding. The arrest warrant on file with the Clerk of the Cook County Circuit Court bears the handwritten notation "Inf (?) Officer Waters—defendant is a fugitive. 3/29/21." He remained underground until the right people had been paid off and the case was nol-prossed.

Spring rolled into summer, whereupon O'Banion found himself in trouble again. At 2:30 A.M. on the morning of June 1, *Herald and Examiner* Circulation Manager George Hartford noticed O'Banion in the newspaper's offices, and told him, "Stick around; we may need you." The gangster replied that he wanted to take a nap but could be found resting at the Fort Dearborn Hotel should he be required later.

Less than an hour later, the watchman at the Board of Trade Building spotted men moving furtively in the offices of the Chicago Typographical Union, housed in the Postal Telegraph Building at 332 South LaSalle Street. He hurried across the street and alerted that building's watchman, who had noticed nothing. Their suspicions aroused, the two men stopped Patrol Sergeant John J. Ryan as he was making his rounds. Ryan posted one watchman in the street while the other accompanied him upstairs to the second floor. They pushed open the union office door just as a small explosion rocked the premises.

O'Banion, Weiss, Reiser, and George Moran were clustered around the smoking safe. The floor was covered with wet blankets they had wrapped around the steel box to deaden the sound of the explosion. They turned at the policeman's arrival, and O'Banion raised his gun, but Ryan was faster and knocked it from his hand.

Ryan covered the burglars with his own pistol, and marched them down to the police station, where all four initially gave false names. O'Banion was Edward Sterling, Weiss was Oscar Nelson, Reiser was John Sibley, and Moran was George Morrissey. Each was charged with burglary and possession of burglars' tools. Money found in their pockets had a singed appearance, causing the police to suspect that the crew was also responsible for a safeblowing that had taken place at Joseph Klein's feed store earlier that night.

Sergeant Ryan earned a three-hundred-dollar-a-year pay raise for collaring the gang, and the *Chicago Tribune* awarded him its one-hundred-dollar "Hero Prize" for the month of May. Ryan, nicknamed "Praying John" by his fellow officers because of his strong religious beliefs, said, "It was Providence and the prayers that saved me," when interviewed by the press about the mass arrest. Chief Fitzmorris was inclined to agree.

"He must have had a guardian angel on every side of him," the chief commented. "Not only were the men armed, but in their possession was found enough nitroglycerine to blow up the whole downtown district."

Chief of Detectives Hughes told reporters, "God must have been with him. Why, this man Reiser would just as soon kill a man as eat."

Bail was set at such a nominal amount (two thousand dollars apiece) that Henry Barrett Chamberlain of the Chicago Crime Commission, a citizens group formed in 1919 to aid the war against crime in the Windy City, stormed into the chambers of Judge Frank Johnston Jr. and charged that there was an organized attempt to "keep bad actors out of jail." Johnston accordingly raised Reiser's bond to one hundred thousand dollars, Weiss's to fifty thousand dollars, and O'Banion's and Moran's to sixty thousand dollars. At Chamberlain's instigation, federal warrants were drawn up charging the four men with possession of explosives in violation of the wartime Defense of the Nation Act.

"This quartet with Charles Reiser at its head is the most dangerous in the city," Chamberlain said. "It would be a crime to allow them to escape by forfeiting their bonds should they be able to make bail. There has not been one safe blown since this gang was arrested, and that condition will exist as long as they are in jail."

They were not in jail long. In the case of O'Banion, Matt Foley from the *Chicago American* posted a five-thousand-dollar bond to free him on the federal explosives-possession charge. The gangsters' attorney, John Byrne, advised State's Attorney Robert Crowe that he was seeking a bail reduction, on the grounds that his clients were the victims of discriminatory treatment. Judge Johnston relented, reducing their bonds on the procuring-explosives charges, and adjusting their bail on the other charges accordingly. O'Banion was required to post forty-five thousand dollars altogether. Two housewives, Mrs. Mary Marubio and Mrs. Edna Casey, acted as sureties.

It cost O'Banion nearly thirty thousand dollars to beat the rap. After making sure that a favorable jury verdict had been bought, he took the stand to give a hilarious performance.

"We had all met at about three o'clock in the morning in the all-night Raklios restaurant here on the corner," he explained earnestly. "We were having hot chocolate and chocolate éclairs. We heard a lot of racket—could have been an explosion in the Postal Telegraph Building. So we climbed the fire escape to see what it was all about.

"Whoever was blowing the safe must have heard us coming. They got away. We stepped off the fire escape through the window and were just looking at the safe when the policeman came in. I always carry a gun in the course of my work. At first I thought it might have been the thieves coming back. But when I saw it was a policeman, I put my gun down and we gave ourselves up like good citizens."

After the not-guilty verdict was officially announced, O'Banion, Reiser, Weiss, Moran, and their comrades hustled off to the Bella Napoli Café, a deluxe restaurant owned by ward boss Diamond Joe Esposito, for a celebratory dinner. Before long, everyone was rip-roaring drunk—even the temperate O'Banion imbibed more than was his custom. One of the gangsters got the idea to re-create the Battle of Bunker Hill, Chicago style. Tables and chairs were overturned and converted into makeshift forts, and the revelers began to discharge their pistols, making sure that the bullets hit anything but one another. Tony "Mops" Volpi, the manager and a tough specimen himself, fought his way through the gunpowder haze and located O'Banion. He pleaded with the North Sider to take the war game elsewhere.

Just as O'Banion began calling the fun to a halt, a beat cop barged in and started threatening all present with arrest for creating a public nuisance. The gangsters converged on him, poked their guns against his uniform, and hustled him outside. Out on the sidewalk, they shoved him aside unharmed and resumed their mock battle. The shaken officer ran for the nearest call box, but by the time the patrol wagon arrived, the merrymakers were long gone.

News of such reckless behavior concerned Torrio, who doubted the stability of his most powerful partner. He had seen Monk Eastman's primal behavior lead to the downfall of himself and his followers back in New York, and harbored concern that O'Banion was headed down the same route, which would also spell trouble for the combine that he was such an integral part of. What Torrio did not understand about Chicago at that time was that the rogue gangster was an accepted, even applauded, ingredient in the energetic, brazen spirit that the city embodied. Whatever scandalized New York amused Chicago at worst.

Nineteen twenty-one brought more disturbing news to the little Big Man. Big Bill Thompson, the patron saint of the underworld, was in a political squabble that was tearing his machine apart and threatening his chances of re-election in 1923. He and Fred Lundin, his flamboyant campaign manager, had quarreled over Thompson's appointment of Charles Fitzmorris as chief of police, a move about which Lundin had not been consulted. Thompson in turn resented Lundin's excessive spending of the political machine's money and tight control over patronage. The onetime medicine man justified his actions by telling all who would listen that Big Bill owed him everything, and that the cowboy mayor had only been elected due to his, Lundin's, skillful management.

There might have been some truth to his claim. In the judicial election of 1921, Thompson advocated a slate that emphasized loyalty to him above all else, which offended the intelligence of the candidates and the public. His crushing defeat by a bipartisan ticket led to predictions that Big Bill was through and had no chance at another term.

Torrio evaluated the situation and decided to strengthen his suburban and village holdings, in case a reform mayor made things difficult in Chicago. He also decided to raise the bar on his current political value, seeking to make friends in the state governor's office.

In July 1921 Illinois Governor Len Small was indicted for embezzling $819,690.31 of state funds during his tenure as state treasurer. Small, a former banker-farmer from Kankakee, had deposited the money entrusted to him into a fictitious bank. He and Bill Thompson were political allies, Thompson having backed him during the gubernatorial election in 1920.

Torrio had good reason to want to see Small acquitted; the former farmer was notorious for pardoning convicted criminals. The anti-Small *Tribune,* over a period of months, printed names, dates, and details of the pardons the governor had granted during his time in office. Wiseacres looking to lampoon Small sang a popular song of the day, "Oh Promise Me," with the title switched to "Oh Pardon Me."

Len Small's trial was to be held in Waukegan, Illinois. Torrio sent a team of emissaries with instructions to bribe the jury first, then resort to violence if need be. The effort was rewarded with success; the jurors acquitted Small on two ballots. The governor's gratitude was manna to Torrio, who would need a friend in such a high place if a reform candidate were elected Chicago mayor in 1923.

In the late winter of 1921 O'Banion's friend and former mentor Gene Geary wandered into Harry J. Reckas's Chicago saloon, a confused and angry expression on his pig-like face and a pistol in his hand. When his unsteady gaze settled on one of the saloon customers, attorney T. J. Fell, he raised his arm, took aim . . . and paused. Fell stared back, the color draining from his face. Seconds passed. Then suddenly, unexpectedly, Geary shifted his arm and pulled the trigger, missing Fell but killing Reckas instantly.

Geary was arrested for murder, and there had been too many witnesses to his crime for him to evade punishment as smoothly as he had in the past. After a brief trial, a jury found him guilty, and the judge sentenced him to hang on June 17, 1921.

Geary took the sentence with sneering stoicism, either not afraid to meet his Maker or confident that his attorneys would get the sentence commuted. But as the months between his sentencing and the April 10 convening of the Supreme Court (who would hear his appeal) dragged by, the racketeer's bravado and grip on reality gradually dissolved. Crisis erupted at the beginning of February, when jailer George Lee heard unearthly screams issuing from Geary's cell at the Cook County Jail. Hurrying to investigate, he found Geary huddled against the wall, shaking uncontrollably.

"The lights! The lights!" the killer shrieked. "They're blinding me!"

Lee sent for the jail physician, Dr. Francis MacNamara, who examined Geary and diagnosed him as suffering from locomotor ataxia. "The man is in a paretic state," the doctor stated, shaking his head. "It is doubtful whether he'll live through until April 10."

Geary's hysteria, Dr. MacNamara discovered, was brought on by the conviction that his "enemies" had bored a hole in the ceiling of his cell and were sending bright rays of light beaming down for the purpose of blinding him. Said enemies included former gang associates, as well as the ghost of the man he had killed.

Geary's attorneys, Thomas Nash and Michael Ahern (who would later represent Al Capone), obtained the services of prominent Chicago alienists, such as Drs. Hugh Patrick, Archibald Church, and Harold Singer, in an attempt to prove that their client was insane at the time of Reckas's murder, thereby prohibiting his execution. Their initial findings were not in Geary's favor. After much legal wrangling, the execution date was postponed and a sanity hearing scheduled for October. An unconfirmed rumor is that Dean O'Banion contributed heavily to a defense fund used to sway both witness testimony and jury opinion. Nash and Ahern's ploy worked; the jury found that Geary was insane and therefore not responsible for his actions.

On the day of his sentencing, everyone in the courtroom wondered whether the insanity plea might not be appropriate after all. When Judge Kersten began reading the formal order committing Geary to the Chester penitentiary for the criminally insane, the racketeer interrupted him from the defense table.

"Wait a minute there, you!!" he shouted at the startled judge. "Who is this Eugene Geary you're talking about?"

Judge Kersten composed himself quickly. "Why, you are the Eugene Geary I'm speaking of."

"I'm not Eugene Geary," the prisoner insisted.

"Well, who are you then?"

"I'm Mattison Eugene Geary," was the indignant and puzzling response. "I'm not Eugene Geary at all."

Kersten attempted to calm Geary, but the latter began to rail at him and insist that "they" were "stealing my heart and my name." He begged to be allowed to go to Springfield. "I want to see the Supreme Court there and get a square deal," he explained.

Judge Kersten reminded him that he had nothing to complain about, as Nash and Ahern had succeeded in saving him from the gallows. "If they hadn't, you might have marched off with Wanderer this morning." (Carl Wanderer, a homosexual former soldier, had murdered his pregnant wife.)

"Well, I didn't get a square deal," Geary replied stubbornly. When asked by the judge if he were insane, he began yelling. "No, I'm not!! I want a square deal. I don't want to go to Chester!"

First Assistant State's Attorney Edwin S. Day commented that he was about ready to agree that the racketeer was not insane after all. Delighted, Geary turned to him and exclaimed, "Of course I'm not!! Let's you and I go down to the Supreme Court and get a square deal."

Judge Kersten finally read out the commitment order and nodded for the bailiffs to take the prisoner back to his cell. As he was being led out, Geary suddenly stopped and turned to face his attorney.

"You talk up there, Nash," he pleaded. "They've got something in my ears. I'm all stuffed up, can't talk." He continued to ramble as he was escorted out of the courtroom. His reign of terror was finally at an end.

Dawn had just broken on the chilly morning of October 11, 1921, when Charles Reiser received visitors. A car pulled up outside his home at 1704 Otto Street and honked twice. Reiser looked out the window and said to his wife, Madeleine, "I think that's somebody I know—I'll go and see." She watched as he left the house, approached the vehicle, and started talking to the occupants. Suddenly guns barked and spat orange fire in the morning air. Reiser collapsed to the sidewalk with fourteen bullets lodged in his body.

Neighbors rushed the injured man to Alexian Brothers Hospital, where a painful examination revealed that one bullet had struck the spine. The doctors assured Reiser that he would live but, because of the spinal injury, would be paralyzed from the waist down. He took the bad news surprisingly well. "He was as game as could be," the attending surgeon commented.

Game or not, the police were concerned that his assailants would try again. (Reiser had claimed to not know them after all.) A guard was placed in his hospital wing, and Detective Sergeant Lawrence Cooney was assigned the task of escorting Mrs. Reiser and the two children to and from their daily visits.

On October 18, Reiser asked his wife to bring him a gun that he had secreted in their house. She agreed, after he insisted that he wanted it for protection in case his enemies made it past the police guard. When she and Verna, their fourteen-year-old daughter, returned for their customary visit, she brought in the weapon.

Sergeant Cooney waited downstairs, as usual, while the visit was in progress. Eventually Verna joined him, saying, "Mother's nearly ready." No sooner had she spoken when gunfire sounded above their heads, followed by hysterical screams from Madeleine Reiser. Cooney raced up the stairs and into the room. Reiser, a faint smile on his lips, was lying back, the still-warm pistol clenched in his fingers. The officer blanched at the sight of his head, which had been cracked open like a gory egg.

Madeleine Reiser could not be consoled. "He shot himself!!" she cried. "I was kissing him goodbye when—oh, why did he do it when he was getting along so nicely?" She was taken home in a state of near collapse.

Police investigators became suspicious, especially after hospital staff insisted at the inquest that Reiser had been in good spirits. When the widow refused to testify during the proceedings, suspicion as to her guilt intensified, and she was placed under arrest. Ernest Schoeps, the dead man's brother, agreed with this turn of events. "He [Reiser] could not shoot himself," he said. "His right hand and left arm were both broken."

Madeleine Reiser was held at the East Chicago Avenue police station until called to tell her story in court. She presented such a pathetic, grieving figure to the coroner's jury that they bought the suicide story. She left the court a free woman and inherited Reiser's hundred-thousand-dollar estate.

In 1931 a *Daily Times* piece that examined Reiser's death in retrospect suggested another possible killer: Dean O'Banion. Reporter Edward Doherty wrote, "O'Banion . . . climbed up the fire escape of the hospital where Reiser was dying. O'Banion got into the right ward and, seeing Reiser in bed, fired twice and killed him."

There are three serious flaws in this scenario. One, Reiser was not dying. Two, it discounts the fact that Madeleine Reiser was definitely present when her husband died. Three, O'Banion's crippled leg would have prevented him from running fast enough to elude Cooney, who arrived on the scene seconds later. Although O'Banion did not kill his former mentor, he probably would have done so if given the chance.

Charles Reiser killed anyone who was a potential threat, including his first wife and even members of his own gang. A case in point was the murder of Clarence White. Reiser and White, an Eighteenth Ward teaming contractor, stood accused of slaying a man named Marshall, who managed the Golden Rule department store. When police arrived at White's home to interview him, they found him dead, his heart punctured by a bullet. The cause of death was officially suicide, but informers told a different story. They said that a homicidal paranoia had seized Reiser and left him convinced that White would crack under pressure and talk. He hurried to the teaming contractor's place and shot him, careful to make it look like suicide. Unlike O'Banion, Reiser did not bind his followers to him through friendship; he intimidated them into a grudging loyalty. The Reiser camp interpreted White's murder as a universal warning.

Another death hit the Reiser ranks in April 1921. The police caught John Mahoney cracking a safe in the West Side Masonic Temple on March 17. They found burglar tools, two automatic pistols, and four cartridge clips on him, and a search of his home revealed thirty ounces of nitro-glycerine (which experts pronounced "enough to blow up the Loop"), two hundred fuses with the wires attached, percussion caps, two spools of steel wire, two jimmies, and assorted safecracker tools. The police were especially interested in the steel wire, as it was the exact same type that had been used to tie up employees during a robbery at the Western Shade Cloth Company—a robbery in which the watchman had been shot to death.

Mahoney, on being told that a murder charge was a certainty, begged to be taken to State's Attorney Crowe. He offered to tell all he knew about the Reiser Gang's past crimes in exchange for leniency. One of the crimes he ascribed to Reiser was White's murder. He talked of numerous alcohol thefts committed by the gang, such as three barrels of grain alcohol stolen from the Northwestern Barber Supply Company, and twenty barrels lifted from the Dr. Price Flavouring Extract Company. He named Guy Wadsworth, a former policeman, as an active gang member; when rounded up, Wadsworth also agreed to turn state's evidence in exchange for leniency.

Wadsworth's fate for his duplicity is not known, but less than a month after Mahoney was released on a twenty-five-hundred-dollar bond, he was shot to death and his body dumped from a car in the alley at 1814 South Peoria Street.

O'Banion would have sanctioned Mahoney's murder, as informers were despised, but White's death had been unnecessary. It was disturbing proof that Reiser was falling deeper and deeper into a state of murderous paranoia.

"I didn't know Reiser, but I remember Dean saying that he was getting out of control, and that he didn't like Dean running the show," E. Barnett recalled. Reiser appears to have been frustrated by O'Banion's rise in underworld celebrity, thanks to the Torrio connection. O'Banion had a more natural talent for organizing beer and alcohol acquisition and soliciting customers for his product. Although he was an exemplary landlord, Reiser was otherwise too aggressive and paranoid to make much headway in the bootlegging business. Had he not been dispatched when he was, a showdown between himself and his former protégé would have been a real possibility.

The months of 1921 had erased two of O'Banion's wilder influences. Reiser was dead, and Gene Geary was venting his psychotic fury on doctors and orderlies at Chester. The North Sider had a reasonably sound advisory council: Nails Morton, Maxie Eisen, and Hymie Weiss. His future looked promising. By nature he was impulsive, a showoff who hated playing second fiddle to anyone, but his arrangement with Torrio was profitable, and he planned to play ball as long as he perceived that the game was fair.

10

In a Reform State of Mind

THE GANG LEADERS WHO ACCEPTED Torrio's plan were sitting comfortably by 1922. In Chicago, a referendum had been held on an adjustment to the Eighteenth Amendment to allow beer and wine, and it had passed by a five-to-one margin. Although it had merely been a popular vote and had no legal backing, the results assured the city's bootleggers that customer shortage would never be a concern.

Despite his Detroit connections and brewery holdings, O'Banion continued to hijack whenever the opportunity presented itself. On April 12, 1922, he and Dan McCarthy were having breakfast in the Hotel Sherman coffee shop when an associate, Hymie Levin, who ran a nearby speakeasy, came hurrying up to their table. He told the North Siders that a driver for the Walter Powers Warehouse was having a drink in his saloon at that very moment, and that Levin had overheard him telling another customer that he was in the process of delivering some bonded liquor to West Side drugstores.

Like everyone else, Levin knew that O'Banion paid well for tips, giving informants 10 percent of whatever he was able to sell the booze for. The speakeasy owner had no sooner finished talking when Vincent Drucci and Harry Hartman, an O'Banion associate and sometime boxer, joined the group. Levin made a worried comment about there not being enough for five to profit from the haul, but Drucci and Hartman denied any interest in sharing in the spoils, merely offering to go along to provide muscle.

O'Banion, McCarthy, Drucci, and Hartman jumped into O'Banion's car and followed the liquor-laden truck, which had just started resuming its journey west. When it slowed down at Canal Street, O'Banion stepped on the gas and drew up alongside it. He, Drucci, and Hartman jumped out of their car, surrounded the Jackson Express & Van Company truck, and ordered the driver, Joseph Goodman, out at gunpoint. When they told him to get lost, he did so gratefully. O'Banion drove the truck to a hiding spot a block away, where McCarthy and the others picked him up so that they could return to the coffee shop to finish their breakfasts.

"My coffee was still hot," O'Banion recalled with pride, pleased at how quickly and easily he'd pulled off the heist. "But I had the girl bring me another order of wheatcakes."

The total take was 225 cases of bottled whiskey intended for the Susquemac Distilling Company. The gangsters conveyed it to Nails Morton's garage, where Morton bought the entire load for $22,500, or $100 per case of twenty-four pints. O'Banion later reminisced, "Hymie Levin and McCarthy and me split that money three ways—seven thousand five hundred apiece for twenty minutes' work. You can't beat that."

Joseph Goodman, after being relieved of his cargo, had run to the nearest telephone to report the theft. At the police station, he looked through photographs and picked out O'Banion, Drucci, and Hartman as three of his assailants. They were arrested for robbery. O'Banion's ten-thousand-dollar bond was posted by Titus Haffa, a real-estate broker and alderman of the Forty-third Ward, which was O'Banion territory. None of the merry trio went to trial on the charge, as O'Banion secured a nol prosqui for the case.

Months later, in June, the safe at the Parkway Tea Room at 725 North Michigan Avenue was blown open and twenty thousand dollars' worth of cash, jewelry, and bonds stolen. Sergeant Shanley removed some clean sets of fingerprints from the steel box, compared them to those already on file at the identification bureau, and determined that Dean O'Banion and Vincent Drucci were the culprits. Nicholas Tice, a night watchman, recalled seeing two young men perched on a refuse box outside the Tea Room at 3 A.M., singing a popular melody. An automobile was parked nearby, its driver chuckling at the spectacle. Officers arrested O'Banion and Drucci, but the charges, like so many others in both of their careers, were dropped with leave to reinstate.

Thompson's administration, and particularly his police force, came under a barrage of criticism for such laxity with criminals. Nineteen twenty-two was barely a month old when a scandal broke that revealed how deeply the corruption ran. A squad of policemen under the command of Lieutenant John W. McCarthy raided a gambling house and sent the prisoners to the Warren Avenue Station. McCarthy requested that Lieutenant James Doherty send them on to the Bureau of Identification. Doherty instead booked them at his station and bypassed the bureau, where their fingerprints would have brought up long and violent records.

To make matters worse, six men were recruited from flophouses and saloons and offered money to impersonate the prisoners. Harry Shelton, an unemployed worker, was approached in a ramshackle restaurant by a plainclothes cop who offered him ten dollars to temporarily pose as "James Albert" in a police holding cell. By the time the ruse was discovered, the real prisoners had long since sauntered out the door to freedom. Chief Fitzmorris ordered Lieutenant Doherty, two sergeants, and three patrolmen suspended pending a grand jury investigation, but it came too late to avert a public relations disaster.

To remove some of the tarnish from the department's image, Mayor Thompson announced in early February that he was appointing the Reverend John Williamson, a Methodist-Episcopal minister, to the post of law enforcement commissioner of Chicago. The office, so the press release trumpeted, would be conducted "in accordance with the teachings of Christ." Thompson assured the public that the minister's investigations and punitive decisions would be final whether they hit the "highest city official or the lowest crook on the street."

"In seeking the causes of crime," the mayor continued, "we must not close our eyes to the fact that many persons who were in the habit of drinking intoxicating liquors and who are not in sympathy with the Eighteenth Amendment now drink moonshine, or anything in the nature of intoxicating liquors, and under the influence of it become utterly irresponsible."

Bootleggers merely chuckled at his halfhearted interpretations, but they laughed out loud when Thompson suggested that war service was another cause of criminality.

"We must also face the fact that during the last four or five years, many young men of the city, as a result of the teachings of war, have been educated to value human life cheaply. Some of these young men are not mentally capable, on account of the war strain, disease, and shell shock, of making the distinction between robbing and killing for private gain and doing the same thing on the battlefield in the name of patriotism."

If anyone had checked the saloons and war records more thoroughly, they would have noticed that two major players in the spread of corruption neither drank intemperately nor fought in the war: John Torrio and Dean O'Banion. Thompson knew well that the scandals and the dilapidated condition of his political machine had nullified his chances of being re-elected in 1923, but he believed he might have another shot in 1927 if he made a good impression during his last months in office. Reverend Williamson's appointment was a piece of political fool's gold, showy and impressive, but of little consequence. The law enforcement commissioner hurt nobody important. Thompson would not bite the hands that had fed him so well over the years.

Nineteen twenty-two was also the year that Al Capone received his first mention in the press. Early on the morning of August 30, Capone was driving his car at breakneck speed along Randolph Street, heading east. He and his three passengers, two men and a woman, were raging drunk from a night of wild partying. At the corner of Randolph and Wabash, their car crashed into a taxicab, injuring the driver, Fred Krause. Blood boiling, Capone stomped out of his car, brandished a deputy sheriff's badge and a gun, and threatened to shoot Krause.

The motorman of a southbound streetcar stopped his trolley when he saw what was happening and tried to persuade Capone to put the gun away. The young Italian responded by threatening to shoot him, too. Arriving police officers sent Krause to the hospital in an ambulance and hauled Capone to the nearest station (his companions had long since fled). The cocky hoodlum boasted that his connections would make the arrest a waste of time, not to mention something that the police might regret later. He was speedily bailed out, and the case never went to court.

The *Tribune*, in covering the arrest, identified him as "Alfred Caponi, 25 years old, living at the notorious Four Deuces, a disorderly house at 2222 South Wabash Avenue." The story was considered so unimportant that only the *Tribune* bothered to print it, relegating it to an inside page.

Alphonse Capone's press debut was a humble one. Seven years later, at the zenith of his fame, reporters would be clamoring to interview him, but the reading public of 1922 noticed him only as a murderous drunk who had nearly killed one man and would likely have finished that job and one other had the police not arrived in time.

O'Banion's celebrity, in contrast, was growing steadily. His safecracking and burglary stunts had already graced the Chicago dailies on several occasions. The April 1922 liquor hijacking case made the front page of his old employer, the *Examiner*, albeit not as a headliner. He was a newsman's dream come true, being a persistent and unrepentant sinner who maintained a friendly smile and ready quip for reporters.

Not all gangsters were equally forthcoming with journalists. If anything, they feared press coverage, not wishing to draw the notice and ire of the reform element. Hymie Weiss, when approached by news photographers, always fixed a cold stare on them and warned, "Take a picture of me and I'll kill you." Although O'Banion would have been wise to share that wariness, he didn't. Many of the newsmen who approached him were former cronies from his slugging days.

It was a combination of quick wit, sensational escapades, and friendly accessibility that made Dean O'Banion fantastic copy. He was becoming the archetypal gangster of the early 1920s, typifying the new, cocky breed the way that Big Jim Colosimo had represented the noisy glitter and glamour of the pre-war Levee.

At the start of 1923, Big Bill Thompson announced that he would not be a candidate in either the Republican primary or the April mayoral election. His official withdrawal coincided with mass indictments for fraud against key members of his machine. Ex-Thompson campaign manager Fred Lundin; Lundin's nephew Vitus Rohm, who was the dispenser of city hall patronage; and twenty-two others were charged with defrauding the board of education of an estimated one million dollars. The brilliant lawyer Clarence Darrow was hired to defend them, and Thompson himself cut short a vacation in Hawaii to testify on their behalf.

While the fate of the conspirators was being decided, the candidates for the mayoral election were declared. The choice Republican contender was Arthur C. Lueder, Postmaster of Chicago, who was backed by Senator Charles Deneen, Attorney General Harry Brundage, and State's Attorney Robert Crowe. Lueder's Democratic opponent was William E. Dever, a sixty-one-year-old jurist who had served a term as alderman in 1902 and currently served as a judge in Superior Court, Criminal Branch.

Thompson sulked about his forced withdrawal from the race, complaining, "I have, of course, been opposed by all the forces of grasping wealth and aggrandizement." The pot was calling the kettle black. He pointed out the good he had done while in office, namely his "Chicago Beautiful" plan, which had widened Roosevelt Road (formerly Twelfth Street), opened the Michigan Boulevard link, and built the Franklin Street Bridge. However practical and aesthetically appealing these improvements were, they were not enough to gloss over the many outrages and embarrassments that had come to light under the Thompson administration.

A shooting committed by Dapper Dan McCarthy focused negative attention on organized labor. On the frigid evening of February 18, 1923, he and Ray Schalk, a professional baseball player, were having a drink in Al Tierney's popular café when union official Steve Kelliher strolled in with his wife on his arm. Mrs. Kelliher spotted McCarthy at once and recognized him as one of her husband's more persistent rivals in the plumbers union. She stormed over to his table and let forth with a barrage of abuse, calling McCarthy a rat and other names. When Kelliher joined her, the arguing intensified to the point that Tierney tried to intervene by asking McCarthy and Kelliher to take the discussion outside. The latter drew a gun, warned Tierney away, and began shooting wildly. McCarthy pulled out his own weapon and fired back, hitting the rival union man between the eyes and killing him.

McCarthy was found not guilty on the grounds of self-defense, but State's Attorney Crowe was so besieged by an angry public (it was the twenty-fourth labor-related killing in Chicago in twelve years) that he suggested that labor leaders should be searched every time a police officer encountered them. Gang and union murders did not endear Thompson to the voting public of 1923.

As the election drew nearer, the mudslinging by the competing factions intensified. Dever was accused of accepting a hundred-thousand-dollar campaign contribution from William Randolph Hearst in exchange for supporting Hearst's intended bid for the U.S. presidency. Dever's Roman Catholic faith became a means of deriding him to Protestant voters, but his supporters struck back by denouncing Lueder's German antecedents. They could have spared themselves the effort, as Chicago residents were in that rare frame of mind where reform was an attractive prospect.

Dever won the election by over one hundred thousand votes. One of his first moves as mayor was to allow the Democratic machine boss, George Brennan, to handle the patronage system. Although almost fanatical in his pursuit of law and order, Dever granted this privilege to Brennan as repayment for the latter's support during the election. Had he not relinquished his supervision over patronage, he might have given the Chicago underworld an even worse time than he did.

Dever was born in Woburn, Massachusetts, but had lived in Chicago since 1887. He had worked in one of the tanneries on Goose Island and had become quite skilled at the trade, but he felt that his calling was as a lawyer. He studied nights after days of hard work in the tannery and eventually passed the bar exam. In 1902 he ran for and was elected alderman of the chaotic Seventeenth Ward. He soon earned a reputation for being honest, sympathetic to the plight of the common man, and a fierce fighter for causes that he believed in.

Although he became the implacable foe of the Chicago bootleggers, Dever was actually anti-Volstead. "I have never intended to be, and am not now, a Prohibitionist," he said. Another time he commented, "I am not engaged in an effort to mold public opinion for or against the Volstead Act or the Eighteenth Amendment. If the people desire the law amended or modified, they know the place to look for relief—in the Congress." But while Prohibition remained on the law books, he would enforce it with every means at his disposal. "The one way to get rid of a bad law," he told an interviewer, "is to enforce it."

Under Dever, Charles Fitzmorris was replaced as chief of police by Captain Morgan A. Collins. Collins, a former medical student and saloonkeeper, was a dedicated policeman and the perfect attack dog for the Dever administration. Money and power did not interest him; like the mayor, he scorned crooks who made a joke out of the law. Enemies sneered that when he was attached to the Chicago Avenue precinct, the district was crawling with gamblers. Collins snapped that he would need several more cops posted on the front and back doorsteps of every gaming house to get rid of the gamblers.

Becoming chief of police was a boon to a man who rankled at the gang rule that gripped Chicago. He and his raiders began striking all over the city, and netted over 1000 prisoners within a month. He warned his captains that if bootlegging was not stamped out, they would be looking for new jobs, and fast.

Torrio tried to deal with Collins via the usual means. After the chief had raided and padlocked the Four Deuces, Torrio offered him a thousand dollars a day to lay off. Collins showed him the door. The next offer was one hundred thousand dollars a month. Collins refused that, as well as another offer of five dollars per barrel merely for his permission to move 250 barrels of beer a day through the city. For the first time since coming to Chicago, Torrio was worried.

At seven o'clock on the morning of Sunday, May 13, 1923, Nails Morton arrived at the Brown Riding Academy at 3008 North Halstead Street, immaculately togged out in a green sport coat, cream-colored jodhpurs, and well-polished riding boots. He had purchased a horse the previous Friday, a regal bay whom O'Banion had named Morvich after the famous racer, and was boarding it at the facility. Morton had made plans to meet Dean and Viola O'Banion and Peter Mundane, a commission broker friend, on the Lincoln Park bridle paths.

He saddled Morvich, mounted, and rode out of the stable. Suddenly, the spirited animal bolted and ran south on Clark Street at a mad gallop. Morton stood in the stirrups and tugged on the reins with all his might in an effort to stop the horse, but to no avail.

His plight was spotted by officer John Keys of the Sheffield Avenue station, who was standing at the corner of Clark and Diversey Parkway. The policeman rushed to catch the horse's bridle, and as he did so, saw the left stirrup break. Morton regained his balance by crouching down and wrapping his arms around his mount's neck. The gangster attempted to leap to the ground but in mid-jump was struck by the horse's foreleg. Morvich tried to leap over his rider's sprawling form but kicked with his back legs, striking Morton on the head.

Officer Keys and a bystander, Joseph McCauley, ran to the gangster's aid while Yellow Cab drivers stationed farther down the street caught the horse. When Keys knelt beside Morton, he gave a cry of recognition.

"Why, it's Nails Morton! He was my lieutenant in France!"

Morton and McCauley carried the injured man to a cab and rushed him to the hospital. Dr. L. A. Beaton was preparing Morton for surgery to reduce the basal skull fracture inflicted by the horse when the Jewish mob boss died, without ever regaining consciousness. A veteran of the Great War, the police courts, and the underworld battles, he met with a bizarre end.

The O'Banions and Mundane had no idea what had befallen their friend until they saw the riderless horse being led back to the riding academy. When informed of the accident, they hurried to the hospital, where they received the bad news.

Morton's funeral on May 15 was an illustration of grief in both the Jewish and underworld communities. A *Herald and Examiner* story, headlined "TRIBUTE TO NAILS MORTON: FIVE THOUSAND JEWISH PEOPLE ATTENDED THE FUNERAL PROCLAIMING HIM PROTECTOR," described how he had made the West Side safe for those of his religious background. Rabbi Julius Levi officiated at the service. Morton's army comrades saw to it that he was buried with full military honors. Also present in the crowd were police officers whose opinion of Morton was not so glowing, but, naturally, they were not invited to speak at the service. "The other side of the career that ended," the newspaper article noted, "was not even mentioned."

His friends and admirers felt Morton's loss so keenly that they planned a memorial service a year later. A printed announcement listed the names of Rabbi Felix Levi, attorney Frank Comerford (who was to deliver the principal address), Hymie Weiss, Dan McCarthy, Maxie Eisen, Terry Druggan, Frankie Lake, Johnny Torrio, and the Miller brothers. Complaints from reformers led to the service being postponed.

According to Chicago legend, Louis Alterie was so maddened by grief that he went to the riding academy after the funeral, removed the guilty horse, and shot it to death. He then called the stable owner and said, "We taught that goddamn horse of yours a lesson. If you want the saddle, go and get it." No proof exists that this event ever took place; in fact, no mention of it was made until two years later, in a *Daily News* story. But anyone acquainted with Alterie would have believed him capable of the deed.

Later writers claimed that Morton had held the wild and impulsive O'Banion in check, thus guaranteeing the North Side Gang's adherence to Torrio's rules for alliance. O'Banion did value his friend's counsel, but it in no way motivated him to stay in an arrangement he supposedly disliked. O'Banion's complaisance of 1920-24 can be linked to one simple reason: He was making money and had no intention of rocking a boat on which he was a co-captain. Torrio meant nothing to him in the personal sense, but he did not harbor bitter feelings toward the Italian either before Morton's death or for months after it.

What ultimately drove a wedge between Torrio and O'Banion was the latter's perception of betrayal. But that lay in the future.

11

The Carmen Avenue Love Nest Murders

In the summer of 1923 one of Johnny Torrio's bitter enemies returned to Chicago after a short term in prison. Spike O'Donnell, the fireball of the gang from Kerry Patch, had been pardoned by Governor Len Small after several pleas for clemency had been received from friends in high places. He walked out the gates of Joliet Penitentiary with his mind on just one thing—getting even with Torrio for the belittlement his slower brothers had suffered in his absence.

O'Donnell gathered a small force of beer runners, strong-arms, and "salesmen" who backed up their pitches with guns and muscle. In addition to brothers Walter and Tommy, Spike's camp included paroled Joliet lifer Jerry O'Connor and two tough gunmen, George "Spot" Bucher and George Meeghan.

The newly rejuvenated South Side O'Donnell Gang sounded the call to war by hijacking Torrio beer trucks and selling the spoils in Kerry Patch saloons. Then they began importing beer from a Joliet brewery and pushing it into both Torrio and Saltis-McErlane territory. They didn't always have to force their product on the saloonkeepers; the beer they peddled was of higher quality than the re-strengthened needle beer that most of the gangs sold because of its low production cost. The O'Donnell beer was cheaper, too—forty-five dollars a barrel as opposed to fifty dollars for the Torrio brew. When Torrio learned about the undercutting, his initial attempt at retaliation was to reduce his rate to forty dollars a barrel, which the O'Donnells could not match. That was when the situation degenerated from petty to ugly.

When the O'Donnells solicited trade, many saloonkeepers would stick with Torrio out of loyalty or fear. Then Spike's men would go through their more intense sales pitches. Tough characters such as Bucher, Meeghan, or Phil Corrigan would fix icy stares on the stubborn target and suggest that buying their beer was the most effective health insurance on the market. If he wavered under the implication and begged for time to think it over, they would grant him a short respite and came back later. If the final decision went against them, they would whip out the brass knuckles and spray the bartender's teeth all over the floor. Then they would smash the premises into kindling.

On September 7, 1923, their enemies fired a return shot. That night, Steve, Walter, and Tommy O'Donnell, accompanied by Bucher and Meeghan, strolled into Jacob Geis's speakeasy at 2154 West Fifty-First Street. They had a bone to pick with Geis, the latter having thrown out a couple of O'Donnell beer drummers during a previous sales call. They told him he had one last chance to switch to their beer, but Geis told them in no uncertain terms that he was not interested. The three seized the saloonkeeper, dragged him over the top of the bar, and beat him so brutally that his skull was fractured. When the bartender tried to intervene, the O'Donnells left him lying unconscious in a pool of blood. Destructive instincts now in full swing, the O'Donnell men visited five more places selling Torrio or Saltis beer and, breaking bones and fixtures.

Word of the rampage reached Torrio when one of the saloonkeepers telephoned the police. Four gunmen tracked down Spike O'Donnell and his followers while they were consuming beer and sandwiches at Joe Klepka's Fifty-third Street saloon, one of their strongholds. One was the youthful killer Ralph Sheldon; another was Danny McFall, a Ragen's Colts triggerman and deputy sheriff. McFall shouted for the shocked O'Donnells to raise their hands or be blown to hell, and fired a shot over Walter O'Donnell's head when the latter challenged him to take the fight outside.

The gunfire jolted the besieged gang members into action. They scattered, attempting to reach the saloon's side and rear doors. McFall collared Jerry O'Connor before the ex-convict could escape and herded him out the swinging doors into the rainy street, where the corpulent, murderous Frank McErlane was waiting with a sawed-off shotgun tucked under his gray raincoat. When O'Connor appeared, McErlane raised the barrel of his weapon and blew the O'Donnell thug's head off.

Torrio hoped that the bloody warning would scare the upstarts back into line, as further killings would only make Mayor Dever more determined to put pressure on the gangs. But when Spike showed more fight than ever, Torrio and his allies struck again. This time, Frank McErlane and Danny McFall riddled Bucher and Meeghan with shotgun fire when the two O'Donnell men slowed their Ford at the intersection of Laflin Street and Garfield Boulevard. The killings took place in full view of several horrified commuters.

An hour after word of the double slaying reached his ears, Mayor Dever summoned Chief of Police Morgan Collins. "Collins," the elderly judge declared, voice tight with anger, "there's a dry law on the nation's books. This town will immediately become dry. Tell your captains I will break every police official in those districts I hear of a drop of liquor being sold." One police official whom he broke right away was Captain Thomas C. Wolfe, who had actually made sales pitches for O'Donnell beer in Torrio saloons. He was suspended and replaced with the tough, gangster-hating Lieutenant William Schoemaker.

Dever told the press, "Until the murderers [of O'Connor, Bucher, and Meeghan] have been apprehended and punished and the illegal traffic for control of which they battle has been suppressed, the dignity of the law and the average man's respect for it is imperiled, and every officer of the law and every enforcing agency should lay aside other duties and join in the common cause—a restoration of law and order. The police will follow this case to a finish as they do all others. This guerrilla war between hijackers, rumrunners, and illicit beer peddlers will be crushed. I am just as sure that this miserable traffic with its toll of human life and morals can be stamped out, as I am mayor and I am not going to flinch for a minute."

The South Side beer war continued despite the threat. On the night of December 1, two O'Donnell beer trucks en route from Joliet were ambushed outside the village of Lemont by thugs in two sedans. Frank McErlane and William Chandell, an ex-con, forced the truck drivers, Morrie Keane and William "Shorty" Egan into their car. After driving some distance, McErlane pumped several blasts from his double-barreled shotgun into the captives and kicked them out of the speeding car into an icy ditch. Miraculously, Egan survived. He dragged himself to a nearby golf club, where the caretaker found him and alerted police. McErlane and Chandell were arrested after being identified by both Egan and the attendant of the garage to which the murder car had been sent for repairs. Both witnesses later recanted their testimony, and State's Attorney Crowe was forced to nol-prosse the case.

Danny McFall was indicted for the murder of Jerry O'Connor but was acquitted after experts testified that a shotgun, not the .38-caliber revolver McFall had been carrying, had killed O'Connor. He faced another indictment, along with Frank McErlane, for the double murder of Bucher and Meeghan. That case also ended up being nol-prossed.

Phil Corrigan was the next O'Donnell man to fall, shotgunned while behind the wheel of his truck. Spike continued to do battle, but with his forces severely decimated, he was more of a nuisance than an actual threat. However, his potential as a troublemaker earned him the dubious honor of being the first intended gangland victim of a Thompson submachine gun, also known as a Tommygun. On September 25, 1925, Frank McErlane's car sped by the corner of Sixty-third Street and Western Avenue, where O'Donnell was standing. The obese killer fired a round at him, but McErlane was unfamiliar with the new weapon and the spray of bullets hit everything but O'Donnell. Spike took it all in weary stride.

"Life with me is just one bullet after another," he sighed. "I've been shot at and missed so often that I've a notion to hire out as a professional target."

After the close call, O'Donnell left Chicago and did not return for two years. But before leaving, he made one last, desperate threat. Knowing that Al Capone had been Torrio's field general in the beer war that had obliterated his gang, Spike blurted during an interrogation at the detective bureau, "I can whip this bird Capone with bare fists any time he wants to step out in the open and fight like a man." He probably could have—O'Donnell stood over six feet tall and was powerfully built. But the day of knuckle-to-knuckle combat was over. So was the rise of the South Side O'Donnells.

While Capone dealt with the Irish upstarts, Torrio took a trip to Italy with his wife and mother in the fall of 1923. While there, he bought his mother a villa, hired fifteen servants, and left her to live out the rest of her days in queenly pomp. He remained in Europe until early 1924, in no hurry to return to the States. Business was good, despite the fiery statements made by Dever and Collins in the Chicago press, and Capone was containing the O'Donnell threat effectively.

Little did Spike guess at the time that he was beholding the calm before the storm.

In 1922 Dean O'Banion and Nails Morton bought interests in William F. Schofield's florist business. There was one shop on Devon Avenue on the far North Side, but O'Banion made his offices in the main location at 738 North State Street, which stood in the shadow of Holy Name Cathedral. He and Schofield had known each other for almost thirteen years, having been friends in their youth.

O'Banion was not merely an absentee owner; he worked most days in the shop, potting plants and arranging flowers along with the employees. Anyone accustomed to seeing the tuxedoed, dapper figure who escorted his gowned wife to opening nights and Gold Coast restaurants was surprised to see him puttering around the store, stained shirtsleeves rolled up and an apron tied around his waist. He had no formal training in the art of floral arrangement, but his natural eye for design and color gave him all the expertise he needed. He became gangdom's official florist, supplying flowers for weddings, funerals, dinners, and other occasions where blooms were a required touch.

None of his harsher traits were in evidence when he dealt with the shop's customers. He frequently gave away day-old blooms to schoolchildren from Holy Name Parochial, suggesting that their mothers would be tickled to receive them. He consulted with Gold Coast matrons over dinner table centerpieces with a courtesy and deference they found gratifying. He sent his floral designers to the homes of his wealthier customers to create mesmerizing layouts based on the theme of the house. To those ordering funeral pieces, he was always gracious and respectful of their grief. Womens associations from Holy Name Cathedral sized him up as a soft touch and regularly approached him for donations. On Saturday, November 8, 1924, two days before he was murdered, O'Banion gave twenty-five dollars to each of four women who, unbeknownst to one another, had all solicited funds for the same charity. He smiled and gave each time without ever mentioning the other donations. "It was such a shame," one of the matrons sighed when discussing the murder. "He was such a nice man."

H. J. Pitts of Chicago remembers patronizing the shop as a boy. "My uncle, J. Pitts, was an ear, nose, and throat specialist, with an office just around the corner from Schofield's. He used to send me there all the time to pick up flowers for Thanksgiving, Christmas, and other holidays. Mr. O'Banion remembered me every time and was always friendly to me."

Every Memorial Day, O'Banion made up a jungle of wreaths and bouquets, piled them in his Cadillac, and drove to Maroa to visit his mother's grave. "It gave Dean a lot of comfort to do that," Schofield commented later. He always knew when the North Sider was getting ready to make a pilgrimage to his birthplace, for O'Banion would prowl moodily through the upstairs offices, sobered by twenty-year-old memories of Emma O'Banion's illness and death.

The job gave O'Banion's daily routine a normalcy he had not known in years. While working for the *Examiner*, his hours had been irregular and the job description varied. Schofield's was open six days a week, from 9 A.M. to P.M., and anyone calling the shop might have O'Banion answer their inquiries or take their orders. (There was a nighttime phone number, which was called by the frantic beer runner the night that two greedy cops held up a Torrio combine beer truck.)

Charles O'Banion later estimated annual revenue generated by his son's shop at somewhere between two hundred thousand and three hundred thousand dollars. Most of the income came from the gangster community, which rarely spent less than thousands of dollars in giving a departed pal an extravagant sendoff.

Soon after the death of Nails Morton, O'Banion began to feud with the Miller brothers. Morton had been partners in various enterprises with Hirschie Miller, and O'Banion wanted to pick up where he had left off. The Millers resisted. He was not from the West Side and he did not share their religious background. Their personal relationship with him, which had always been cordial if not exactly friendly, cooled.

Julius "Yankee" Schwartz tried to benefit from the dissolving friendship. Schwartz came to Chicago from New York in 1919, escaping investigation for his role in the fixing of the 1919 World Series. A second-rate prize fighter, he became a hanger-on in the camp of lightweight boxing champion Benny Leonard, and through Leonard developed a casual friendship with the Miller brothers. (Davy Miller was not only a redneck and white supremacist, but also a prizefight referee.) Schwartz benefited from his association with the Millers—he got a piece of West Side bootlegging action and within a matter of months moved from a flophouse into a permanent suite in a luxurious downtown hotel.

By January 1924 the friendship had soured. Schwartz supposedly double-crossed one of Davy Miller's friends in a liquor deal and refused to make amends. The Millers expelled him from their company. Fuming, Schwartz made his way to O'Banion's camp and cultivated the North Sider's confidence by repeating all the derogatory things he'd heard the Millers say about him. O'Banion believed what he was told and nursed his hostility until things came to a head on January 20.

On that freezing Sunday night (the temperature had dropped to minus-eight degrees Fahrenheit and showed no sign of rising), O'Banion, Weiss, and Schwartz went to the La Salle Theatre to see *Give and Take*, a comedy. Also in attendance were Davy Miller, who had just returned from refereeing a prizefight in St. Louis; Maxie Miller, the youngest of the clan; and Maxie's wife. Davy's wife was home nursing a bad cold. The O'Banion and Miller parties were unaware of the others' presence in the packed theater until the play ended and the audience was filing out into the icy street.

O'Banion, Weiss, and Schwartz noticed Maxie and Davy as they were coming out of the La Salle. The two groups stood together and exchanged cool greetings. Davy Miller made it clear that he despised Schwartz, refusing to even acknowledge his presence. O'Banion took offense at the insult directed at his friend and gestured for Miller to step aside.

"What's the trouble between you and Schwartz?" he demanded.

"He's no good, and I want nothing to do with him," Miller replied tersely. Maxie had just hailed a cab, so Davy turned away without another word and walked toward the curb. O'Banion caught him by the arm and snapped, "He's as good as you are, you bastard."

Miller's fighting instincts flared, but he was not prepared to create a spectacle. He just glared at O'Banion, Weiss, and Schwartz collectively and said, "I can lick all three of you fellows, but this isn't the place."

It was a good enough place for O'Banion, who shoved him. Miller pushed his arm back and raised his own. O'Banion yanked out his revolver and fired repeatedly into Davy's stomach. Maxie rushed to his brother's rescue, whereupon O'Banion shot at him, too. Incredibly, the bullet ricocheted off of the younger Miller's steel belt buckle and only damaged his nerve. As a horrified crowd gathered around, the three North Siders made a quiet but hasty getaway.

Davy was rushed to the nearest hospital, where police investigators demanded to know who had shot him. Despite his weakened condition, Miller replied that he would take care of the assailants himself. When doctors examined his wounds and told him that his chances of recovery were not good, he called his brother Hirschie to his bedside and told him what had happened. Hirschie surprised everyone by talking to reporters who had flocked to the hospital. An operation saved Davy's life, but his recovery was overshadowed by the field day the press had with the story. The *Herald and Examiner* headline trumpeted, "GANG WAR OVER MILLER FEARED."

Some reporters took Hirschie Miller's story at face value and suggested that O'Banion, instead of being angered at Schwartz's snubbing, had been out for blood because the Millers had shorted him sixty thousand dollars in a booze deal. O'Banion denied that allegation and also took exception to being named the aggressor in the incident.

"If I had wanted to bump this Miller off, do you think I'd have done it in the middle of the Loop?" he demanded with some logic. As an afterthought and probably a veiled warning to the Millers, he added, "I'd have fixed him out in some dark alley on the South Side." He insisted that Miller had been the first to draw a gun but was silent when asked for a motive. "I'm sorry it happened," he finally said. "It was just a piece of hotheaded foolishness."

The public shooting of Davy Miller tagged O'Banion forever after as a mad dog, a daredevil killer who took pleasure from inflicting pain. One writer later described him as "a casebook psychopath, with a nerveless indifference to risking or administering pain." It's worth taking a moment to investigate the validity of such a label.

The question of whether O'Banion displayed psychopathic tendencies was addressed by Dr. R. Evans, a British psychiatrist with a large practice. After examining several primary documents, such as news clippings and interviews with O'Banion associates, he wrote:

> There is a great deal of misunderstanding and controversy over the use of this term [psychopath], and it is not presently used in psychiatry. Essentially, what would be referred to as a psychopath is what we now know as a "personality disorder" of an anti-social type. Anti-social personality disordered individuals every often become involved in criminal and violent behavior and appear to have no sense of feelings for others or remorse for their actions. It would seem to me from first glance that O'Banion was not typical of this kind of person and that he does appear to have had a sense of empathy for others. It may well be that he simply was a very emotionally charged and impulsive individual who acted before he thought things through.

Dr. Evans was of the opinion that O'Banion's impulsiveness and occasionally violent actions were linked to his turbulent childhood. In this regard, he wrote:

> Dean's early behavior suggests to me that he was a child with a difficult temperament. It makes you wonder whether or not he suffered from a condition known as Attention Deficit Disorder, which we recognize now, but which was never a concern in the early part of this century. Children with Attention Deficit Disorder, or "hyperactivity," very often go on to have behavioral problems in adulthood.

> It may well be that O'Banion was angry at the loss of his mother and being immersed in an anti-social subculture in Chicago, therefore adopting and using the prevailing morals of the location and the day. There is no doubt that his mother's death and the unusual socializing effect that he was exposed to would likely have led to him developing as an anti-social young man.

Childhood causes aside, all the signs show that O'Banion was not psychopathic. His attack on Davy Miller was motivated not by the desire to inflict pain but the protective instinct of a gang leader. Yankee Schwartz had become a casual member of the North Side Gang by 1924, and O'Banion could hardly stay silent when a vassal was being snubbed in front of him. Part and parcel of maintaining a gang's loyalty was the leader's willingness to stick up for his followers. O'Banion was not an iron-fisted autocrat like Charles Reiser had been; his strong support of his men earned him a respect and affection that crime historians have remarked on at length.

O'Banion initially handled the tense situation outside the La Salle by demanding to know what the trouble between Miller and Schwartz was, and then defending his man against the spiteful answer. Miller unknowingly sealed his fate when he did not back off then and there. If he had, gunplay might never have ensued. Instead, he retorted that, in more favorable circumstances, he would thrash all three North Siders himself. O'Banion shoved him; Miller pushed his arm away. There may be some truth to Dean's assertion that Davy pulled a gun, or that O'Banion thought he was going to. O'Banion responded by shooting fast and unsteadily—physicians attending Miller after the attack commented on the ragged messiness of the wound. There had been no premeditation at any time.

Months later, Al Capone was embroiled in a similar confrontation, this one with lethal results. On May 8, 1924, he stormed into Heinie Jacobs's saloon on South Wabash, just a few doors away from the Four Deuces, looking for one Joe Howard, a small-time booze hijacker who liked to hang out there and brag to the impressionable regulars. Earlier that evening, Howard had slapped around a flabby pimp named Jake Guzik, who, though a coward when it came to physical altercations, was the Torrio–Capone Gang's financial brain. What Guzik did to offend Howard has never been clear, but he came out of the confrontation with a bloody face and hurried off, wailing, to Capone.

Capone found Howard at the bar. Witnesses said that Howard declared cheerfully, "Hello Al!" and thrust out his hand for Capone to shake. Capone grabbed him and demanded to know why he had assaulted Guzik. To save face among his fan club at the saloon, Howard sneered, "Go back to your girls, you dago pimp!" Capone released him, took a step back, and shot him in the head.

Joe Howard's murder was held up as an example of what Capone would do to avenge a friend. Robert Schoenberg wrote in *Mr. Capone*:

> It was probably the most strategically important killing of Capone's career, coming eight months before he assumed leadership of the outfit. Now, the scruffiest gang member could tell himself, *If Al would go the limit for that pig, Guzik, what wouldn't he do for me?*

O'Banion wounded Davy Miller for similar reasons and was labeled a psychopath. Capone actually killed his foe and emerged as a great leader. The discrepancy, not to mention the injustice, is obvious.

Chicago crime historian and author John Binder agrees that the Miller shooting was not the unique result of an unsound mind. "These were tough guys who did not take insults easily and were quick to fight and shoot." He counters the assertion of past writers who suggest that even after being guaranteed bootlegging riches, the North Side Gang (in particular O'Banion) continued to commit high-risk crimes like robbery and safecracking because of mental instability. "Lots of the non-Italian gangs did similar things. Some of the Saltis guys as well as Fur Sammons [a Capone associate] either did or were chief suspects in various high-profile armed robberies."

O'Banion had been watching the Sibley Warehouse at Sixteenth and Peoria Streets for some time. He was determined to seize its contents, a million dollars' worth of pre-war bonded Kentucky whiskey. An armed guard patrolled the premises twenty-four hours a day, making a midnight theft too risky. After giving the matter much thought, O'Banion approached a professional forger, a member of a counterfeiting ring that had stolen the certifying apparatus of a well-known bank. He requested and paid for some forged withdrawal permits for the Sibley liquor. After his death, the rumor arose that he had shelled out an additional hundred dollars for a fake forty-one-thousand-dollar check, which he allegedly used to pay an accomplice for his role in the booze heist.

Early on the morning of December 19, 1923, teaming contractor John Coleman received a phone call requesting him to send a truck to the Sibley warehouse. He drove the vehicle himself, arriving just before noon. "I met a lame man there who seemed to be in charge," Coleman later testified. "He was a good dresser and a nice fellow."

"Do you mean Dean O'Banion?" he was asked, to which he replied, "Yes, I found out later it was O'Banion." Coleman also spotted a small man wearing thick spectacles, a description fitting Terry Druggan, but Druggan's complicity was never confirmed.

Another truck, this one from the Mayer Warehouse Company, was already at the loading platform. As soon as Coleman's vehicle had been backed into the proper position, O'Banion directed the loading of 250 cases of whiskey onto each one. After the cargos were secured and concealed beneath heavy tarpaulins, O'Banion told both Coleman and the other driver, "Go right along with this stuff. We needn't have any fear; we've got protection."

The North Side Gang leader and a team of solid men armed with shotguns climbed into a touring car and drove out into the street, followed by the two trucks and a police squad car. Lieutenant Michael Grady and a five-officer team, all of whom were on O'Banion's payroll, had agreed to provide additional protection during the transportation to a warehouse at Forty-seventh Street and Evans Avenue.

When the theft became public knowledge, twenty-six people were indicted. They were O'Banion and ten bootleggers in his gang; Sackett H. Verral, president and treasurer of the warehouse; Walter and Sheridan Clinnin, whose brother was once a first assistant U.S. district attorney; Lieutenant Grady and his men; and a handful of others who played lesser roles. The federal grand jury also suspected several high-ranking Prohibition officers and officials with the local Department of Internal Revenue. The case never amounted to anything, however, and Grady was subsequently made a captain.

O'Banion used his share of the proceeds to buy the Cragin Distillery, then set out to replenish his coffers. At 11 A.M. on January 22,

Lieutenant William O'Connor and his patrol squad were driving around the South Side, having been ordered to keep an eye out for O'Banion, who was wanted for the Miller shooting. At Indiana Avenue, near 19th Street, they saw a stalled truck with a motorcar pulled up beside it.

O'Banion and the officers saw one another at the same time. The North Side Gang leader, who was behind the wheel of the car, hit the gas pedal and raced down the icy thoroughfare of Indiana Avenue with the police in hot pursuit. The chase continued onto State Street and finally ended when O'Connor's vehicle forced the gangsters' car to the curb near State and Twentieth. Lieutenant O'Connor and his men closed in and arrested O'Banion, Hymie Weiss, Dan McCarthy, and two men who'd been huddling in the back seat and seemed relieved to see the policemen. The duo claimed they had been kidnapped.

Charles Levin and Sam Baer, both Chicago truck drivers employed by the Sterling Transfer Company, told their rescuers they had been trucking 251 cases of Haveland Rye whiskey from a warehouse at East Thirty-sixth and Cottage Grove Avenue to the Chicago and Rock Island railroad yards, where the booze be would shipped to the Corning Distillery Company in Peoria. Seven loads had already reached the yard safely, but somehow O'Banion had gotten wind of the eighth and hijacked it. Two of his men had just gotten behind the wheel of the seized trucks when the police stumbled upon the scene. They drove off in the vehicles when the officers pursued O'Banion's car, and the cargo was never recovered.

O'Banion, Weiss, and McCarthy surrendered their guns in glum silence and were uncommunicative during the trip to the detective bureau. A grand jury indicted the trio for "conspiracy to possess, transport, and sell intoxicating liquors." Bond was set at ten thousand dollars each and a trial date was scheduled for July 7.

Chicagoans loved mystery and drama, so a combination of the two was irresistible. On February 21, 1924, a former motorcycle cop discovered the body of a man lying in a snow bank off Nottingham Road. Coroner's Physician Joseph Springer determined that the victim had been shot three times in the head by a .38-caliber revolver. A large sum of money and a gold watch found in the corpse's pockets ruled out robbery as a motive for the killing. The investigating officers initially presumed that the man was another casualty in the Torrio–O'Donnell beer war.

The dead man's identity was traced via a tailor's label in his clothes, which were expensive and well made. He was John Duffy of 1216 Carmen Avenue. His fingerprints showed that he had a criminal record in Philadelphia, where he had lived until last July. Duffy, whose real name was John Dougherty and who happened to be the nephew of Jimmy Dougherty, referee of the famous Dempsey–Gibbons prizefight, was being sought back home for two murders and a countless number of holdups and robberies. Philadelphia police described him to their Chicago counterparts as one of the most desperate characters they had ever encountered.

Police found no one home at 1216 Carmen, so a guard was mounted outside the door. When no resident showed up by evening, the door was broken down. Inside, the officers found another dead body, that of a woman about twenty-three years old who had been shot twice in the head. Her killers had positioned her body on a divan and covered her with a white sheet.

Her death sparked intense public interest in the case. She was identified as Maybelle Exley-Duffy, wife of the slain man. Her past was almost as sordid as that of her husband; before coming to Chicago, she had been an inmate at a brothel in Louisville, Kentucky. She and Duffy met in October 1923, when he visited the brothel in the company of a Chicago buddy who was in love with another prostitute there. Duffy fell in love with Maybelle and brought her to Chicago in January 1924. They married on Valentine's Day, and were dead a week later.

Anyone who had known the couple in the slightest capacity was questioned. Few had glowing words for John Duffy. Freddie Curtiss, a casual acquaintance, said, "You'd be talking to Duffy, quiet and peaceable, and—*bam*!—you'd be picking yourself up with a black eye or half your teeth knocked out. He called me up one night and said he was going to croak me the minute he sees me." All expressed sympathy for Maybelle.

The police favored the theory that John Duffy had incurred the wrath of a Chicago gang, either through unsanctioned bootlegging or his own belligerent nature, and been lured out of the apartment for a one-way ride. They theorized that Maybelle had seen the faces of the killers, who returned after murdering Duffy to silence her forever.

Gradually, the details of Duffy's relations with Chicago gangland came to light. His connections with the sporting world (through his uncle) had earned him the admiration of Yankee Schwartz, who in turn introduced him to the Miller brothers. They had sized him up as a mad dog type who might prove to be dangerous company, and edged away from him. Duffy went at it alone, assembling a small crew of rumrunners and earning enough as a freelancer to support himself and Maybelle in style. When Jack Horton, one of his partners, was asked if the Duffy Gang had run their liquor in from Canada, he replied, "No need to go to Canada. We could buy plenty of it—all we wanted—close to Chicago." Investigators believed that the booze the gang had acquired had been hijacked, not bought, and that the wronged gangsters had finally taken revenge.

A breakthrough in the case occurred when William Engelke, a former Lincoln Park motorcycle cop, was tracked down on the advice of those already questioned. He had been seen acting strangely on the morning that the bodies of Duffy and Maybelle were found, pestering friends for money and insisting that he needed funds to get out of town quickly.

Engelke admitted to having been a witness to the murder of Maybelle Exley. He said that on the night of February 20, he had been at the Carmen Avenue apartment, drinking with the Duffys. The couple, once totally drunk, started quarreling. Engelke couldn't recall the reason for the argument, but while he watched, Duffy yanked out his pistol and fired, hitting his wife in the head. Two tears slid down her nose as she lay dying, which shocked Duffy into sobriety. Stricken with remorse, he lifted her body onto a divan, crossed her hands over her breast, and covered her with a sheet. He and Engelke then left the apartment and sought out Julian "Potatoes" Kaufman.

Julian Kaufman, whose nickname stemmed from regular dealing in potato futures, was the son of Edmund Kaufman, millionaire commission broker. Although his upbringing had been a privileged one, he, like O'Banion, knew tragedy early in life. In 1911, when Kaufman was thirteen, his mother Hattie died during a holdup that turned deadly. The young man joined his father in the brokerage business, but found his true calling as a gambler who catered to

Chicago's wealthy. Potatoes had been a friend of Nails Morton and now did business with the Miller brothers and the North Siders.

Duffy told Kaufman that he had killed his wife, and pleaded for a car in which to dispose of the body. The Jewish gambler promised to see what he could do. He drove Duffy and Engelke to a restaurant at Lake and Clark Streets and left them there, promising to meet them later that night. The two men hid out in the Broadway Arms Hotel until early evening, when Duffy telephoned Kaufman and arranged an 8:30 P.M. meeting at the corner of Twenty-Third and Wabash.

Both parties met at the scheduled time and place. Engelke, shivering in the evening cold, watched as Kaufman and Duffy walked away a short distance and spoke for a few minutes before heading for a Studebaker parked further down the street. Two men were already seated in the car. Duffy stepped into the vehicle, and when Engelke attempted to follow, Kaufman put an arm out to stop him.

"Come on, that's a bad guy to monkey around with," he said in a low voice. "He's a maniac. He ought to be croaked. . . . Do you want to be mixed up in any murders? You'd better beat it." Engelke said nothing, just remained on the curb with the Jewish gambler while the car drove off. It was, he said, the last time he saw Duffy alive.

Kaufman was arrested immediately, and released on bond just as quickly. Acting on a tip, the police arrested James Monahan, husband of Hymie Weiss's sister Violet, whom they'd been informed had been the driver of the death car. Officers located three cars registered to Weiss, one of them a Studebaker, in a public garage a few doors away from Monahan's home at 3808 West Grand Avenue. The Studebaker was seized because of Engelke's claim that Duffy had taken his last ride in such a car, and removed to the detective bureau to be examined for bloodstains. When all tests came back negative, Monahan was released. Weiss himself was in Hot Springs, recuperating from a series of violent migraine attacks.

A *Tribune* reporter, knowing that Duffy's slaying had all the earmarks of a gangland assassination, and that both Schwartz and Kaufman were associated with Dean O'Banion, resolved to interview the gang leader. He went to the flower shop, and was admitted into the upstairs office where O'Banion was working on his monthly business statement. When told that the police sought him for questioning as a result of Schwartz and Kaufman's implication in the affair, he shrugged.

"I saw that in the papers," he said. "I suppose the idea got about that, because Schwartz was mentioned with me in that affair in the La Salle Theatre lobby, he is a friend of mine. That [shooting] was a misfortune. It was a hotheaded affair, and I hoped it would blow over. But a fellow can't lose a bad break, I guess."

He continued, "I saw in the papers that Schwartz's name was connected with Kaufman's and that I might know something. Well, I don't. I know Kaufman about as well as a hundred other casual acquaintances. I wouldn't be fool enough to get myself mixed up in a criminal affair for him or anyone else. And I haven't seen Schwartz since that affair in the theater. I know him, yes, but that's as far as it goes.

"The police don't have to look for me, I'll go and look for them. I'll be in the state's attorney's office at 2:30 P.M. Monday afternoon. I'd go there tonight if it wasn't that I have to finish up my business statement.

"I can tell the state's attorney anything he wants to know about me. I'm not looking for notoriety. Whatever happened to Duffy is out of my line. I never even saw Duffy. I don't mix with that kind of riffraff.

"Schwartz is only an acquaintance. You know how that is? You hear someone called "slim," or "shorty," or "Yankee," and the name sticks in your memory, or at least comes to your mind again when you meet him. That is how well I knew him, just to nod and call him "Yankee" when I'd meet him somewhere in the Loop."

"How about Julian Kaufman?" the reporter asked.

"Oh, everybody knows Potatoes," O'Banion answered. "But my acquaintance with Kaufman is only of the theater lobby kind. When he'd see me going into some show or I'd run across him in a theater or hotel lobby, I'd shake hands or nod. That's all."

"Did you know Kaufman well enough to do a favor for him?"

O'Banion smiled. "I can tell you candidly, that I can count on the fingers of this one hand"—he elevated it for the reporter's inspection—"the men I would do a favor for." He concluded the interview with an ironic comment. "The floral business, if there is any in the world, certainly teaches you who your friends are."

Hirschie Miller, when interviewed, admitted to having known Duffy as a "tough guy from Philadelphia" but denied that the knowledge had any sinister implications. "You know, I know a lot of people," he said. "It pays in business, and I've traveled around town a lot all my life." When reporters asked him to confirm the rumor that he'd offered to cut Duffy in on some action, he was visibly amused.

"Who? Me? Do I look like Santa Claus? Do I walk around with the coconuts dropping off my shoulders?"

On March 7, Engelke, who was still in police custody after being charged as an accessory to Maybelle Exley's murder, suddenly expanded on his story. He confirmed that after the woman's death, he and Duffy had gone to Kaufman's apartment, but changed his version of events from that point on.

"We [Kaufman, Duffy, and himself] went out to Maxie Eisner's place at Roosevelt Road and Newberry Avenue, and there we met Dapper Dan McCarthy," said Engelke. "Kaufman left word for Dean O'Banion to call him."

O'Banion had been casually mentioned as a suspect before; Duffy's liquor route had been in his territory. But there had been no direct evidence to link him to either murder, until Bill Engelke told his story.

At about eight o'clock on the night of March 21, Engelke and Duffy met O'Banion and Kaufman at Twenty-third and Wabash. Duffy relaunched his litany of pleas, only this time insisting that he needed not only a car but also money to get out of town. Engelke heard O'Banion say, "Sure, I'll give you a grand. I'll give you more than that if you need it." He and Duffy then crossed the street and got into a Studebaker that had been parked at the corner. Engelke was prevented from following by Kaufman, who said to him, "Do you want to be mixed up in any murders? You better beat it." Engelke and Kaufman remained on the curb while the Studebaker drove away.

Having made his statement, Engelke was visibly frightened. He accepted that he would be tried as an accessory to the murder of Maybelle, and said, "I hope I get a nice long term. I don't want to get out for awhile." He told Judge David, in whose court he had fingered O'Banion, "You might as well take my carcass out to Twelfth and Newberry now and bury it."

Strangely, the state's attorney's office had heard the story of O'Banion's suspected involvement in the affair a week before, but did nothing. Reporters demanded to know why. State's Attorney W. W. Smith replied rather lamely, "Well, we figured that if O'Banion didn't think he was suspected, he would come in and surrender himself. He's that sort of fellow."

The newsmen refused to back off. One of them demanded, "When he didn't come in, why wasn't he brought in?"

"We still hoped he'd surrender himself and didn't want to frighten him," Smith answered.

Why the state's attorney's office decided to postpone "frightening" O'Banion for a week is anyone's guess. He had already talked to the press about the killings (as did Al Capone and Hirschie Miller) and pleaded ignorance. "I'm a respectable business man," he told one reporter. "My florist store keeps me busy all the time."

The order to pick up O'Banion was finally issued, but he had gone into hiding. Dan McCarthy surrendered himself, but Bill Engelke denied knowing him, despite his earlier claim that they'd met at Eisner's. Already the star witness was showing signs of selective amnesia.

The North Side Gang leader was nowhere to be found. The police traced him to the Congress Hotel, but upon raiding his room, found Louis Alterie instead. The cowboy hoodlum was grilled, but smirked his way through the entire interrogation. He said, "The *Wolverine* pulls out at 10 A.M. See what you can make out of that." Desperate enough to risk a wild goose chase, a dozen detectives boarded the *Wolverine Limited* passenger train as it left Michigan Central Station at 10 A.M. but failed to find O'Banion.

The chase ended on Wednesday, March 12, after four days of exhaustive searching. O'Banion called his friend John Sbarbaro, an assistant state's attorney (and undertaker) and said that he was ready to surrender himself for questioning. Detective Joseph Geary took him into custody at the flower shop. O'Banion admitted that he had known he was wanted but deliberated evaded the police so that he could arrange his affairs in the event of arrest. He denied all knowledge of the murders and swore that Engelke and the Duffys were strangers to him.

The acid test came when Engelke was brought face to face with O'Banion at the detective bureau and asked to identify him as the man who had taken John Duffy on his last ride. As predicted, the witness faltered. He could not make the identification. "If that's O'Banion, he ain't the fellow I thought he was," he babbled. "I never met O'Banion, but I understand he was the man I saw climbing into a sedan with Duffy. This ain't that guy, though."

O'Banion, who was wearing an expensive pinstriped suit, stared at Engelke for a minute before announcing that he had never seen the other man before. The state's attorney's office justifiably suspected that the sudden recant was fear-motivated, and ordered O'Banion held in technical custody in a hotel room overnight to give Engelke time to reconsider.

The hotel chosen was the Briggs House, where O'Banion's fellow *American* slugger Vincent Altman had been gunned down in 1911. Once sequestered in suite 1618, he relaxed and responded to questions with an arrogant ease that his interrogators found infuriating. He insisted that he hadn't been up to anything sinister during his spell of hiding. "Just attending to some business," he smiled. "Wonder you fellows didn't run across me." All the solid facts they could get out of him were that his name was Dean O'Banion, he owned shares in Schofield's flower shop, and that he was interested in buying into an automobile sales agency.

Captain John Stege once commented that anyone could take a pen and paper and correctly figure out any gang murder in Chicago, but that you couldn't go into court with just a piece of paper. With a terrified Engelke refusing to cooperate, the state's attorney's office was forced to release O'Banion. In the wake of the recant, Potatoes Kaufman and Dapper Dan McCarthy escaped prosecution, too.

After O'Banion went free, public interest in the Carmen Avenue murder case waned, and it was crowded out of the headlines by newer, more lurid events. Bill Engelke was held for trial, charged as an accessory after the fact in both murders. In November he was convicted and sentenced to a prison term of ten years to life, but the prosecutor stunned everyone by requesting a new trial for Engelke and modifying the charge to a minor crime punishable by only one to ten years in jail. It was a move almost without precedent, and set tongues wagging over the possibility that O'Banion was rewarding him for his recant. An effort was then made to have Engelke placed on immediate probation, but Judge Lindsay refused.

"You've already made this case farcical enough," he said severely.

The episode added something to the O'Banion legend. Edward Dean Sullivan claimed that O'Banion had imported Duffy from Philadelphia to kill the Miller brothers. But if the facts are examined closely, it becomes obvious that Duffy came to Chicago in 1923 to escape questioning in a murder case. Sullivan suggested that once O'Banion saw what a fool he had hired, he told Duffy to pack his bags, but Duffy refused to leave. Friends of the Philadelphia gangster told the police that he had actually come to Chicago to hide out, was discovered by Yankee Schwartz, and introduced around the underworld. O'Banion and Duffy must have become casual acquaintances through Schwartz.

Schwartz and Duffy eventually fell out, and Duffy was motivated by greed and spite to make a dangerous offer to Hirschie Miller. When Davy's life was hanging by a thread, the Philadelphian went to Hirschie and offered to kill both Schwartz and O'Banion for ten thousand dollars. Miller refused. Duffy seemed proud of himself for having offered, and boasted of it when drunk. Naturally, word of it reached O'Banion, who did not seem worried. "I can take care of myself with a dozen 'tough guys' like that," he told a friend. "Rods or fists."

His dismissive attitude was deceptive. Duffy's murder proves that he had been biding his time, waiting for his chance to get even. It was an important killing for O'Banion, for he proved that he was willing and able to cut down anyone who posed a threat to him, and get away with it. It was not a mindless murder committed to satisfy bloodlust or an imagined insult. He'd been publicly targeted, and went hunting his hunter first.

Torrio could understand such a motive. He had ordered killings himself when reasoning with the offender had failed. But O'Banion had chosen a bad place to rendezvous with Duffy and Bill Engelke on the night of the murder. Twenty-third and Wabash was in the vicinity of the Four Deuces, Capone's old haunt, and suspicion arose that the Torrio Gang was involved in Duffy's execution. Capone, accompanied by his lawyer, surrendered himself for questioning and convinced the police that he did not know John Duffy or Bill Engelke, and that he hadn't spoken to O'Banion in three weeks. It was an indignity which he and Torrio felt would not have been necessary had O'Banion (1) not left Bill Engelke alive to tell tales and (2) not brought his plan into action so close to the Four Deuces. The murder of John Duffy was understandable, but O'Banion's handling of it wasn't.

O'Banion himself was not upset by the experience. What was important to him was that he had gotten away with it. He had proved that he could kill an enemy, have a witness name him, have his name splashed all over the front pages, and still walk away without so much as an indictment.

He did suffer a minor embarrassment after all the publicity. In mid-February he had visited a life insurance company. "I'd like to take out a life policy for ten thousand dollars," he told an agent. "I am carrying quite a bit now, but one can never be too careful in these matters." He gave his occupation as florist, and the policy was issued. But when the Duffy scandal hit the papers, the company realized what a blunder they had made. Representatives scurried frantically to the state's attorney's office to learn how the policy could be canceled.

"Here we insure for ten thousand dollars a guy who talks about bumping off people like I talk about buying a loaf of bread!" the agent moaned.

There is no record of whether or not the policy did get canceled. If so, the loss was a minor one because he did have other policies totaling $150,000 in value. Although he had yet to make a will, he had insured himself in his wife's favor to make certain that she would be provided for in the event of his death. Husbandly concern, not a sense of imminent doom, prompted O'Banion to make the arrangements. Had he worried about dying young, the events that were to shake gangland in the latter half of 1924 would never have happened.

After being released from custody in the Duffy case, O'Banion appeared in Judge A. S. Trude's South Clark Street courtroom with Hymie Weiss and Dan McCarthy. O'Banion and Weiss were answering charges in relation to the January assault on Davy Miller. They and McCarthy were also scheduled to draw bail in the robbery and kidnapping charges based on the hijacking they had pulled after Miller was shot.

Maxie Miller was the sole prosecution witness. He told Judge Trude that Davy was in Los Angeles, slowly recovering from his injury. When a squad of policemen escorted the three North Siders into the courtroom, Miller glared at them so hatefully that three husky policemen planted themselves squarely between him and the trio.

Some were surprised that Miller came to court at all, as brother Hirschie had been dodging one attempt on his life after another. The day before, Hirschie had been fired upon by a passing automobile and narrowly escaped death. The rumor circulated that O'Banion gunmen launched the attack to dissuade the Millers from pressing the assault charge against O'Banion and Weiss. No sooner had Hirschie calmed his nerves after the attack when he learned that his cleaning and dyeing establishment at 2832 North Clark Street had been bombed. For days afterward, Miller rode with two plainclothes cops and an escort car that checked the street for potential drive-by attempts. The *American* commented, "President Coolidge, out for a drive, was never more carefully guarded."

Hirschie Miller quickly discounted O'Banion as the source of his woes. "O'Banion," he told the press, "plays no part in this. Forget him. There is no enmity between the Millers and O'Banion." He blamed the recent violence on the competing Master Cleaners and Dyers Association, who had been after him to raise his cleaning and dyeing prices to what they charged.

Maxie Miller was less sure about O'Banion's blamelessness in the matter. "If anyone thinks they can intimidate me," he declared, "they've got another guess coming. I'd have been here today if I'd had to crawl up Clark Street on my hands and knees in the face of all the bombs and bullets in Cook County."

State's Attorney Joseph McCarthy moved for a continuance until April 11, and the motion was granted. The three North Siders were then taken to Grand Crossing Court, where they were permitted to draw bail in their various charges.

The Miller assault case never came to anything. Davy refused to press charges. The family was busy keeping thugs from the Master Cleaners and Dyers Association off Hirschie's back, but without much success. On April 19, 1924, one of Miller's drivers was beaten and a truckload of garments stolen. O'Banion was the least of their worries as 1924 progressed.

12

Cracks in the Foundation

Al Capone came to O'Banion in March 1924 with an intriguing proposition. He said that there was an election coming up in nearby Cicero in April and that a deal had been made with the local bosses there. If the Chicago gangs could ensure the re-election of Town President Joseph Z. Klenha, they would be free to operate their bootlegging and gambling businesses in Cicero, out of reach of Dever's crusading clutches. It was a sweet offer that Torrio and Capone leaped at, but they needed more muscle than they currently had at their disposal. Ragen's Colts pledged support, but the rough and experienced North Siders made attractive slugger prospects as well.

O'Banion saw the golden possibilities to be achieved by playing an active role in the takeover of Cicero. The prospect of operating freely in a jurisdiction out of Dever's control was irresistible, as was the chance to expand his operations beyond the North Side. He agreed to lend two hundred of his most hardened fighters to assist in the planned Election Day mayhem.

Torrio had been cultivating Cicero, which laid to the southwest of Chicago, as a second headquarters since 1923. It had long been under the joint control of the West Side O'Donnells, Eddie Vogel, who ran a huge slot-machine concession, and Eddie Tancl, an ex-boxer who ran the Hawthorne Park Café. Town President Klenha was merely a mouthpiece for their unofficial government. Torrio recognized the setup as amenable to his operations, and started moving in.

Prior to 1923, Cicero had its share of gambling houses and speakeasies. There were, however, no brothels, as none of the unofficial leaders wanted anything to do with prostitution. Torrio tested the waters by opening a bordello on Roosevelt Road. The town police raided it and locked up the girls. Other attempts to set up women in other parts of Cicero met with the same result. Vogel, Tancl, and the O'Donnells were behind the raids, fearing that flagrant prostitution would upset the citizens and plant the seeds of reform in their minds.

Torrio reacted to the bum's rush treatment with his usual bloodless but effective style. Since Cicero was part of Cook County, he called upon Sheriff Peter B. Hoffman to lead a squad of deputy sheriffs through the town and seize every slot machine they came across. Vogel got the message; no women, no gambling. He and Torrio had to talk.

The two parties reached an agreement. Torrio ordered the slot machines returned to Vogel, and promised the O'Donnell brothers that they could maintain exclusive beer distribution rights in the town. The only leader he did not settle with was Eddie Tancl, who hated him and held out from the negotiations out of spite. To further promote good will, Torrio agreed to respect the sensitivities of the townspeople and open no brothels in Cicero.

The gang set up headquarters in the Hawthorne Hotel at 4823 Twenty-Second Street, a three story building constructed from blackened brick. Its use was apparent from the steel shutters on the windows and the armed guards who patrolled the lobby.

Cicero was never the same thereafter. Steely-eyed characters poured in from Chicago like refugees, which in a sense they were as long as a reform mayor was in power. The newcomers included Capone's brothers, Frank and Ralph; Francesco Nitto, alias Frank Nitti; financial genius and former pimp Jake Guzik; and "millionaire newsboy" Frankie Pope.

O'Banion was a partner in some of the gambling houses that the mob opened or bought into, such as The Ship at 2131 South Cicero Avenue, in which he owned a 15 percent interest. The North Side Gang had no controlling interest in any Cicero action; it was strictly a Torrio–Capone stronghold.

The Cicero election was scheduled for April 1. Ward boss and Republican committeeman Ed Konvalinka, a native Ciceronian whose political career had started behind the counter of his popular soda fountain, was not so confident that Klenha's slate would be victorious without help. He conferred with Eddie Vogel, and Capone was approached. Capone didn't need much persuading, nor did O'Banion.

The Democrats took precautions to ensure a Klenha victory. The Election Commissioner went so far as to strike over 3000 names of Klenha-friendly election clerks and related personnel from the staff list and replace them with more neutral officials. The gangs responded predictably: The Democratic candidate for town clerk, William K. Pflaum, was attacked in his office the night before the polls opened and savagely beaten before the thugs trashed the office.

The moment the polls opened, a collection of black limousines cruised around the booths, on the lookout for any anti-Klenha voters. Gangsters prowled along the lines of citizens waiting to cast their ballots. Those who did not vote as suggested were dragged out of line and stomped into a bleeding pulp in front of their horrified fellow voters. Honest election officials didn't fare much better; Democratic campaign worker Michael Gavin was shot through both legs and dumped in the basement of a Chicago hotel until the voting was over. An election clerk was beaten and kept tied up in a Torrio–Capone roadhouse.

The Democrats, recognizing gangster support as a necessary evil, had secured the services of local hoodlums who'd been covetously eyeing the same Cicero advantages that the Chicago gangs had. But these mercenaries were hopelessly outnumbered by the opposition, although they fought valiantly. Two killings near the Hawthorne Hotel, a third in Eddie Tancl's saloon, and a fourth whose throat was slashed were the end result of gang-to-gang clashes. The police—those officers who were not being paid to be oblivious—were powerless to stop the carnage. One officer required hospitalization after attempting to quell polling-station violence.

The terrified Ciceronians appealed for outside help. Word of their plight reached Cook County Judge Edmund K. Jarecki. The law stated that Chicago policemen could not act in an official capacity outside the city limits, but Jarecki deputized seventy patrolmen, five detective squads, and nine squads of motorcycle cops as "special agents" of the county court, and dispatched them to Cicero. The intervention came too late; Klenha and his Republican ticket won the election by a staggering majority. Cicero had been taken.

For Al Capone, the victory was bittersweet. His older brother Frank had been killed in a gun battle with police officers outside a polling place on Cicero Avenue.

O'Banion's mood must have been jovial. He had played an instrumental role in the thrashing of Cicero, and earned himself a position on the unofficial board of directors. He had also earned a tidy profit on the flowers ordered for Frank Capone's funeral, some twenty thousand dollars' worth. For the Chicago Heights boys, he put together a six-foot-tall heart composed of hundreds of red carnations, and for the Hammond, Indiana crowd (who looked after Torrio's brothels on the state border) he created a lyre of lilies and orchids. O'Banion's effusive floral arrangements filled every nook and cranny in the Capone house, and some had to be hung on the trees and lampposts outside for want of space.

Hymie Weiss and Potatoes Kaufman were among the mourners. So were union boss "Dago Mike" Carrozzo and other high-profile gang leaders. In Cicero, blinds were drawn and saloons locked for two hours as a sign of respect.

Klenha's victory afforded some consolation to the grieving Al Capone. Although prostitution remained off limits by mutual agreement, bootlegging and gambling went on everywhere one looked. The Chicago mob was more absolute in its Cicero rule than it had ever been in Chicago. When Klenha made the mistake of passing legislation Capone disapproved of, the gangster went to city hall, asked the president to step outside, and then kicked him down the steps in full view of a policeman who watched the proceedings, shrugged, and walked away. A rebellious newspaper editor ended up in the hospital and had controlling interest in his paper snatched by Capone.

Despite these bursts of brutality, the townspeople had some good things to say about their new overlords. Capone and his men waged a war against burglars, holdup men, and petty thieves whose activities upset the people more than any gambling oasis. Presented with a diminishing level of street crime, Ciceronians acquired a grudging tolerance for the newcomers.

Capone and his partners were only too pleased to offer such cleanup services if it made their presence in the town more tolerable. They had a lot invested in Cicero; besides the saloons that sold the combine's liquor and beer, there were gambling houses such as the Hawthorne Smoke Shop (next to the Hawthorne Hotel), the Subway, and the Radio. Floating handbook games moved all over town, sometimes shifting locations on a daily basis. Gamblers bought gang beer at twenty-five cents a stein, wine at thirty cents a glass, or whiskey at seventy-five cents a shot, and wagered away up to fifty thousand dollars a day. In places that they did not outright own, the Chicago combine claimed a cut of 25 to 50 percent. The tribute was not unreasonable in terms of the immunity that it paid for. Token police raids were broadcast well in advance, and the lieutenants that the combine posted in each independent joint not only collected the percentage agreed on, but kept out the troublemakers.

Not everyone went along meekly. Eddie Tancl let one and all know that he intended to keep going his own way. He had always gotten along with the West Side O'Donnells, buying their liquor and associating socially, but their alliance with Torrio, whom he hated, cooled their relationship. He observed that his beer deliveries were of increasingly poor quality, in some cases not real beer at all but the needled stuff. When Tancl bellowed that he would buy from someone else, he was told to get out of town. The pugnacious ex-boxer laughed and defied them to make him. The O'Donnells and Ralph Sheldon sent a two-man squad to plant dynamite outside of Tancl's saloon, but they were discovered before the fuse could be lit. One was later shotgunned at the wheel of his beer truck, and the other went into hiding for months. The matter of Eddie Tancl rested there for awhile, as the spring was to provide more important problems that required solving. His enemies finally caught up with him six months later, in November, when Myles O'Donnell and Jim Doherty, an O'Donnell gunman, killed both Tancl and his bartender, Leo Klimas, in the former's saloon.

O'Banion's compensation for his role in the Cicero takeover was a beer concession in the town. To fatten his income, he allegedly persuaded fifty Chicago saloonkeepers to relocate to his Cicero territory, where he supplied them at a competitive cost. He did acquire new Cicero customers, but not exactly through perfidy.

"I remember reading somewhere that Dean stole customers from these West Side gangs," E. Barnett said, "and that's not true at all. A lot of saloonkeepers on the West Side and other places started closing up because there was a reform mayor in Chicago and they knew they'd have it better in Cicero. At least that's what a couple of them told me when I made deliveries. Most of them went there voluntarily, because there weren't as many saloons in Dean's Cicero territory, so there was less competition. It wasn't just guys on the West Side either, they came from all over. I don't know how these stories get around."

O'Banion's new customers found that his product was superior quality and the troublemakers were kept out, so business boomed. The concession, which Torrio had evaluated as being worth twenty thousand dollars a month, rose to one hundred thousand dollars under O'Banion's direction.

The gangs who had formerly been supplying the relocated saloons complained to Torrio, resenting the fact that O'Banion had absorbed some of their former income. Torrio went to O'Banion and suggested that in the name of fairness, he split the profits with the offended parties. O'Banion refused; the new customers had come to him of their own free will and he failed to see how he owed anyone anything. Short of all-out war, there was no way to force the issue, so the matter of O'Banion came to a hostile halt.

Blond, pert Margaret Collins was the darling of the Chicago underworld. She was a well-known figure in the cabarets, and was normally seen with John Sheehy, the tough safecracker who had been O'Banion's partner when both operated under Charles Reiser's wing. On December 7, 1923, Margaret and Sheehy visited the infamous Rendez-Vous Café to celebrate her birthday. By the end of the meal, Miss Collins was drunk enough to demand that their waiter bring her some ice to throw at the drummer on the club's stage. When he refused, she complained to her escort and cooed, "I think we ought to do something about it."

Johnny agreed. At that moment, the headwaiter, a rugged man named Guth, appeared at their table and told them to behave; their rowdiness was annoying the other patrons. Sheehy told him where to go. When Guth warned him again, the gangster drew his pistol and fired two shots, killing both Guth and the waiter who had initially refused to bring Margaret ice. Sergeant John O'Malley, alerted by the gunfire, rushed onto the premises. Sheehy tried to shoot him, too, but the policeman was faster, and the gangster fell dead with several bullets in him. Margaret mourned her lover briefly. In April 1924 she began to see John "Jew" Bates, also known as "Big," an O'Banion lieutenant. Speculation ran rampant that she and O'Banion were lovers, which both denied.

The pale, over-rouged young woman appeared to attract misfortune. Originally from New York, she was for years the sweetheart of a hoodlum named Thomas. When he was murdered in 1921, Margaret ventured to Chicago and the arms of Johnny Sheehy. She genuinely grieved over his death, and even bought an expensive monument for his grave. When she began seeing Bates, trouble drifted to the O'Banion camp as well.

Not long after Cicero was taken, O'Banion, Louis Alterie, Bates, and Margaret sat down to dinner at the Friar's Inn Cabaret with Mike Carrozzo and his wife. Carrozzo, president of the street cleaners union, had been a suspect in the February 1920 murder of labor slugger Mossy Enright. The dinner was to precede a business meeting, but the meeting never came to pass, at least not that night. During the meal, Margaret drank herself into a nasty mood, took exception to something that Mrs. Carrozzo said, and slapped the other woman's face. Before the offended party could fight back, the hot-blooded Mike Carrozzo leaped out of his chair, seized Margaret, and began pounding her with his fists. Bates lunged to her defense, followed by O'Banion and Alterie, who were not about to let a woman get manhandled in front of them. The three of them threw Carrozzo to the floor, sending the table and its contents crashing in all directions, and kicked him into a bleeding pulp. The staff broke up the brawl and persuaded the North Side and Carrozzo parties to leave separately.

O'Banion and Carrozzo made peace afterward, agreeing to put the incident behind them. But gunfights erupted all over Chicago, and informers told the police that despite their outward civility, the followers of both men were fighting it out in dark alleys and shadowy side streets. Since the combatants escaped before police arrived, such a feud was impossible to prove, but it is not unlikely.

While O'Banion was acquainting himself with the needs and wants of a growing (and some said stolen) Cicero clientele, he himself was being encroached upon. The Genna brothers were reaching beyond Little Italy and sending their shadowy salesmen into the North Side.

O'Banion cut his liquor with water, liquefied sugar, and other substances to increase product volume and therefore profit. What he declined to do was manufacture rotgut, which caused alcohol-poisoning deaths. As a result, his wares were much more expensive. An O'Banion bottle averaged six to nine dollars, a price beyond many of the North Side's more destitute residents, who had to go south of the river to get their alcohol fix. The Gennas targeted these consumers and sold their poison at three dollars a bottle, undercutting O'Banion by at least half. When he found out about it, he was outraged.

Barnett recalled coming into the smoking room over Schofield's flower shop after O'Banion switched headquarters, and finding O'Banion in a rage. "He found bad bottles being sold on the North Side by these Sicilians, and he went to the Capone boys to back him up, and they told him they couldn't do anything. I remember that Weiss was in the office with him. As Dean was paying me my money from the cash box, he was saying to Weiss, 'So Johnny [Torrio] tells me that he can't do nothing with these guys. They won't listen.' And Weiss says, 'Let's talk about it later.' I guess he didn't want to discuss it when I was there."

He went to Torrio to complain about the treaty violation. Torrio felt no sympathy, in view of the brush-off O'Banion had given him over the Cicero issue, but for the sake of diplomacy agreed to speak with the offenders. Whatever he advised the brothers fell on deaf ears, because their rotgut continued to infiltrate the North Side. O'Banion took matters into his own hands, hijacking a thirty-thousand-dollar truckload of Genna whiskey.

He also resolved to get back at Torrio. From O'Banion's perspective, Torrio's outfit and the Genna brothers were one huge Italian conspiracy out to take him down. He'd seen it happen in the Little

Hell of his childhood, the incoming Sicilians swarming in, choking out the Irish and Swedish who had occupied the district for years. He had nothing against Italians or Sicilians as a people, but he feared and hated the way they operated as a gang. It was common knowledge that they befriended their enemies right up until the moment of execution. In a fit of paranoia O'Banion convinced himself that the polite mask was starting to crack, that the Gennas' infiltration into his territory would only increase. The fact that Torrio did nothing to stop them added to his suspicion.

In the middle of May 1924 he received a tip from a police informant. The Sieben Brewery, in which he owned a huge interest, was targeted for a raid during the early morning hours of May 19. All those found on the premises, as well as the owners, would be arrested.

The Sieben, which had opened in July 1876 at 1470 North Larrabee Street, was situated in the heart of the German community. Connected to the brewery itself was the Bier Stube, a popular beer garden. The Sieben family, rather than go out of business or produce the pathetic near beer, subleased it to the Mid-City Brewing Company, which was really a front for Torrio and O'Banion. The authorities caught their first whiff of illegal suds in August 1923 and sent an investigator to check the premises out. The officials found something more potent than legal near beer being produced, and revoked the Sieben's license. Undaunted, Torrio and O'Banion resumed operations after a brief waiting period, provoking the government to go after them a second time.

The logical thing for O'Banion to do with the tip was warn Torrio, who could not afford to be arrested. He had already been fined in December 1923 for ownership of a West Hammond Brewery, and the law stipulated that a second offense carried a mandatory jail sentence.

The North Side embraced this opportunity to get Torrio thrown behind bars and tumble him off his throne. It was a great time for it, as Capone was currently in hiding, having murdered Joe Howard on May 8.

O'Banion went to Torrio with a proposal that surprised and delighted the Italian. He spoke wearily of his battles with the Gennas, and admitted to a fear that they would eventually get him. He must have been as convincing as he was eloquent, for the normally shrewd Torrio was completely taken in by his claim that he wanted to sell his various bootlegging holdings and retire to Colorado, where Louis Alterie had a ranch. O'Banion had been a guest at the ranch before, and said that he was looking at buying a spread of land himself. He suggested that if Torrio would buy his share of the Sieben to begin with, he could start planning his departure from Chicago.

It is curious that Torrio took the bait so easily. Perhaps he was so relieved that a solution to the O'Banion–Genna conflict was being offered that he swallowed any misgivings or suspicions and agreed to buy O'Banion's stake in the Sieben for five hundred thousand dollars.

To make the ruse more convincing, O'Banion said that a large shipment of beer was due to move out early on the morning of May 19, and he wanted Torrio to be present with him so that Torrio could reassure the remaining North Siders that everything would go on as usual. The Italian agreed.

O'Banion's actions were predictable, for after childhood he rarely did anything without making the undertaking dangerous. He could only derive satisfaction from deeds that few would dare. He didn't want to be netted in the planned raid merely to throw suspicion off himself in the eyes of the Torrio mob, but also to see Torrio's face when he realized the loss of half a million dollars and his freedom to boot. O'Banion knew that he would be charged along with everyone else and fined, but it was a minor price to pay to witness his own triumph.

It was close to 5 A.M. on May 19 when several squads of policemen led by Chief Morgan Collins and Captain Matthew Zimmer stormed the Sieben Brewery. The thirty-officer crew had been lying in wait outside the building for hours, hoping to intercept the beer shipments as they were being trucked out. They raided as the dawn broke, their first prisoners being the armed gangsters on sentry duty. Inside, they found five trucks loaded with beer barrels and a multitude of drivers, brewery employees, and gangsters. O'Banion and Louis Alterie were standing to one side with Torrio, overseeing everything. Also present, for reasons never determined, was Daniel J. O'Connor, a Democratic politician aligned with the Prohibition interests.

Reactions to the sudden influx of policemen varied. Torrio was silent, hiding the shock and confusion that he must have been feeling. Some workers surrendered quietly, while others struggled with their captors. Torrio and O'Banion tried to calm the volcanic situation by ordering the men not to resist arrest, and the raiders later admitted that the two gang chieftains were instrumental in preventing violence.

O'Banion's reaction to the raid was jovial. He smiled pleasantly at Captain Zimmer and remarked, "You ought to get a raise." He was observed approaching Sergeant Michael Vaughn and greeting him like they were old friends. Torrio missed none of it; his eyes narrowed as the truth slowly sank in.

The Dever administration praised the raid as a major victory against the underworld. Chief Collins had seized 128,500 gallons of beer, and thirty-four prisoners. Among those arrested were two policemen, Joseph Sonnenfeld and Joseph Warszynski, who had been stationed at the brewery to ensure that the 1923 closure was not circumvented. Collins ripped their badges off on the spot.

Also found in the raid was a black notebook, which had been flung under the loading platform. Prohibition Agent Brice Armstrong retrieved it. Flipping through the pages, he saw that it was an account book whose contents spelled out the tight arrangement the Torrio-O'Banion mob had with the police. Six police sergeants were on the payroll, with two men working eight-hour shifts twenty-four hours a day. They assisted with the delivery of the Sieben product to its various destinations and provided a protective escort to thwart potential hijackings.

When Thomas Nash, O'Banion's attorney, learned of his arrest, he immediately filed a writ of habeas corpus, but it was invalidated when O'Banion and the other prisoners were turned over to the federal authorities, who had promised full cooperation in prosecuting them.

O'Banion's demeanor remained cheerful. While a sullen Torrio, who gave his name as Frank Langley, sat in a holding cell at the Federal Building and fumed, O'Banion treated the whole affair as the minor setback that it was . . . for him. After two detectives interviewed the prisoners in the holding cell, O'Banion maneuvered past them and strolled toward the exit, whistling cheerily. He was almost out of the building before he was spotted and returned to the cell, where he paid a janitor to fetch breakfast for his fellow prisoners.

As soon as the arraignment was over, Torrio produced a roll of cash and peeled off seventy-five hundred dollars to free himself and five thousand to free O'Connor, who had been booked as "James Casey." In his haste to get O'Connor out before he could be recognized, Torrio left everyone else to await the arrival of bail bondsmen Billy Skidmore and Ike Roderick.

Torrio suspected that he had been double-crossed. O'Banion argued that he had not been able to foresee the raid, and therefore not obligated to return the money paid for now worthless property. His logic was sound enough, but he betrayed his guilt by backing out on his promise to leave Chicago.

The O'Banion legend claims that he and Hymie Weiss had a confrontation about the treachery he'd shown. Weiss, the thinker, knew that Torrio would not forgive such an insult, especially since he would be going to jail over it. He pleaded with his friend and leader to make peace overtures to Torrio before the situation developed into a gang war. O'Banion sneered at the thought and declared, "To hell with them Sicilians!!" The phrase rippled through gangland like waves through a pond, and both Torrio and the Genna brothers took it as a mortal insult. Brimming with murderous fury, they started plotting O'Banion's execution.

In actuality, Weiss backed O'Banion in the Sieben swindle—its perfection suggests that he was the driving force behind it. He believed that the North Side 's position in the Chicago underworld hierarchy was at the top, not as Torrio partners at best, satellites at worst. Unlike Torrio and Capone, both comparatively new arrivals to the town, O'Banion, Weiss, and their followers had cut their criminal teeth there. Their sentiment was not unlike that of the North American Indians, who first greeted the white settlers as bringers of good fortune, then grew increasingly resentful as the white society began dominating their own.

O'Banion's celebrated "Sicilians" comment, if he had said it at all, would not have been sufficient provocation to drive the Italian gangsters to murder. The parties concerned would have heard far worse in their time. In truth, the Gennas were seething over O'Banion's hijacking of their North Side liquor shipments, and Torrio was livid at the realization that the North Sider was trying to push him out of the way. He'd been hoping that O'Banion would settle down and be content with the bootlegging wealth that the city-wide gang agreement had given him, but it was now obvious that he did not trust his partners and was trying to rid himself of them. Left unchecked, he would destroy everything Torrio had worked so hard to build. His actions, not his words, were responsible for his death warrant being drawn up.

It remained unexecuted for the time being, because Torrio's way to order the hit and deal with the consequences was not clear. Capone, his right arm, had killed Joe Howard two weeks earlier and was in forced hiding until the witnesses could be dealt with. Torrio himself had legal trouble and could expect to be in and out of court repeatedly until he finally went to jail.

The Genna brothers also wanted O'Banion's blood and were too headstrong to worry about revenge on the part of his successors. But they, too, restrained themselves at the order of Mike Merlo.

Merlo headed the Chicago branch of the Unione Siciliana, a national organization that had been formed to better the lot of impoverished Sicilians in America. In practice, the Unione was an exploitive machine that corralled Sicilian votes and sold them to the highest political bidders, but it masked this ulterior motive by performing a litany of good works among the people. Mike Merlo in particular had a genuine concern for his compatriots' welfare and did what he could to assist them in finding employment and housing. O'Banion was similarly inclined in his North Side territory, earning respect from Merlo, who also frowned at the thought of the war that would erupt should such a well-connected gang leader be killed. Therefore, when there was talk among the Gennas of assassination, he intervened. At his insistence, Torrio and the Gennas backed down. They had a healthy respect for him, and not only because of his reputation for wisdom. He had been a prominent figure in the Nineteenth Ward's aldermanic war of 1921 and had numerous gangster allies, making it risky to challenge his pronouncements. In 1924 he was battling cancer, which had weakened him physically, but his word remained law.

The Merlo–O'Banion relationship is an interesting one, because it is a testimony to O'Banion's merit as a gang leader and his significance in the underworld hierarchy. If he had been a mere Torrio vassal, as some have insisted, or a mad-dog type whose death would have promoted the common good, Mike Merlo not only would have supported his murder, he probably would have insisted on it. After all, he had done nothing to stop the extinction of the O'Donnells. Merlo knew that O'Banion was just as powerful and well connected politically as Torrio or the Gennas, and there would be no easy way to remove him.

While Mike Merlo lived, the North Sider was beyond the reach of his enemies, but in view of Merlo's declining health, the injunction would only be temporary. They could wait.

On June 13, bandits held up a train on the Chicago, Milwaukee, and St. Paul route near Rondout, Illinois. They escaped with forty-two sacks of registered mail whose value was estimated at close to three million dollars. The modus operandi was brazen: Two masked men crept into the engineer's cab and forced him at gunpoint to stop the train at a site where two automobiles carrying more gunmen laid in wait. When the clerks in the mail car tried to barricade themselves inside, they were pelted with gas bombs until they came out, choking. The robbers seized them and made off with the car's valuable contents as soon as the air cleared. Chief Post Office Inspector Germer told the press that while a Philadelphia-based gang was believed to have committed similar train robberies recently, he had it on good authority that the gang had had help from Chicago thugs on the Rondout job.

O'Banion, Weiss, and Alterie were arrested on suspicion of having "fingered" the train for the heist, if they did not do the job themselves. The charges ended up being dropped, and the actual criminals were rounded up later, but the Rondout business was a tough entanglement for O'Banion while it lasted.

On July 7 O'Banion and Dan McCarthy appeared in court to face charges of conspiracy to violate the Volstead Act, robbery, and kidnapping, all related to the hijacking they had attempted two days after Davy Miller was shot. (Weiss was granted a separate trial.) Although State's Attorney Robert Crowe had nol-prossed the charges, the government had been less inclined to overlook the incident, and a federal grand jury indicted the trio. O'Banion was not too concerned; he knew that his reputation shielded him from easy prosecution. The government had a frustrating task in assembling a jury. Most prospective jurors admitted that fear might override their sense of civic duty. O'Banion, amused, periodically played court jester. "Say," he drawled at one point, "it's gonna take them longer to get a jury than it'll take the Democrats to pick a candidate for president."

Charles Levin, one of the truckers whom the gang had kidnapped, was the star witness. To cripple the government's case, North Side emissaries approached him and gave him some sound advice. "They warned me," Levin recalled. "I was told to keep my mouth shut or get it closed for good. And there is reason to believe that something like that might happen."

When he changed his original story on the witness stand, pleading poor memory due to shock, he was jailed on charges of perjury.

Ten of the twelve jurymen believed that the gangsters were guilty as charged, but two seemed unconvinced. They refused to listen to anything that the other jurors said to dissuade them. At midnight, after the jury had been out for eight hours, one juror actually knelt on the floor of the conference room and prayed that the two holdouts would see reason. After more than twenty-four hours of arguing, the jury reported that they were unable to reach a unanimous verdict, being deadlocked ten-to-two for conviction. Judge Cliffe was forced to discharge them.

Assistant District Attorney Edwin L. Weisl announced that the government was going to seek a new trial right away. "The breakdown of law and order is caused not by officials, but the jurors' lack of a sense of duty to their government," he said.

The rumor circulated that the two stubborn jurymen had been offered twenty-five thousand dollars apiece to vote for acquittal. An attorney told of how one of his colleagues, who worked for O'Banion, said, "O'Banion is all through running beer—he's made his pile and he intends to get out and be a good citizen. That's why he doesn't want to go to jail in this case." The man drew a fat roll of cash from his pocket and said, "Here is fifty thousand dollars. I'm going over to the Federal Building and make sure that he doesn't go to jail."

While government investigators scrambled all over Chicago, interviewing the jury and searching for the unethical lawyer, O'Banion moved on. He knew that he would be tried again, but not until early 1925 at the earliest. That gave him plenty of time to raise more bribe money and keep Levin scared.

13

The Handshake Murder

FOR THE REST OF THE SUMMER, O'Banion laid low, allowing the storm he had stirred up to settle. At the end of September, he and Louis Alterie went to the latter's ranch near Jarr Canyon, Colorado, for a month's vacation. They were accompanied by their wives, O'Banion's chauffeur, and Alterie's niece. By all reports, O'Banion thoroughly enjoyed the visit. He hunted, went horseback riding, and took life with an ease he had not known in years. Alterie's cowboy neighbors put on rodeos, which he filmed with a motion-picture camera. While the cowboys roped cattle or rode bucking broncos, O'Banion perched on a fence, waving his hat and cheering lustily. The local ranchers loved him. "He smiled a lot and was very friendly," one of them told a Colorado reporter a month later.

It is easy to see why O'Banion was happy in such an environment. The strong sense of community was a comforting throwback to his Maroa boyhood. The ranchers liked him, and he was gratified by their easy acceptance of him. One of many photos taken during the Colorado sojourn shows the O'Banions, the Alteries, and their Chicago companions posing with their newfound friends against a wooden fence, garbed like cowpunchers.

O'Banion did not relax so much that he forgot about the situation back home. He took advantage of his comparative anonymity in Colorado to collect a miniature arsenal. Going to a local weapons dealer known to Alterie, he bought a machine gun, hundreds of shells, and dozens of rifles and pistols. The Chicago elections were slated for November, and he wanted to make sure that his candidates were victorious. The Forty-second and Forty-third Wards, which composed his North Side territory, had always been staunchly Democratic; his objective was to get Bob Crowe and the Republican candidates into office. It was the sort of challenge that the Maroa daredevil loved.

Before leaving Colorado on October 20, O'Banion staged a rodeo extraordinaire and invited cowboys from miles around. They were thrilled when he offered as a prize the finest rifle they had ever seen. Little did they guess that it had come from a collection intended to wreak terror on the Chicago streets in November.

Soon after the North Sider party returned to Chicago, a testimonial dinner was held in O'Banion's honor at the Webster Hotel at 2150 Lincoln Park West, in the heart of the North Side's ritziest neighborhood. The town Democrats had heard the disturbing rumor that O'Banion was intending to support the Republicans this time around, and hastened to rekindle his favor.

The guest list would have whitened the faces of the law-abiding element. On one side of the long banquet table sat O'Banion, Weiss, Drucci, Alterie, Maxie Eisen, and Frank Gusenberg, one of the three deadly Gusenberg brothers; Jerry O'Connor, a gambling house operator and vice president of the Theatre and Building Janitors Union; William Scott Stewart, former assistant state's attorney and now legal counsel for Louis Alterie; and Cornelius N. Shea, a murderer, labor racketeer, and secretary of the Theatre and Building Janitors Union. Just across the table sat Colonel Albert A. Sprague, commissioner of public works and Democratic nominee for U.S. Senator; County Clerk Robert M. Sweitzer; Chief of Detectives

Michael Hughes; Lieutenant Charles Egan; and an assortment of lesser public servants.

Tissue streamers of red, white, and blue, decorated the walls of the banquet hall, and the guests enjoyed the finest quality wine, beer, and pre-war Scotch. Colonel Sprague, Robert Sweitzer, and the other Democrats took turns standing up and praising O'Banion. Then the North Sider was ceremoniously presented with a diamond-and-ruby-clustered platinum watch, a gift from the Democratic Party for services rendered.

During the congratulations and general hobnobbing, Alterie saw a waiter passing a hat among the guests for tips, as was customary at the Webster, and leaped to his feet with both maple-handled pistols drawn.

"Hey, you!" he bellowed. "None of that racket stuff goes here!" Facing the distinguished company, he asked, "Shall I kill him?"

Jaws dropped. For a split second there was silence. Then O'Banion burst out laughing. "Naw, let him suffer," he said, whereupon Alterie dismissed the terrified waiter with a playful shove.

When Mayor Dever found out about the "Belshazzar Feast," as the clergy dubbed the gathering, he exploded. Chief of Detectives Hughes and the other officials who had attended were called into his office to explain themselves. Hughes claimed that he had thought the dinner was for Jerry O'Connor. "When I recognized a number of notorious characters I had thrown into the detective bureau basement a half-dozen times, I knew I had been framed and withdrew almost at once," he insisted.

The Webster Hotel gathering marked a change in the way that gangsters and politicians related to one another. Previously, they had associated in closed offices or at underworld functions the general public rarely got wind of. (The only exceptions were the public gatherings of gangsters and lawyers, police officials, and judges of Italian descent, but it was commonly understood that a social bond existed between such people that transcended whatever side of the law they existed on.) Now gangsters and public servants were socializing in the open, unconcerned about the demoralizing effect their actions were having on their fellow office holders and the citizenry. Such open fraternizing, wrote Fred Pasley, "became an institution of the Chicago scene and marked the way to the moral and financial collapse of the municipal and county governments in 1928–29."

O'Banion accepted the platinum watch with pleasure, but he had already decided to go Republican. His primary reason for the allegiance swap was the bootlegger-friendly slate of candidates the Republicans offered, but another motive, detrimental to his current political allies, existed as well: He had his eye on a political career for himself.

Viewed from several angles, Dean O'Banion had the makings of an excellent politician. He was Irish-American, an ancestry shared by most politicians of the day. To the common folk, he was friendly and engaging, so much so that the voters who had been roughed up by his election terrorists in the past might have been inclined to let bygones be bygones. (If they were not, they could merely receive more of the same treatment.) His criminal record posed no real impediment. Ex-mayor Fred Busse had been a barroom rowdy for years, Anthony D'Andrea was a convicted counterfeiter, and Aldermen Kenna and Coughlin had sponsored the First Ward Ball, which had offended public sensitivities to a larger extent than any of O'Banion's bootlegging and robbery charges ever did.

In Dean O'Banion, the two most influential figures in Chicago politics—the politician and the gangster—would be melded into a single entity, concentrating both his clout and his effectiveness. O'Banion hadn't yet decided whether he would actually run for office, but he reasoned that he had to walk before he could run. First he would show his power by bringing the Forty-second and Forty-third Wards, Democratic fiefdoms for many years, into the Republican fold. Campaign speeches of his own would come later.

Earlier in the year, the North Sider had looked over a spread of land outside of Chicago and fantasized about building a suburb there, something he could own and manage as thoroughly as Torrio controlled Burnham or Forest View. It was a potential next step should he be successful in his own back yard.

O'Banion was not alone in thinking himself a perfect match for public office. Those already serving in city government thought so, too, and became concerned when the rumor circulated that he had political ambitions. The extent of their anxiety would be investigated after his death.

On November 3, the night before the election, O'Banion and the other shareholders in the Cicero gambling joint The Ship met for the weekly split of the profits. As part of a compensation package for the use of his sluggers in the Cicero takeover, Torrio had given the North Side Gang leader a 15 percent interest in the place. Present were O'Banion, Hymie Weiss, Vincent Drucci, Al Capone and bodyguard Slippery Frank Rio, and Frank Maritote. As they divided the money, Capone remarked that Angelo Genna had incurred heavy losses at The Ship that week and had left an IOU for thirty thousand dollars. He suggested that to maintain good relations with the Gennas, they should tear up the note.

O'Banion reacted angrily. He personally didn't care about the Genna goodwill, and definitely not enough to forfeit 15 percent of thirty thousand dollars. He grabbed the first opportunity to locate a telephone, call Genna, and demand that he pay up within a week, or else.

It was the second time in recent history that the North Side Gang leader had clashed with Torrio and Capone. Just before his departure for Colorado, O'Banion was informed by Capone that his friend and ally Jew Bates would have to be removed from his position as day manager of Cicero's Hawthorn Smoke Shop. O'Banion, Alterie, Torrio, Capone, and Frankie Pope had bought out the gambling parlor's original owner the previous spring and set Bates up, first as night manager and then as day manager. At first the Jewish gangster did his job diligently, but soon gambling fever seized him just as fiercely as it had any of the Smoke Shop's patrons, and he began betting against the house himself. By following the best tips, he made almost fifty-five thousand dollars in one month alone. That particular month, the Smoke Shop failed to pay its usual handsome dividend to the owners, and an incensed Capone called a meeting of all six men, Bates included.

"The Jew is through," Capone declared. Torrio and Pope, who'd also been aggravated by the situation, nodded their agreement.

"Not on your life," O'Banion retorted. "He's going to stay." He had no intention of seeing a friend thrown out into the cold or losing an ally in the Capone-dominated Cicero stronghold. The matter was dropped for the time being, but O'Banion's stand against the Torrio–Capone combine was becoming more aggressive as time progressed.

When Torrio heard about the threat to Genna, he knew that O'Banion had to go, regardless of what Merlo had decreed. The Sicilian leader was now on his deathbed, and doctors predicted that he would not last another week. If O'Banion were not eliminated soon, an explosive war between the North Siders and the Gennas would erupt, destroying the lucrative alliance and machine that Torrio had worked so hard to build. The gun battles and murders that were sure to ensue would create a public outcry and intensify the already simmering pressure being exerted by Mayor Dever.

Killing O'Banion would have its own consequences, namely vengeful successors. There undoubtedly would be bloody headlines and a period of police crackdowns. But it would all pass, and the North Siders might be persuaded to see reason.

November 4 was no more peaceful an Election Day than previous ones. Voters and precinct officials were slugged, shot, and even kidnapped. Running gunfights between gangsters in automobiles terrified pedestrians. One notorious character, John Mackey, was cut down by eleven bullets in front of a polling place at 405 South Hoyne Street. Two companions—Claude Maddox, who captained the microscopic Circus Gang, and Anthony "Red" Kissane—were injured in the fusillade that killed Mackey.

The mayhem at a Fourteenth Ward precinct was typical of what went on all day. The polling station had barely been open for half an hour when voter Anton Rudzinski was shot in the back by gangsters speeding by in an automobile. Bullets from the same attack grazed the head of one voter, tore the coat off of another, and caused a third to be cut by flying glass.

O'Banion kept busy in the Forty-second and Forty-third Wards. He had already put the local voters into a pro-Republican frame of mind by wandering into speakeasies and pool halls and announcing himself by shooting out a few of the lights. Once he had everyone's undivided attention, he would tell them how they were expected to vote and hint that if the Republicans lost, he would come back and shoot more than just light fixtures. The tactic spawned an election-day refrain: "Who'll carry the Forty-second and Forty-third Wards? O'Banion, in his pistol pockets!"

When the polls opened in his territory, O'Banion and an estimated two hundred hard-boiled sluggers went to work. Chief Collins, remembering past elections, sent squads of police riflemen into the North Side. Pitched battles broke out between the cops and O'Banion thugs. Several arrests were made. The steadily filling paddy wagons had little effect on the intensity of the general violence.

At one point during the voting, O'Banion learned that Domenic "Libby" Nuccio, chief of the tiny Gloriano Gang, had taken over the polling station at the corner of Wells and Division Streets and was forcing the voters to mark the Democratic candidates on their ballots. Furious, O'Banion drove to the scene, leaped out of the car with pistol in hand, and chased Nuccio away. The two gangsters exchanged curses and threats so vicious that bystanders stood frozen in shock. Those ugly words would be remembered six days later, and would briefly turn Domenic Nuccio into a murder suspect.

O'Banion attained his impressive goal: The Republicans won the Forty-second and Forty-third Wards. Colonel Sprague, who had courted the North Sider's favor at the banquet, lost to his opponent, Charles S. Deneen, by 5,938 votes. Robert Crowe defeated Democrat Michael L. Igoe, who had been Torrio's attorney during the 1923 beer-war murder investigations, by almost ten thousand votes.

O'Banion was so pleased that he could barely contain himself. "I turned the trick!" he boasted afterward to City Sealer Carmen Vacco.

Success went completely to his head. O'Banion had proven that he had the power to make thousands of people vote the way he wanted them to. This time, he had directed the benefits of that influence to others, but next time, it would be his name on the ballot.

It seemed as if his star were rising, but in reality, his sun was beginning to set.

On Saturday, November 8, 1924, Mike Merlo died, succumbing to the cancer that he had fought for so long. Frankie Yale arrived from New York for the funeral, scheduled for November 13, and approved young Angelo Genna as successor to the Unione Siciliana presidency in Chicago.

Yale had also come for another reason. Capone had told him that he was needed to perform a killing, similar the Colosimo hit in 1920. It appeared that no local killer would do—the victim was too smart and alert for intended assassins.

From the moment that news of Merlo's passing became known, O'Banion's energies were concentrated on the copious flow of orders that were placed at his flower shop. Merlo's friends wanted only the best, so the work was time-consuming. O'Banion and his partner, William Schofield, were in the shop all day Sunday, November 9, and most of the night. They wove blooms into horseshoe, pillar, and quilt patterns, attaching to each finished piece a gilt ribbon bearing a weepy message. Torrio had left an order for ten thousand dollars' worth of flowers, and Capone had commissioned an eight-thousand-dollar rose sculpture. It was the busiest day O'Banion had known in his career as a florist.

Sunday evening, Jim Genna and City Sealer Carmen Vacco visited Schofield's. O'Banion was gone for the evening, so Genna paid Schofield $750 for a floral piece. He was scanning the premises, and memorizing the layout, and he requested that upon completion, the arrangement be sent to the Merlo home on Diversey Parkway.

Later the same night, Frankie Yale called. He gave Schofield an order for two thousand dollars' worth of blooms and mentioned that he and some friends would be coming to pick it up Monday at around noon. Schofield scribbled the order down in the shop's book, worked for a few more hours, then went home.

O'Banion spent Sunday night hitting the cabarets with Louis Alterie, and the two did not stumble home until 3 A.M. Before they parted company, Alterie asked his friend to give him a wakeup call at nine o'clock, so they could go to the shop together. The business would be swarming that day with O'Banion's enemies as well as friends, and Alterie wanted to be around in the event of trouble. O'Banion agreed, and after a few hours' sleep at his home, he left for work. He either forgot or neglected to call Alterie.

O'Banion dove into the volume of work that awaited him at the shop. The morning passed quickly, and at eleven-thirty he was still hard at it, clipping chrysanthemums in the workroom.

The phone rang, and O'Banion answered it. It was Schofield, who said, "I'm at Mount Carmel Cemetery, fixing up graves for Armistice Day. Can you stay there until around one o'clock? I'll be in then."

"Sure," O'Banion replied. He hung up, and glanced out into the main shop, which was empty of customers for the time being. "Bill," he called to the Negro porter, William Crutchfield, "the floor's littered with petals and leaves. Better brush them up."

Crutchfield complied, and O'Banion resumed his work on the chrysanthemums. Victor Young, the shop manager, and bookkeeper Vincent Galvin were nearby, and the delivery driver had arrived to pick up another pile of orders.

The front door opened, and three men walked in. Crutchfield glanced up from his cleaning and noted that they were well dressed, and that two looked like Italians. The third was taller, less swarthy, and gave the impression of being Jewish or Greek.

The tall man was Frankie Yale. The other two were John Scalise and Albert Anselmi, the merciless Genna hitmen who gave about as much thought to snuffing out a life as they did to turning out a light. O'Banion glanced out of the workroom at the sound of their entry, and his face lit up. He knew that they had come for the two-thousand-dollar order Yale had placed the night before.

O'Banion set the flowers on a worktable and approached the visitors, his right hand extended for a shake. He still held the florist shears in his left. Crutchfield had finished his sweeping and was headed for the back room. As they passed each other, O'Banion asked the porter to close the backroom door. Crutchfield complied, understanding that his boss must have private business to discuss with the men. As he turned to close the door, he caught a glimpse of the tall man taking O'Banion's outstretched hand in an apparently friendly clasp.

Fifteen minutes later, gunfire erupted. All of the shop employees except for Crutchfield ran out of the workroom and into the alley, terrified. When the noise subsided, the porter emerged in time to see the three men run out the front door, knocking over two schoolboys who had been peering in the shop window. The trio escaped in a waiting Jewett sedan, their safe departure ensured by six defense cars that had obstructed traffic on State and Superior Streets until they could get away.

O'Banion was lying on the floor in front of the glass showcase, which was now splintered by a bullet hole. Crutchfield knelt beside him, but there was nothing he could do. The North Sider laid on a pile of crushed flowers, his blonde hair spilled across his forehead and hands twitching, as if still seeking a gun. Blood streamed from an ugly bullet hole in the back of his head, and his work clothes were slowly turning scarlet via a heavy influx from more wounds to his neck and chest.

One of the shaken employees called the Chicago Avenue station to report a shooting. The first officer to arrive was Captain Daniel Murphy. Captain William Schoemaker, Chief of Detectives Michael Hughes, and Assistant State's Attorneys John Sbarbaro and William McSwiggin joined him minutes later. They had to fight through a swelling crowd to get inside the shop.

Father Morrison and Father O'Brien from Holy Name Parochial School were already on the premises when the police arrived, having been alerted to the shooting by the schoolboys who had seen the killers flee. When their ministrations were finished, the officers lifted O'Banion's body carefully and carried it to a table in the back room. While the Coroner, Dr. Joseph Springer, was performing a cursory examination, William Schofield returned from Mount Carmel Cemetery.

Initially puzzled by the crowds outside his shop, his reaction quickly turned to grief when informed of the murder. He and O'Banion had been friends as well as business partners. While a hearse was backing up toward the delivery entrance, the telephone jangled. Schofield picked it up.

"You want a floral wreath?" he said slowly. "I'm sorry, but we can't take your order. We've had an . . . accident here. And I guess we'll want all our floral wreaths at that."

He hung up and stared at the floor. In the background, O'Banion's body was zipped into a canvas bag, placed on a stretcher, and carried out to the hearse. The flowers he had been working on before his killers walked in were still on the worktable, but now they were crushed from the weight of his body and soaked with his blood.

Out in the main shop, amid the hubbub, Crutchfield resumed his cleaning duties. This time he mopped blood instead of floral debris, cleaning up after the tragedy he had been unfortunate enough to witness.

William Schoemaker, a tough-as-nails cop who liked gangsters just slightly less than Mayor Dever did, headed the murder investigation. He rounded up Torrio, Capone, the Miller brothers, Libby Nuccio, the Genna brothers, and anyone else who might have wanted to see O'Banion dead, but they all denied having anything to do with the killing. Davy Miller went so far as to say that he was glad O'Banion was dead. Torrio and Capone insisted that they had been friends with the deceased, holding up their recent flower purchases as proof.

Mike Carrozzo, whom O'Banion had soundly beaten at the Friar's Inn, was questioned and released. So was Margaret Collins, ex-paramour of O'Banion lieutenant Jew Bates. She had just returned to Chicago after a brief absence to place a monument over the grave of Johnny Sheehy, the only one of her many lovers to actually touch her heart. She denied any inside knowledge about O'Banion's murder.

Officers picked up Frankie Yale and his bodyguard Sam Polaccia while they were preparing to board a train back to New York. Yale had been netted earlier in a general roundup of suspects and charged with carrying concealed weapons, but he was released after a brief court appearance. Chief Morgan Collins, when he learned of Yale's arrest, linked him immediately with the list of Colosimo murder suspects from four years earlier. He ordered Yale's detention until witnesses could be brought in to look at him.

Yale claimed that he had not even arrived in Chicago until Tuesday, the day after O'Banion was killed. He had come for Mike Merlo's funeral on November 13 and delayed his return to New York because of a banquet that Diamond Joe Esposito had held for him.

Chief of Detectives Michael Hughes, who had attended the dinner for O'Banion at the Webster, commented wistfully, "Though we know that we are on the right track, I do not believe we can get far enough for a trial with these three men [Yale, Scalise, and Anselmi]." He was right. William Crutchfield was brought in to view them, but could not or would not make a positive identification. Yale and Polaccia went free and caught the next train home.

In their thoroughness, the police investigators also spoke to O'Banion's friends. Weiss, Drucci, Moran, and McCarthy fended off all requests for cooperation; they had their own plans about how to get even. Only Alterie talked, and most of what he said was superficial nonsense.

Viola O'Banion answered only a few essential questions posed by officers, and then fled into tearful seclusion. She was so hysterical in her grief that her family detailed a nurse to help her make it through the funeral.

Charles and Margaret O'Banion had been in Hot Springs, where Dean had sent them on vacation, when they were notified of the murder. They caught the first train back to Chicago, and were met at the station by Viola's sister Vivian and a bodyguard. Another guard helped the couple into a limousine, but not before they expressed their grief and shock to a brace of reporters.

Margaret O'Banion had not married Charles until Dean was in his twenties, but stepmother and stepson had been extremely close. She had often told friends that he was so good to her that she thought of him as her own son.

"My boy!" she wailed. "Where is my boy? I want to see him. I can't imagine who would kill him. He didn't have an enemy in the world. He was . . . he was the best son any mother ever had."

One reporter asked Charles O'Banion where he was going. "Going?" the distraught father echoed. "What does it matter where I go? I can't say anything except that he is dead now, and I'm going to spend the rest of my life trying to avenge his death."

Charles O'Banion's torment was considerable. He had lost his first wife and his two sons, when the natural order of things dictated that women outlived their men and children survived to take care of aging parents. Emma O'Banion had coughed her life away into a bloody handkerchief, a raging fever took his son Floyd, and now Dean had been shot to death in an obvious gangland assassination. Charles was still living with the memories and wondering why.

Valiantly, he struggled to defend the memory of his errant son. "He was never a gun-toting youngster," he snapped to *Daily News* reporter Maureen McKernan. "Fighter he was, as any kid has to be to get along, but hard working and peaceful. This saying he was a gang fighter makes me tired. I know what he was doing when he was a kid. . . . Four years he was an altar boy at Holy Name and good in his catechism."

Charles was the first witness called at the November 12 inquest. Standing before the jury, a newspaper shielding his face from cameras, he mumbled answers about Dean's family history. When asked where his infamous son was born, he was heard to reply, "In Aurora; he had been in Chicago twenty years."

It is possible that the real answer, Maroa, was misheard as Aurora, but Charles never corrected the mistake as he signed the death certificate. He either did not notice it, or wanted to shield his former neighbors and friends from the prying Chicago press.

There was some confusion over whether O'Banion had known his killers. The controversy exists even today.

Captain William Schoemaker declared, "O'Banion, of all things, knew he was marked for death. He knew it might come at any moment. A handshaker, yes, but not with strangers, when any stranger might mean death. He knew them, at least by sight, and he did not suspect them." He explained that whenever approached by someone he did not know, O'Banion stood with feet apart, hands on hips, thumbs to the rear and fingers down in front, enabling him to seize a pistol at the slightest hint of danger.

Those who knew O'Banion claim that they never observed such wary behavior. "Dean had his hand out to people all the time," Barnett recalled. "He was a backslapper. Unless he had good reason to be on his guard around someone, he was more forthcoming than a kid." There is no reason to believe that O'Banion had ever met Yale, so the friendly approach that he made to his killer invalidates Schoemaker's theory, and does not prove that he knew his assassins.

Some reports quote him as saying, "Are you from Mike Merlo's?" which would suggest that he did not know the men and wanted to make sure that they were the ones coming for the noon pickup. But other reports claim that what he actually said was, "Hello boys! You want Merlo's flowers?" which denotes less uncertainty. Crutchfield, the porter, claimed that O'Banion had asked him to close the door between the work area and the shop proper, cutting off his view of those in the back room. The porter said O'Banion gave him the impression that he wanted to speak to the men privately.

Had O'Banion been expecting Yale for reasons other than the flower pickup? If so, he never got to discuss it. The killing was accomplished quickly, and the murderers escaped so smoothly that *The New York Times* marveled over the feat. "The existence of a master mind was revealed," one editorial said.

O'Banion's killing, dubbed the "handshake murder" by the press, seized the public's imagination for three reasons: (1) the victim was a high-profile gangster, the most important Big Shot to go down since Big Jim Colosimo; (2) it had taken place at noon on Chicago's busiest thoroughfare; and (3) the whole episode unfolded like some elaborately staged play whose finale featured the murderers' escape into the crowded streets. *The New York Times* discussed the third factor at length in a November 12 editorial:

> Murder is such an ancient art, and has had so many practitioners, not a few of them highly ingenious, that a really novel variant in the manner of its commission is nowadays next to impossible. Yet the task has been accomplished in Chicago. The use of automobiles in the carrying out of criminal plots of all kinds became an old story long since, and yet it was by means of these vehicles that originality was accomplished.

The notion that six automobiles could block noontime traffic on a street that was hectic at the best of times focused curiosity on the victim, whose murder had been important enough to require such elaborate preparations. O'Banion's death became front-page news not only in Chicago but in other North American cities as well. The intense interest initially was inspired by the audacity of the deed itself, but gradually the focus of attention shifted to O'Banion. While waiting for their chance to interview his mourning family, reporters wrote at length about his criminal past, making up more than they actually researched. The police contributed to the creation of an underworld legend when Collins called the departed gangster "Chicago's arch killer, who has killed or seen to the killing of twenty-five men."

It was an extreme description that would spawn equally intense stories. Those claiming to be in the know said that one of O'Banion's favorite pastimes had been to dare suckers to fire clay-packed shotguns and laugh when the resulting backfire took out the victim's eye. Others talked about finding his car seats splattered with blood and gore on many occasions. The speculation snowballed until the resulting tales became part of Chicago underworld lore. Dean O'Banion was on his way to becoming a grotesque star.

"Once in a while, I'll read a book about the Chicago gangsters and can't believe some of the stuff written about Dean," Barnett said. "He wasn't a plaster saint; if he thought you were interfering with his business, you had good reason to be scared. He probably did take out a few guys for threatening him or his operation. But he wasn't a goddamn maniac like he was made out to be. He was a good boss to me and the other guys, and a ton of people missed him when he went."

The inquest into O'Banion's death took place from November 12 to November 25 and yielded no results. "Slayers not apprehended," the Cook County Coroner noted in the court record. "John Scalise and Albert Anselmi and Frank Yale suspected, but never brought to trial."

The New York Times predicted that O'Banion's slaying would be followed by retaliatory killings committed by his soldiers but doubted that the motive would be grief. "They [his friends] will not mourn for him particularly; but they will resent the breaking up of his organization and the ending of its profits," an editorial stated.

The Times could not have been more wrong. The North Side Gang had never truly been a business team; it was a union of friends, of blood brothers, who enjoyed the chase and one another's company.

When Big Jim Colosimo was killed, his friends and supporters were wooed by Torrio's promises of prosperity because Big Jim's associates were foremost his business partners. The North Siders had been O'Banion's genuine friends. They would not be swayed except by force.

Hymie Weiss's sense of agony and guilt must have been considerable. He had encouraged O'Banion's rebellion. Edward Dean

Sullivan recalled, "He [Weiss] had been an active influence in getting O'Banion to break with the Torrio–Capone organization. He had urged it long before circumstances made it necessary. . . . When O'Banion was killed, Weiss felt, in a way, personally responsible."

Al Capone agreed with Sullivan's accusation. In a candid discussion of O'Banion's killing, he said, "Dion [sic] was all right and he was getting along, to begin with, better than he had any right to expect. But, like everyone else, his head got away from his hat. *Weiss figured in that.* Johnny Torrio had taught O'Banion all he knew, and then O'Banion grabbed some of the best guys we had and decided to be the boss of the booze racket in Chicago. What a chance!

"When he broke away, for a while it wasn't so good. He knew the ropes and got running us ragged. He was spoiling it for everybody. When we had been paying a cop a couple of hundred dollars, he'd slip them a thousand. He spoiled them. Well, we couldn't do anything about it. It was his funeral."

Hymie Weiss became obsessed with avenging his beloved friend's death. He knew that he could not touch Yale, since any gunmen sent into Yale-dominated Brooklyn would be spotted quickly and sent back feet first. Torrio, Capone, and the Gennas were easier targets.

William Schofield confirmed that retribution was forthcoming. "They [the North Siders] were out fifteen minutes after Dean was killed," he said with grim satisfaction. "They've been out there ever since. They know who did it, and they won't call the police when they catch 'em. You watch."

A framed card found hanging over O'Banion's desk at the flower shop was cloying but accurate in its description of the friendship that existed between the core members of the North Side Gang:

A friend is one
Who makes a speech
You understand;
He's partly kindness
Partly mirth
And faith unfaltering
In your worth
He's first to cheer
You to success

And last to leave
You in distress.
A friend is constant,
Honest, true,
In short, old pal
He's just like you.

A Chicago detective sensed the North Siders' plans, as did almost everyone else in Chicago. "There will be more murder," he predicted glumly. "More murder, and it will come quick."

14

"The Most Nauseating Thing I've Ever Seen in Chicago"

Dean O'Banion's funeral was the most lavish in gangland history, surpassing even the opulent respects paid to Big Jim Colosimo in 1920. The ten-thousand-dollar casket, sent from Philadelphia on an express train that had carried no other cargo, was made of silver and bronze. Intricately carved silver posts were at all four corners, and fastened to the side was a gold plaque bearing the inscription "Dean O'Banion 1892–1924."

O'Banion's body "laid in state," as the press termed it, for three days in Sbarbaro's funeral chapel on North Wells Street. At the head and foot of the casket knelt two silver angels, heads bowed in sorrow and holding solid-gold candlesticks in which ten candles burned softly. Engraved on a marble slab supporting the magnificent coffin was the scriptural passage, "Suffer little children to come onto me."

The vast array of floral offerings turned the chapel into a moist, dusky-scented Garden of Eden. A huge heart composed of two thousand red roses and marked "Husband" was sent by the grieving widow. The North Siders contributed a seven-foot pillar of white carnations, symbolizing the source of strength O'Banion had been for them all, and a wreath of red roses labeled "Our Pal." Prizefighter Micky Walker sent a basket of roses. The effusion of blooms was highlighted by an electric lighting system that shed a ghostly glow across the casket and pews.

O'Banion's face had been restored by the undertaker's art; mounds of talc had covered the abrasions and bruises created by his fall. White satin cushioning lined the casket, with an extra mound added for his left hand to rest upon. A rosary was clasped in what a *Daily News* reporter called "his soft, tapered hands, which could finger an automatic so effectively."

On Friday, November 14, the day of the burial, thousands lined the street outside Sbarbaro's establishment to view the body. When the doors opened at 9:30 A.M., the first contingent of police guards found themselves faced with too big a crowd to effectively control, so they telephoned for reinforcements. It took two hundred officers to shepherd the throng. People climbed on rooftops to get a view of the funeral parade when it began, but the ominous sound of cracking lumber prompted Chief of Detectives Hughes to clear them off.

An estimated thirty thousand people paid their last respects. Many were curiosity seekers, but some visitors felt genuine sorrow. Mingling with the press and sightseers were O'Banion's colleagues, employees, and customers from the flower shop, and slum dwellers who had known his charity.

Viola was in the chapel constantly, insisting on being near her husband's body. Worn with grief and anxiety, she caught snatches of sleep in the small pew at the head of the casket. Charles O'Banion, Louis Alterie, Vivian Kaniff, and a hired nurse took turns watching over her, concerned for both her health and sanity.

She sat, dressed in black satin, tear-stained face and quivering body covered up by a black veil and full-length mink coat. Watching the throngs fill the chapel, gawking at the man she had loved as if he were a curiosity piece, she felt an uncontrollable urge to dispel the bloody illusion. She spotted *Daily News* reporter Maureen McKernan and broke her silence.

"He was all I have in the world," she said, head bowed. "I don't know what to do now that he is gone. I can't think. I don't know what I'll do with my home.

"He was not a man to run around nights, only to take me to a show. And never one of those men with women calling him up. He was home loving, wanting his friends about him, and never leaving without telling me where he was going."

She talked about his disdain for vulgar ostentation, and his love for Colorado. Alterie, who was her moral support at the moment, jumped in with a fond anecdote about the rifle O'Banion had offered as a rodeo prize during the October visit. Viola nodded.

"That [rifle] was the greatest interest he ever showed in guns," she said adamantly. "Carrying one, of course, sometimes, as anyone will for protection against Chicago night streets, but seldom with one at home, and many a day at a time without one in his pocket."

Her words could easily be dismissed as those of a distraught widow blind to a sordid reality. But she could truly attest to a gentle, loyal aspect to his character. She was determined that he not be lowered into his grave without speaking in his favor. She had loved him too much for that.

Having spoken her piece, her strength crumbled. "I can't think, now he's gone. I loved him so and he was all I cared anything about," she added, pulling out a black-bordered handkerchief and burying her face in it.

She and the rest of the O'Banion family had wanted a funeral service to be held at Holy Name Cathedral, but Cardinal George Mundelein, through Bishop Edward Hoban, forbade it. "O'Banion was a notorious criminal," the spokesman explained. "The Church did not recognize him in his days of lawlessness, and when he died unrepentant in his iniquities, he had no claims to the last rites for the dead."

O'Banion's friends gave him a more extravagant send-off than the church could have. When the service began, Hymie Weiss and Louis Alterie, who was dressed in a purple collar and frock coat, sobbed noisily in their seats, not caring who might remark on it. A hired orchestra played a weepy rendition of "Ave Maria," drawing tears from Vincent Drucci, Bugs Moran, Dan McCarthy, and other hardened hoodlums who sat with their wives or perfumed blonde friends a few seats away from the other mourners, among whom were judges, aldermen, and policemen. The chapel windows were opened so that the thousands who lined Wells Street outside could hear the music, and most heads were bowed in repose.

After the service concluded, the orchestra played the "Dead March" from *Saul.* The pallbearers—Weiss, Moran, Drucci, Dan McCarthy, Maxie Eisen, Matt Foley, and Frank Gusenberg—carried the gleaming casket to the hearse. Uniformed cops had to clear a path for them through the crowd. Viola, supported by her sisters, and the surviving O'Banions followed them to the cars parked along the congested curb.

The funeral procession was more than a mile long. It contained twenty-six cars and trucks carrying flowers, vehicles containing the mourners, three bands playing dirges, and an honor guard of uniformed police officers from Stickney. (Chief Collins had prohibited the participation of Chicago policemen.) Every streetcar leading to Mount Carmel Cemetery was jammed with sightseers; five thousand were already there. This open display of fascination for a gangster's untimely passing revolted Judge John H. Lyle, who commented bitterly, "It was the most nauseating thing I've ever seen in Chicago."

The gravesite was highly conspicuous. An awning covered it, and green velvet carpeting coated the ground. Evergreen lined the hole. A mound of earth beside it was concealed by a heap of evergreen branches, from which a silver crucifix protruded. Ironically, flower petals and bits of ribbon from Mike Merlo's burial tributes had blown across the cemetery and littered the ground near the grave. O'Banion had helped fashion them, and now they dotted his final resting place.

In accordance with Cardinal Mundelein's strictures, O'Banion was buried in unconsecrated ground and there was no graveside mass. But as the casket was being lowered into the pine-scented earth, Father Patrick Malloy of St. Thomas of Canterbury Church stepped forward and recited a litany, a Hail Mary, and the Lord's Prayer. He had known O'Banion for years and refused to believe that he had been truly evil. Father Malloy remembered that O'Banion had done much to alleviate suffering in the North Side slums, and would not desert him in the end. "One good turn deserves another," he told the crowd.

Viola O'Banion stood with her father-in-law a distance from the crowds who milled around the grave. She listened to Father Malloy's tribute, weeping quietly, and then returned to her car. Weiss and the other North Siders followed. Eventually, only thrill seekers remained, many of them women who invaded the tent over the grave and snatched blossoms from the flower heap as souvenirs. Watching them seize their mementos, one would have believed that a celebrity had been buried.

The churches and citizens groups feared that impression. Dr. John Thompson summed up their worries in a lengthy statement to the press.

"Here is a man said to have been implicated in twenty-five murders buried with the pomp and ceremony of a king," he complained. "What are the youth of our city to think about it? It is a sad commentary on our civilization that a criminal can become the center of interest in a great city like this.

"The revelations that have come out of the O'Banion tragedy show the influence that the criminal classes, high and low, have in society. No man could go as long in crime without being apprehended and punished if he did not have accomplices and sympathizers."

Mayor Dever was mortified by the city's show of gangster worship. He dragged the press over the coals for what he believed to be their complicity.

"By the time the emotional newspaper reporters had gotten through with the O'Banion case, he was clothed in a veil of romance that made of him a free-hearted Beau Brummel instead of a coarse, brutal murderer, which he was. The press gives to the youthful reader the wrong idea of what constitutes a hero."

Dever conferred with Collins and ordered the formation of a strong-arm squad consisting of the department's toughest officers. These men would not be obliged to send criminals to court, but rather deal out a ferocious justice on the spot, using the gang's own methods. *The New York Times* observed, "Police officials take this to mean that there will be less work for the courts and more for the surgeons and undertakers."

It never happened. The only real inconvenience suffered by the underworld was the December 1924 padlocking of the Four Deuces, but Capone established another business office immediately at 2146 South Michigan Avenue, and the Deuces' regulars found equally accommodating hangouts elsewhere. Several arrests were made during the gangster squad's first few days, but none of those apprehended were treated—in any way—by a surgeon or undertaker. No Wyatt Earp or Pat Garrett was created at gangland's expense.

Torrio, Capone, and the Gennas sent flowers and put in an obligatory appearance at the wake and funeral. Anticipating trouble, Mayor Dever had ordered that a special police squad circulate among the mourners. No violence broke out, but the quiet and order were deceptive, and everyone knew it.

Torrio and his wife slipped quietly out of Chicago and went on an extended vacation, visiting Hot Springs, New Orleans, Havana, the Bahamas, Palm Beach, and St. Petersburg. He had no stomach for violence and wanted to be out of Chicago while Capone and Hymie Weiss battled it out. It has been written that Weiss gunmen pursued the Torrios on their journey, sometimes missing them by hours, but it was unlikely that the North Siders went to such efforts. They knew that sooner or later Torrio would come back to Chicago. He would get his then.

The most vocal presence in the O'Banion tragedy, and also the most enigmatic, was Louis Alterie. He issued a public challenge to the slayers to fight it out, Wild West style, at the corner of State and Madison Streets.

"If I go, I'll go with a smile," he insisted, "because I know that two or three of them will go with me. If I knew who killed Dean, I would shoot it out with the gang of killers before the sun rose in the morning, and some of us, maybe all of us, would be lying on slabs in the undertaker's place."

Alterie confided that he had been receiving death threats over the phone. "I invited him [one caller] to come over to have it out, but he refused to come. He called me a dago and that got me sore. You know, I am half French and half Spanish." He predicted that he would be the next to go if he did not keep on his guard. In spite of his fear of assassination, he kept repeating his challenge to O'Banion's killers in nightclubs and speakeasies, making such a nuisance of himself that Mayor Dever was flabbergasted. "Are we still abiding by the code of the Dark Ages?" he asked. "Or is this Chicago a unit of an American commonwealth?"

One Sunday night Captain John Stege came upon Alterie haranguing the clientele at the Midnight Frolics. The big cop made a beeline for the cowboy hoodlum, took him aside, and slapped him in the face in front of dozens of tough customers who laughed hysterically. Stege hauled Alterie down to the detective bureau, where he was held until Monday without being booked. The gangster's lawyer, William Scott Stewart, made a plea to Judge William Lindsay of the criminal court, asking that Stege either file charges or release his client. Lindsay ruled in Scott's favor, forcing Stege to charge Alterie with disorderly conduct and carrying a revolver. The judge targeted Stege for a scolding that *The Chicago Daily News* detailed in the next day's edition.

> **JUDGE GOOD TO ALTERIE**
> **Scolds Police for arresting Gunman, frees him on 2 charges.**
>
> Reprimanding the police for "wasting their time" in arresting Louis Alterie, Judge William J. Lindsay of the criminal court ordered that Alterie, pal of the late Dion O'Banion, and two others be booked on two charges and released on one-thousand-dollar bonds. . . .

"Why do you waste your time on this kind of stuff?" demanded Judge Lindsay as he acquiesced in the pleas of William Scott Stewart to have Alterie and the others booked. "Why, I have to carry a revolver myself because my neighborhood is so poorly policed. My home has been robbed and that is merely illustrative of the experience of hundreds of others."

The public humiliation deflated Alterie and supposedly disgusted his colleagues enough to expel him from their ranks. George "Bugs" Moran finally confronted him at the Friar's Inn one night and advised him to leave while he could still walk. Alterie took the hint and speedily left Chicago for his Colorado ranch.

The role of Louis Alterie in O'Banion's death has never been closely examined. It has been accepted by crime historians that he was a flaky braggart who was expelled by the North Siders because of his ineptitude and instability. But was it really that simple?

Why was Alterie talking so much while his comrades remained silent?

Why would Hymie Weiss expel a senior gang member when he had a war of revenge in mind? Wouldn't that have been a time when experience and ability with a gun were valuable commodities?

Louis Alterie had been hyperactive and volatile, but no more so than O'Banion or Vincent Drucci. So why was he expelled—unless he figured more strongly in O'Banion's death than merely failing to play bodyguard the morning of the murder?

Alterie, in one of his candid discussions, told a reporter, "John Torrio and Al Brown [Capone] are good friends of ours and had no hand whatsoever in the killing." After exonerating them, he was seen quietly talking with the two on Thursday, November 13, when they came to the funeral chapel. He was the only North Sider seen conversing with them.

Moran confronted Alterie at the Friar's Inn on Monday, November 17, and the next day the cowboy hoodlum caught a train out of Chicago—but it was not bound for Colorado; it was heading for New York. Johnny Torrio also took a train to New York that night, although not the same one as Alterie. The *Herald and Examiner* reporter who uncovered the information calculated that the two men would have reached their destination within hours of each other.

Why would Alterie and Torrio—presumably made enemies by O'Banion's killing—have gone to New York at the same time? Were they planning to meet and needed a place safer than Chicago to confer? Frankie Yale and Sam Polaccia were arrested as they boarded a train that would have gotten them to New York shortly after Torrio and Alterie arrived.

Louis Alterie did eventually return to Colorado. He maintained his position as president of the Theatre and Building Janitors Union in Chicago, but it was an absentee job. In Colorado he resumed the wild schemes and shenanigans that created his Chicago reputation. In January 1932 a grand jury in Chicago indicted him for taking part in a Midwest-based kidnapping ring. Another plot, this one to extort half a million dollars from wealthy Illinois citizens, was exposed around the same time. One of his accomplices was Ward C. Swalwell, a former Cook County assistant state's attorney.

On November 8, 1932, Alterie shot two men in a fight in the Glenwood Springs Hotel in Colorado. He was handed a sentence of one to five years, which was suspended on the condition that he leave the state. Alterie first went to Santa Fe, New Mexico, then back to Chicago, safe in the knowledge that all that remained of the O'Banion heirs was a ragtag bunch led by Bugs Moran.

Being president of the Theatre and Building Janitors Union, Alterie figured in the battles for control of the motion-picture industry that shook the early Thirties. Organized crime, having lost a gold mine when Prohibition ended, saw the movie business as the new bonanza, the Depression-era public being starved for entertainment. Gangsters took control of industry unions, and those who defied them were squeezed out or killed. Alterie was questioned in the murders of Tommy Malloy, a leading motion-picture operator, and Clyde Osterberg, a rebellious union organizer.

Something went wrong for Alterie in 1935. He may have offended Frank Nitti, who took over the Chicago crime syndicate when Capone went to prison in 1931, or rival union members may have had their eyes on the post he had occupied for twelve years.

On July 9, a man named "Sullivan" rented a room facing the Alterie residence at 922 Eastwood Avenue. Nine days later, the cowboy gangster and his wife, Ermina, were leaving their apartment, intending to drive to his union headquarters. Gunfire exploded from Sullivan's window. Alterie, his head, neck, and left arm punctured by twelve bullets, crumpled to the sidewalk. Ermina, her face ashen, knelt over him as he lay dying. "I'm sorry, but I'm going, Bambino," he whispered before losing consciousness. His widow arranged for his remains to be shipped to Burbank, California, where he had been born.

Viola O'Banion, accompanied by her sister Vivian Kaniff, left Chicago soon after Christmas 1924, seeking refuge in Miami from both the press and the Illinois winter. In mid-January 1925, a *Herald and Examiner* reporter, alerted to her presence there, located her on the beach near the fashionable hotel where both women were staying.

"I'm through with that—that case in Chicago," she told the journalist. "There's no use meddling with it. It's too deeply involved, too tangled, ever to be solved, and I don't want anything more to do with it. That is why I have made up my mind to say nothing."

"Then you mean that you are not going back to Chicago?"

"I am going back in around a month, but only for a few days. After that, I do not know what I shall do."

When asked what she would do if subpoenaed by the grand jury investigating O'Banion's death, Viola replied testily, "They would have to find me first." She reflected for a moment and then continued, adding, "I suppose that I could be forced to go before the grand jury, but no one can force me to remember the things that I am trying to forget."

The reporter finally asked her directly, "Mrs. O'Banion, do you know who killed your husband?"

Viola ran her fingers through the hot sand, studied it for a minute, and then answered slowly, "I may have firm suspicions."

She never acted on them, nor did she back up her assertion that any return to Chicago would only be temporary. She came back to stay, a decision that a few police officers eventually regretted.

In May 1926 motorcycle policeman Ralph Fjellman from the Ridge Avenue Park district, caught her speeding through the North Side and pursued her sedan for more than three miles before she stopped. "She was doing seventy if she was doing a mile," he told reporters. "But she's a good sport. Once I caught her, she didn't make a fuss." With her was none other than the exiled Louis Alterie, who was back in Chicago to attend to union affairs. Viola was arraigned at the town hall and fined five dollars plus court costs.

Fjellman's encounter with her was painless compared to what his brother officers had to endure during similar arrests. When Lincoln Park policeman George Carlson arrested her for speeding and tacked on a disorderly conduct charge when she displayed aggression, she paid a twenty-five-dollar fine and warned him, "You'll be sorry for this." A few days later, Larson was taken off of motorcycle duty and assigned a foot patrol route in Lincoln Park. His superiors denied that Mrs. O'Banion's "pull" had brought about the transfer, saying that such changes were routine.

She was arrested again in 1927, 1928, and 1929, all on speeding-related charges. Her demeanor toward the officers worsened with each confrontation. When Orville Berkey charged her in January 1932 with running a stoplight and having insufficient taillights, she initially refused to tell him who she was and was taken to the Summerdale station. She insisted angrily that she would not accept the tickets issued on the two charges and relented only when a woman companion persuaded her to do so.

Berkey followed the two women as they left the station and saw Viola throw the tickets out her car window as she drove off. Fuming, he leaped onto his motorcycle, overtook her, and re-arrested her for disorderly conduct. She cursed him, calling him a rat and threatening to have his job. In court she disrupted his testimony with shouts of "It's a lie!" The exasperated judge, aware of her previous traffic violations, fined her fifty-two dollars and issued a reprimand that left the courtroom speechless. She paid it by stalking to the clerk's desk and flinging down three twenty-dollar bills.

Viola O'Banion's romantic life was to prove equally stormy after she became a widow. On April 13, 1926, she and Frank Fisk, president of the Republic Printing Company, accompanied another couple to their wedding in Crowne Point, Indiana, where the unexpected happened.

"Our friends dared us to marry," Viola later testified sheepishly, "and we just did."

The newly married Fisks parted company that very night, Viola going to Michigan City and Fisk returning to Chicago. They never lived together. Viola sued for divorce. Her brother Edward Kaniff testified that he had seen Fisk going into a North Side hotel accompanied by a woman who was not his wife. The bemused Judge Sabath granted Viola the divorce.

She married again, less than a year later. Her third husband was wealthy butcher O. A. Turner, who owned a prosperous shop on Devon Avenue. This union lasted considerably longer than her marriage to Fisk, but it, too, ultimately ended in divorce, whereupon she petitioned to have the name of O'Banion restored to her. "I realized," she told a friend, "that the real love of my life died when Dean did."

In September 1936 she vowed to make a fresh start. She had adopted a daughter, Viola Marie, and petitioned Circuit Court Judge William V. Brothers to change both her surname and that of her daughter to Carter. Brothers granted the request, and Viola disappeared into obscurity.

15

The Bootleg Battle of the Marne

HYMIE WEISS REFRAINED FROM immediate retaliation against O'Banion's killers. The murder itself had resulted in scathing press coverage and even the removal of Mike Hughes from his post as chief of detectives (Hughes went on to become head of the Cook County Highway Police). Launching an offensive against Torrio, Capone, and the Gennas too soon after the event would intensify the police and public pressure that Louis Alterie's war cries had aroused.

He waited.

Journalists acquainted with the North Side Gang wrote that there would be no single leader to replace O'Banion, that Weiss, Moran, Drucci, Alterie, Maxie Eisen, and Dan McCarthy intended to rule the gang as a unified "board of directors." If that was the original plan, it soon changed. McCarthy, having no stomach for war, gradually dropped out of the gang's inner circle, immersing himself instead in union activities. Alterie talked too much and was shown the door. Maxie Eisen, like McCarthy, decided that union work posed fewer health hazards. Moran and Drucci, although loyal to

O'Banion and competent fighters, lacked leadership qualities. The top spot fell to Weiss by default. Since he had been O'Banion's right hand and advisor, as well as an essential player in the North Side Gang's bootlegging, gambling, and union successes, assuming the leadership role was natural for him.

Weiss injected his personality into the gang, making it a dedicated war machine. The rip-roaring Robin Hood spirit that O'Banion had created dissolved as the aim of the gang changed from getting by to getting even. Weiss did not neglect day-to-day business in favor of revenge schemes. If anything, he expended more energy than O'Banion had in making profitable connections with other gangs, in Chicago and in other large U.S. cities such as Cleveland and Detroit. One such alliance, made with Cleveland bootlegger Harry Goldman in the summer of 1926, netted Weiss a tidy $134,000 in a single liquor-smuggling deal alone.

Edward Dean Sullivan described Weiss as one of only four great leaders in Chicago gangland, the others being O'Banion, Torrio, and Capone. Others, with equal accuracy, proclaimed him the only gangster that Al Capone ever really feared; Weiss would be the reason why Capone would recall 1925 and 1926 with a shudder.

On January 12, 1925, the North Siders fired the opening shot in what the press dubbed the "Bootleg Battle of the Marne." A sedan, curtains drawn and license plates covered , pursued Capone's car through the city's icy streets, and forced it to the curb at State and Fifty-fifth. North Side gunmen poked their weapons through the curtains and blasted their quarry. They did a thorough job, striking the chauffeur, Sylvester Barton, in the back with a slug and nearly killing Capone's cousin Charlie Fischetti, who was in the back seat. A police sergeant who viewed their handiwork commented, "They let it have everything but the kitchen stove."

Capone was not in the car when the attack occurred, but he was scared enough to order from Cadillac a twenty-thousand-dollar automobile equipped with steel armor, bullet-proof glass, and doors secured by combination locks that would bar any attempt to break into the car and plant a bomb. In addition to this fortress on wheels, he had a scout car drive a half-block ahead and a touring car loaded with armed bodyguards bring up the rear whenever he went out.

Torrio, on the other hand, took no special precautions. He arrived in court on January 17 and withdrew his not-guilty plea in the Sieben Brewery case. Because this was his second offense under the Volstead Act, he definitely would be going to jail. Delays and continuances had kept him a free man for more than eight months, but imprisonment now seemed a safe haven from Weiss's North Siders. He said nothing as the judge sentenced him to nine months in the DuPage County Jail in Wheaton and fined him five thousand dollars plus court costs. Four other prisoners, including the two officers arrested in the Sieben raid, also drew jail terms. Twenty-one defendants were released. In the cases of Louis Alterie and brewer George Frank, continuances were granted.

Torrio was given until January 27 to settle his affairs. The prospect of jail did not bother him at all, as Sheriff Peter Hoffman, who had impounded Eddie Vogel's slot machines when Torrio wanted to teach the Cicero gambler a lesson in humility, was in charge of the DuPage County Jail. Hoffman could be relied upon to make Torrio's stay as comfortable as he dictated. Torrio had faith in Capone's abilities as a battle general, and felt sure that by the time he got out of jail, his young protégé would have cowed or eliminated the North Siders.

At about four o'clock on the afternoon of January 25, Torrio and his wife, Anna, returned home after a busy day. He had been conducting business, and she had been shopping. The Lincoln town car, driven by one Robert Barton, whose brother Sylvester was Capone's chauffeur, was laden with packages. After Barton stopped the car in front of the Torrio home at 7011 Clyde Avenue, Anna stepped out, arms loaded, and walked to the front door. As she turned to push it open with her back, she saw her husband and Barton standing by the car, gathering parcels into their arms. Movement in the background caught her eye, and she saw Hymie Weiss, clutching a shotgun, and Bugs Moran, armed with a .45, charging toward the two men.

Weiss, Moran, and Drucci had been sitting in a parked Cadillac for over an hour on nearby Seventeenth Street. They readied themselves as the Lincoln bearing their quarry pulled up to 7011 Clyde, and waited until Anna Torrio was out of harm's way. Then Weiss and Moran stepped out and moved in for the kill while Drucci waited behind the wheel.

The North Siders fanned out, Moran going to the front end of the Lincoln and Weiss to the rear. Their opening shots went through the body of the car and nicked Barton in the leg. Torrio dropped everything and ran for the apartment building as fast as his legs could carry him.

Moran and Weiss fired again, this time striking Torrio in the right arm. As the impact swung Torrio around to face his attackers, the pair pumped more buckshot into him, shattering his jaw and peppering his body. He crumpled to the sidewalk, blood from his wounds darkening the pavement.

Weiss, clutching a now-empty shotgun, stood motionless beside Torrio's car, ignoring the terrified Robert Barton. Moran raced up the walkway, straddled Torrio, and trained the muzzle of his .45 on the Italian gang leader's head. Anna Torrio watched, paralyzed, sure that she was about to become a widow.

When Moran pulled the trigger, nothing happened. The .45 was empty. Moran, cursing, fumbled for another clip just as a laundry truck rolled onto Clyde Avenue.

When Drucci spotted it and honked the horn, Weiss ran back to their car. Moran took one last look at his victim's injuries and decided that a slow death would be as effective as an instant one. Hurrying back to the Cadillac, he and Weiss jumped inside and Drucci drove off.

Anna Torrio flew to her husband's side. She seized him under the arms and dragged him to the safety of their apartment building. Robert Barton limped back to the punctured Lincoln and drove away. He stopped at a drugstore a short distance from the Torrio home and placed a call to Al Capone at his Cicero headquarters.

The laundry truck driver who had interrupted the North Siders pursued their car as it zoomed westward on Seventieth Street. As the Cadillac turned north on Stony Island, it eluded him. Thanks to the slowness of his truck, his valor did not get him killed.

At Jackson Park Hospital, Torrio begged his doctors to cauterize his wounds. He was terrified that the North Siders had rubbed their bullets with garlic, a practice many gunmen followed because of the belief that garlic would induce gangrene in victims who did not die immediately. The attending physicians complied, not willing to take any chances. The injuries were terrible: a shattered jaw, a broken arm, and three ragged holes in his chest and belly. He developed a raging fever when his neck and jaw became infected.

Capone, alerted by Robert Barton, arrived at the hospital. "Did they get Johnny?" he demanded frantically. When gently advised that his mentor might die, he blurted, "The gang did it! The gang did it!" Intense emotion eroded his natural inclination to be silent. He eventually collected himself and denied that the O'Banions could have had anything to do with the brutal attack.

Johnny and Anna Torrio both refused to identify the attackers. "I know who they are," the little gangster muttered. "It's my business."

One person was less hesitant in making an identification. Seventeen-year-old Peter Veesaert, son of the janitor at 6954 Clyde, had been lounging on his building's basement steps when the attack began. He voluntarily told the police what he had seen. At the station house, he looked through mug-shot books and picked out Bugs Moran's picture. He recalled Moran's noticeable chin dimple and recounted how the gangster had been the first to leap from the Cadillac and open fire. Three times he selected Moran in police lineups. When brought face to face with him at the detective bureau, Veesaert said firmly, "You're the man."

"Who? Me?" Moran growled.

"Yes," the teenager replied.

The police presented Moran to Mrs. Torrio at the hospital, where she and her husband both denied recognizing him. Three days later Municipal Judge William J. Lindsay released Moran on a five-thousand-dollar bond, despite requests from the police that he be detained pending further investigation. Nothing ever came of it; John and Anna Torrio's denials nullified Veesaert's story.

Hymie Weiss, unfazed, made another attempt on Torrio's life. While Capone was undergoing a late-night police interrogation, three carloads of men pulled up outside Jackson Park Hospital. One man got out and told the night nursing supervisor that he wanted to see Torrio. The woman refused, as Anna had ordered that no one except family and certain friends be allowed to visit. When the nurse mentioned that police guards were everywhere, the visitor departed at once. When Capone learned of the infiltration attempt, he moved into the room adjoining Torrio's. Police guards took up posts at Torrio's door, in the outside hallway, and at every window and fire escape.

Being too ill to do much else, Johnny Torrio did a lot of thinking during those long hours in bed. He knew that the citywide organization he had envisioned and briefly administered was irreparably fractured. Hymie Weiss would not be swayed by promises of partnership and riches; the North Sider wanted revenge. Torrio knew that gangs which had been forced to tolerate his organization in the past would now flock to Weiss. War was coming. Chicago was going to be a battleground, and he did not want to be around to see it.

"Johnny can dish it out, but he can't take it," an associate commented publicly. It was true. Torrio, having always lacked the muscle to inflict violence directly, had cultivated his brain instead and left the rough stuff to hirelings. He did not have the nerve or the stomach for the battle that loomed.

On February 9 he was sufficiently recovered to leave the hospital via a fire escape, surrounded by bodyguards. He appeared before Judge Cliffe and paid his five-thousand-dollar fine without a murmur. He was equally passive when a nine-month jail sentence was imposed. The place of incarceration had been switched to the Lake County Jail, but Torrio didn't mind.

County jails were not known for their severity. In June 1924 the Cook County Jail was exposed as a gangster hotel of sorts. Terry Druggan and Frankie Lake had been sentenced to a year's imprisonment for defying an order to close the Standard Beverage Corporation, a bootlegging front. After shelling out twenty thousand dollars in bribes to the warden and other officials, Druggan and Lake obtained the freedom to come and go as they pleased. A reporter from the *American* discovered the arrangement when he visited the jail to interview the two gangsters and found that both were gone. He wrote a scathing story that blew the whistle. Public outcry prompted an investigation that ended with the jailing of the warden and Sheriff Peter Hoffman.

Torrio was not interested in leaving the prison as long as Hymie Weiss waited for him outside, but he did spread around enough money to turn his cell into a home away from home. Sheriff Edwin Ahlstrom allowed him to furnish it with a brass bed, carpet, dresser, bookcase, radio, and record player. Torrio screened the windows with bulletproof mesh and blackout curtains to discourage a sniper attack, and hired deputy sheriffs as bodyguards.

Sheriff Ahlstrom did not restrict Torrio's visitors to immediate family only. Capone, Jake Guzik, and other business associates came regularly, and it was in March 1925 that a monumental conference took place. Present were Torrio, his lawyers, and Capone. The little gang leader, his lower jaw wrapped in a scarf to hide bullet scars, said that he was leaving Chicago forever and turning his multimillion-dollar business over to Capone. He had thought long and hard about it, and decided that he could not face the storm that was brewing. He was forty-three and had worked hard all his life; now he wanted to get out and enjoy his riches. Al Capone was the one most suited to succeed him as head of the organization. He was young, shrewd, and capable of meting out the violence necessary to restore peace.

In exchange for investing all of his power and assets in Capone, Torrio received a cut of future gang profits for a limited time. He planned to return to Italy with his wife but assured Capone that he would always be willing to provide counsel when necessary.

Capone accepted the crown of thorns. Just twenty-six-years old, the man known as "Scarface" now had complete control of a business that raked in tens of millions of dollars a year. He handled the responsibility well, so well that within five years all of Chicago would be under his control.

Torrio's failure to make his inter-gang alliance plan work does not reflect on his organizational abilities. He was, rather, years ahead of his time. Before his death in 1957 he would see criminal mobs from all over the country form mutually beneficial partnerships. But in the early 1920s, greed and a determination for independence characterized most gangs and their leaders.

Unlike his mentor, Capone was up for the challenge of striking down his enemies. He was the perfect mixture of businessman and battler, preferring to negotiate first but having no compunction about using force to quell trouble. Yet he faced the future with some apprehension. Hymie Weiss was clever and deadly in a way that O'Banion had never been; he had almost gotten Torrio, and Capone was the next natural target.

In early 1925 Weiss was preoccupied not only with revenge but the bootlegging case against him stemming from the April 1924 hijacking. He and Dan McCarthy made a court appearance on April 9,

1925, and for reasons never determined withdrew their earlier pleas of not guilty. Upon receiving their guilty pleas, the judge sentenced both to six months in the Kane County Jail in Geneva, Illinois, and fined them a thousand dollars plus partial court costs. Both were granted thirty days in which to settle their affairs.

U.S. Marshall Palmer E. Anderson took Weiss and McCarthy into custody on May 9 and delivered them to the McHenry County Jail at Woodstock, Illinois, to which the original place of incarceration had been changed. Not long after Sheriff Lester Edinger shut the jail doors behind them, Chicago simmered with renewed violence.

Nineteen twenty-five looked set to be a banner year for the Genna family. In January, Angelo married Lucille Spignola, an eighteen-year-old beauty from a prestigious Italian family. Her brother Henry, a lawyer and politician, had helped the Gennas cultivate their alky-cooking cottage industry. Spignola and his family had secretly been dismayed by Lucille's engagement to Angelo, because the Gennas were street level gangsters while the Spignolas regularly hobnobbed with the likes of opera star Desiré Défrère and conductor Giacomo Spadoni. But the Gennas were dangerous to oppose, so the bride's family put on brave faces and planned a lavish wedding.

The reception was held in the Ashland Auditorium and attended by more than three thousand guests, most of who had responded to published announcements to "Come one, come all." The cake occupied center stage. It had taken four days to bake and contained four hundred pounds of sugar, four hundred pounds of flour, several buckets of flavoring, seven cases of eggs, and equally huge quantities of other ingredients. At its multi-tiered top was a doll-sized replica of the newlyweds. Angelo Genna, described by the press as a "young importer," beamed at his newly acquired "respectability."

Anxious to escape the shadowy stigma of Little Italy, he and his wife took rooms at the Belmont Hotel on the North Side. It stood across the street from Big Bill Thompson's house and was down the road from the J. Ogden Armour family abode. There they planned to stay while they shopped for a house.

The couple finally decided on an attractive suburban bungalow. On the morning of May 25, 1925, Angelo hopped into his flashy roadster and headed downtown to put down fifteen thousand dollars on the property. He had not gone six blocks before a sedan with four men inside swerved out of a side street. Shotgun fire let Genna know that he was in trouble. He stepped on the gas and pulled out his own gun.

Pedestrians thronging the sidewalks of Ogden Avenue were stunned as they watched Genna fire out his window at the pursuers. Both vehicles were now rocketing down the city street at more than sixty miles per hour. When the sedan drew up beside his roadster, Angelo jerked the steering wheel and tried to swerve onto Hudson Avenue too quickly. His car careened out of control and crashed into a lamppost. Genna was too dazed and entangled in the wreckage to escape as his assailants screeched to a halt beside him. Shotguns boomed again, this time with fatal results. His body torn by slugs, Angelo died at a hospital later that afternoon.

After burying their brother in style and with full Unione Siciliana honors, the surviving Gennas declared open season on the alleged culprits, the North Side Gang. They could think of no one else who would assassinate Angelo, although later events would prove that they might have been too trusting of the wrong party.

Vincent Drucci and Bugs Moran, who were in command of the mob while Weiss served his sentence, approached Samoots Amatuna, the eccentric but deadly bodyguard, and offered him a bribe to deliver John Scalise and Albert Anselmi, O'Banion's slayers, into their hands. One has to wonder why they believed they could trust him, for in addition to killing on behalf of the Gennas, he also ran a café, Citro's, with Scalise as a silent partner. John Citro, another partner in the business, was the brother of Frank Foster (Citro), an O'Banion satellite, so the connection may have given them more confidence in their ability to shift his loyalties. They also may have offered to back him in his bid for the presidency of the Chicago chapter of the Unione, a post he wanted, thereby appealing to his sense of ambition. Amatuna's smile hid treacherous intentions as he agreed to lure the Sicilian torpedoes to the corner of Sangamon and Congress Streets, where waiting guns could pick them off.

Moran and Drucci arrived at the prearranged spot on June 13, 1925. Suddenly a limousine streaked past their Hupmobile and pelted it with shotgun fire. Moran escaped injury, but Drucci was grazed by flying lead. The two North Siders attempted pursuit, but their car was too badly damaged and they abandoned it. When police traced it to Moran later and questioned him, the gangster feigned shock and insisted that the car had been stolen earlier.

Four policemen in an unmarked car spotted the assailants—Mike Genna, Scalise, and Anselmi—driving south on Western Avenue. Suspicions aroused, the officers sounded their police gong and initiated pursuit. Genna, who was driving, hit the accelerator, but when he tried to swerve onto West Sixtieth Street, his car crashed into the curb. The officers pulled up beside them and were getting out of their car when the three gangsters, who had climbed from their wrecked vehicle unhurt, opened fire.

Detective Charles Walsh, a father of three, and Detective Harold Olsen, who supported a widowed mother and four young brothers, were killed instantly. Officer Conway fell with his jaw shot away. Only Sweeney, the youngest policeman, was unhurt. He traded fire with the gangsters until their ammunition dwindled, then lunged at them, a pistol in each hand. They fled, still clutching their smoking weapons.

Patrolman Albert Richert, an off-duty cop, saw the battle from his seat on a trolley car. He came running to Sweeney's aid. George Oakey, a sixty-year-old retired officer, also joined the chase when his wife saw the shooting and alerted him.

Mike Genna and his companions parted company at the mouth of an alley. While Scalise and Anselmi kept running, Genna swung about and fired a shotgun volley at Sweeney, who shot back and severed the femoral artery in Genna's leg. The wounded gangster staggered down the alley, smashed a basement window, and crawled inside, where he took refuge on a coal heap, his lifeblood puddling onto the filthy floor. Sweeney, Richert, and Oakey entered the building, broke down the basement door, and rushed him. In his weakened state, he was powerless to resist as they disarmed him.

Mike Genna was not destined to face justice for murdering Detectives Olsen and Walsh, or anyone else. His wound was too serious. But as ambulance attendants were placing him onto a stretcher, he mustered up enough strength to kick one of them in the face and snarl, "Take that, you son of a bitch!" He fell back, unconscious, and died hours later at the Bridewell Hospital.

A policeman whose suspicions had been aroused by Scalise and Anselmi's hatless, disheveled state hauled the pair off a trolley car and charged them with the murders of Walsh and Olsen. Enough witnesses had observed the deadly shootout that their conviction on murder charges appeared to be a certainty. State's Attorney Crowe, Chief Collins, and Chief of Detectives Schoemaker trumpeted that the deadly duo would go to the gallows.

But that was not to be. A defense fund was raised via contributions forced from Little Italy residents. In the fall of 1925 they stood trial for the murder of Detective Olsen. The defense attorneys charged that their clients were, at worst, guilty of manslaughter, insisting that they had been defending themselves against unwarranted police aggression. The jury obliged by returning a verdict of manslaughter, and the judge sentenced both gangsters to fourteen years in Joliet.

Scalise and Anselmi were tried for Walsh's killing in February 1926 and found not guilty after the prosecution, strangely, left the jury with little alternative for another verdict. Assistant State's Attorney Gorman declared, "Either this is a hanging case or a case of justifiable homicide." The jury voted for the latter.

The Sicilian torpedoes passed the months in Joliet with calm indifference, confident of a re-trial on the Olsen case and a more favorable verdict the second time around. Their chance came in June 1927, when the Illinois Supreme Court granted them a new trial. As expected, they were found not guilty and walked away free men.

A Little Italy resident claiming to be privy to gang secrets told detectives that Mike Genna had been scheduled to die on June 13 anyway. Scalise and Anselmi had secretly shifted their loyalty to Capone and actually were taking their former boss for a one-way ride under the guise of hunting down the North Siders. This information makes it obvious that Angelo Genna's slaying was also a Capone job instead of a North Side assault, as previously believed. It was by sheer accident that the detectives had seen Scalise and Anselmi foiled their plan to kill Mike Genna. He died anyway, but under much more sensational circumstances than intended.

Tony Genna was terrified that he was next. The Genna tiger had been declawed by the deaths of Angelo and Mike, and the next logical step would be to blow out its brains. Tony hid out in the Congress Hotel for weeks, sending his mistress out for supplies, but on July 8, Dean O'Banion's birthday, he drove to the corner of Curtis Street and West Grand Avenue to meet with Guiseppe Nerone, a Genna torpedo who had originally left their employ after complaining of being undervalued. What he said to persuade Genna to meet him is not known, but as they stood on the sidewalk shaking hands, two men approached. One said, "Hello, Genna." Tony turned, but not before he was shot five times in the back. Nerone and the assassins fled, and Genna staggered into an Italian grocery store, where a policeman alerted by the shots found him.

At the hospital, Genna refused to name his assailants until doctors told him that he was dying. Then, at the urging of his brother Sam and his mistress, he muttered three times a name that sounded like "Cavarello." The police turned Chicago upside down looking for a gangster of that name, not realizing that they had misheard. What Genna had actually said was "*Il Cavaliere*," or "The Cavalier," a nickname for the genteel and educated Nerone.

Tony's death finished the Gennas as a gangland power. Sam and Pete went into hiding, and Jim Genna fled to Sicily. While there, he was arrested for a jewel heist and did two years in prison. Sam and Pete eventually returned to Chicago but chose to live obscurely as importers of cheese and olive oil. A few of their more ambitious gunmen attempted to reorganize the gang, but their efforts ended in their own deaths, likely at the hands of Little Italy residents who had grown tired of the exploitation and forced tributes such as the Scalise–Anselmi defense fund.

Capone and the Genna brothers had never been more than business associates temporarily united by O'Banion's assassination. Angelo Genna's aggressive seizure of the Unione Siciliana presidency after Merlo was buried shattered the fragile alliance. Capone, being of Neapolitan descent, was barred from that post, but he had intended to maneuver his Sicilian associate Tony Lombardo, who would promote his interests and prevent the Unione from being used against him, into Merlo's vacated position. He did not trust Angelo Genna to administer the organization as honorably as Mike Merlo had.

Angelo's murder did not drop the Unione into Capone's lap. Samoots Amatuna, the silk-gloved torpedo with a passion for both music and murder, barged into the Unione offices with West Side saloonkeeper Eddie Zion and gunman "Bummy" Goldstein (his "campaign managers") at his side and declared himself president. Capone, who had once again advocated friend Tony Lombardo for the post, was furious. He did nothing until November 1925, however, as he was busy trying to get Scalise and Anselmi off on the cop-killing charges. On November 10, one year to the day after O'Banion's murder, Amatuna was shot to death in a Roosevelt Road barbershop.

His killers were initially thought to be Vincent Drucci and West Side O'Donnell gunman James Doherty, but the style suggested Capone. When Eddie Zion and Bummy Goldstein followed Amatuna to the grave in gangland style, it became obvious that Capone was reaping his revenge for the spring takeover of the Unione headquarters.

Capone took over the alky-cooking operations and installed Tony Lombardo as president of the Unione. Scalise and Anselmi worked for him until May 1929, when their greed got them killed.

Spike O'Donnell acquired a fresh sense of fight in the spring of 1925. He geared himself up for battle by importing a New Jersey gunman named Harry Hassmiller and recruiting local fighters to his gang. Spike had timed his return well, for O'Banion's death had disintegrated the old united front among the gangs, and he now faced smaller crews against whom he stood more of a chance. O'Donnell first went after the Saltis–McErlane and Sheldon Gangs, his longtime enemies. Those two mobs, once allies, were now fighting each other, and when O'Donnell threw his hat into the ring, the South Side turned into a battleground. Cook County averaged a murder a day.

All participants suffered heavy casualties. In June, Sheldon gunmen killed Walter O'Donnell and Harry Hassmiller in a roadhouse outside Chicago. Spike retaliated by trying, and failing, to murder Sheldon's close friend Walter Stevens. Frank McErlane wounded another O'Donnell brother, Tommy, in October. In November, Joe Saltis was peppered with assassins' bullets but managed to survive.

On September 25, 1925, Spike O'Donnell achieved a dubious notoriety as the first intended victim of a machine-gun attack. He was standing in front of a drugstore on Western Avenue and Sixty-Third Street, chatting with a newsboy. A sedan pulled up, and someone yelled, "Oh, Spike!" O'Donnell looked, seized the boy, and threw both himself and his companion to the pavement. Shotgun blasts destroyed the drugstore window, while machine-gun bullets raked the brick wall. Frank McErlane was later named as the machine-gunner.

Never before had a Thompson submachine gun been put into service as a gangland weapon of war. The gun, which weighed about twenty pounds when fully loaded and could fire eight hundred rounds per minute, had been designed for use by the Allies in the Great War, but the Armistice had been signed before the weapon could be shipped overseas and the Thompson was sold domestically. By 1925 only three thousand guns had been sold. Its obscurity led police and reporters to blame the drugstore damage on a "machine rifle" or more than one weapon fired in unison.

It wasn't until October 4 that the Thompson claimed its first Chicago victim. Frank McErlane sped past the Ragen Athletic Club, headquarters of the Sheldon Gang, in a black touring car and opened fire, killing a man named Charles Kelly and wounding one Thomas Hart. Captain John Enright confirmed that a machine gun had been used and that "the same gun had been used in an attack on Spike O'Donnell at Sixty-third Street and South Western Avenue."

William "Klondike" O'Donnell chose 1925 as the year he would rise up against Capone, for whom he had only a grudging tolerance. Reasoning that Capone's strength was divided by his battles with the North Siders and systematic elimination of the Gennas and their successors, he and his ace enforcer James Doherty began pushing their beer into Capone's Cicero saloons and bragging about it.

Capone had to do something while he still had time—Hymie Weiss had just come home from the McHenry County Jail and could be counted on to keep the war going as soon as he regained his bearings. Weiss was also occupied with the upcoming April primary, when all of gangland would be forced to work together to get Robert Crowe's slate elected. So all was comparatively quiet until April 27, almost two weeks after a Crowe victory at the polls.

That night, Capone received word that an O'Donnell contingent was driving in the vicinity of Roosevelt Road. He assembled a strike force of five cars—one to carry himself and three gunmen, the other four to run interference—and sallied forth to deal with the upstarts. The Capone squad caught up with their quarry's green Lincoln outside Harry Madigan's Pony Inn at 5613-5615 Roosevelt Road and opened fire, blasting the car for several seconds before speeding off into the night. It was not until the next day that Capone—and everyone else—learned who the casualties were. One was Thomas "Red" Duffy, bootlegger, Thirtieth Ward precinct captain, and friend of the O'Donnells. Another was James Doherty, the gang's enforcer. The last was identified as William McSwiggin, assistant state's attorney.

Twenty-five-year-old McSwiggin had been Robert Crowe's star assistant. Many of his cases had been gang-related; he had quizzed Capone about Joe Howard's murder, assisted in the investigation into O'Banion's death, and prosecuted Scalise and Anselmi in their second trial for cop-killing. None of his courtroom successes, however, had involved gangsters.

McSwiggin had been a boyhood friend of both Red Duffy and Jim Doherty, and the association continued even after he chose a career on the opposite side of the legal fence. Such persistent friendships were not uncommon. Policemen, judges, and politicians who played with gangsters as children rubbed elbows with them as adults. McSwiggin's father, a policeman, had begged his son to avoid his gangster cronies, but to no avail. The young attorney prosecuted Jim Doherty and Myles O'Donnell for the November 1924 murder of Eddie Tancl, but the trial ended in their acquittal. Not many saw that outcome as anything but prearranged.

William McSwiggin's boss, Robert Crowe, knew that many Chicagoans would not understand or appreciate the dead man's associations, so he told the press that McSwiggin had been doing undercover work, seeking inside information related to another case. Reporters dutifully repeated the weak explanation and demanded repeatedly in their papers, "Who killed McSwiggin, and why?"

Suspicion fell immediately on Capone, and his activities up to the night up the murder were examined closely. It was revealed that after the April primary, McSwiggin had visited Capone at the Hawthorne Hotel. The young man's father claimed that the reason for the visit was too loaded with political dynamite for him to talk about it. Capone admitted meeting with McSwiggin but insisted that he'd had nothing to do with the attorney's murder. "Of course I didn't kill him. Why should I? I liked the kid."

The killing was never officially solved. Five grand juries came up with nothing that could send the guilty party to the gallows. "Who killed McSwiggin" was cried with less vehemence and frequency as it sank in that the murdered prosecutor had been a friend to the class of men he had sworn to send to prison. Capone washed away any lingering visions of virtue by saying, "I paid McSwiggin. I paid him a lot, and I got what I was paying for."

Al Capone had never intended to kill William McSwiggin. His target that drizzling July night had been the insurgent O'Donnells. The West Side Gang was shaken by the triple slaying, Jim Doherty's loss being no minor one, and gave Capone no further trouble. The way was clear for the Italian gang boss to have his showdown with Hymie Weiss.

Weiss became embroiled in a legal battle of his own while Capone was under scrutiny for his role in McSwiggin's death. On June 23, a U.S. deputy marshal interrupted a party he was holding in rooms 301, 302, and 303 of the Rienzi Hotel, in order to serve a warrant on Eddie Vogel for violation of the Mann Act. Weiss confronted the raider with a shotgun and forced him off the premises. When Chicago police officers Joyner, Seyferlich, and Essig returned in response to the marshal's call for assistance, the revelers were gone, but the officers did find and seize a huge cache of liquor, namely:

48 pints of Cliquot champagne
24 quarts of Cliquot champagne
2 one-gallon glass jugs of whiskey
1 quart bottle of Hill & Hill whiskey
1 pint bottle of Old Crow whiskey
1 fifth-gallon bottle of 3 Star Hennessey brandy
1 pump taken from a beer barrel

The officers notified special intelligence officers Pat Roche and Clarence Converse of their find, and the two government agents promptly arrived with Prohibition agents Jacob Maas and Joseph Dorr in tow. They seized the liquor and charged Weiss, Frank Foster, and Eddie Vogel, who had rented the rooms, with conspiracy to violate the Volstead Act.

Before leaving the deserted hotel rooms, Agent Converse removed some valuables, namely a gold desk pad, a wristwatch, and a matching set of diamond and platinum cuff links, vest buttons, and shirt studs, and held them for safekeeping. The items were returned to Frank Foster, the rightful owner, but the removal prompted Weiss to take a quick inventory of the rooms. He decided that the raiders had taken more than they had returned. In July he, Foster, and Vogel sued for the return of the following items:

5 dozen neckties
3 hats
1 dozen silk shirts
1 pair of field glasses
3 dozen silk hose
1/2 dozen pairs of silk underwear
45 shares of stock in a boat called the *Half Moon*
Sundry keys, books, and papers

They also tried to reclaim the seized liquor by arguing that it had been taken from a lawful residence, which therefore had made its removal unlawful. The government responded by denying any knowledge of the missing items (which may have been stolen by hotel staff or guests after the raiders left), except for the shares in the *Half Moon* (which had formerly been the German Kaiser's private yacht) and the keys, books, and papers, all of which were being held until the rightful owners could be determined. The claim that the hotel rooms were a private residence was rejected, and the liquor was retained. The defendants were released on bonds of twenty-five hundred dollars each, Weiss being bailed out by his Canadian partner, J. J. Stewart of Montreal.

Weiss had been busy since his release from jail. By the summer of 1926 the North Side Gang's bootlegging operations had expanded, and Weiss had partners in Cleveland, Florida, and Canada. He was well on his way to building a syndicate.

In July, while still dealing with the Rienzi Hotel raid, Weiss resumed his attack on Capone. He abducted Tommy Cuiringione, alias Ross, or Rossi, Capone's chauffeur, with the intention of making him spill what he knew about Capone's daily schedule. Cuiringione was tortured for hours before he was shot in the head, weighted down with bricks, and dumped in a cistern south of Chicago. Two young boys discovered his grisly remains when they led their horses to the cistern to drink. The animals shied, the boys investigated, and reported their findings to a policeman.

Capone conveyed his shock and disgust at the brutal killing in angry statements to the press. "They call me heartless, eh? Ross was tortured to make him tell my business secrets. He knew nothing whatever about my affairs."

On August 10, a week after the murdered man's body was fished out of the cistern, Weiss met Drucci in the latter's suite at the Congress Hotel. They ate breakfast together and left at 10 A.M. to stroll south on Michigan Avenue. The weather was sunny and mild, so they'd dispensed with a car. They were on their way to the office of Morris Eller, Twentieth Ward boss and Chicago Sanitary District trustee Morris Eller. Drucci was carrying $13,200 in his pocket.

When they reached Ninth Street, Weiss and Drucci headed for the Standard Oil Building, where Eller had his office. Just as the two gangsters were about to step from the sidewalk into the lobby, a car screeched to a halt and pistol fire cracked. Weiss threw himself to the pavement, as did the other pedestrians. Cars on Ninth Street and Michigan Avenue either halted, their drivers and passengers hugging the floor, or roared away to safety. Only Drucci reacted aggressively; drawing his gun, he crouched behind a mailbox and returned fire.

Two gunmen jumped from their vehicle and closed in on him. Before they could pick Drucci off, or vice versa, a police car appeared. The driver of the assault vehicle took off, leaving his comrades stranded. In the ensuing confusion, Weiss fled into the crowd, as did the two gunmen. Drucci, however, had not had enough. He ran into the street, leaped onto the running board of a stopped car, and pointed his pistol at the terrified driver, one C. C. Bassett. "Take me away, and make it snappy," he ordered. Before Bassett could comply, policemen surrounded the automobile and dragged the gangster off. He initially gave his name as Frank Walsh, but it didn't take long for his real identity to be determined.

"It wasn't no gang fight!" he protested. "A stick-up, that's all. They wanted my roll," he said, referring to the money in his pocket.

In a rare stroke of good luck, the officers caught one of the gunmen as he dropped his pistol and tried to escape. He gave his name as Paul Valerie of 3533 Walnut Street, a fake address. His name was actually Louis Barko—a Capone gunman. But when the policemen brought him before Drucci for identification, the North Sider smashed their victory by saying firmly, "Never saw him before," forcing them to release the hired killer. Drucci obtained his freedom after Mary Weiss, Hymie's mother, signed bonds totaling five thousand dollars (one thousand for the charge of carrying a concealed weapon and four thousand for assault with intent to kill.)

An estimated thirty bullets had been fired in the street battle, with only one hitting a human target, passerby James Cardan, who had been nicked in the leg. The rest had punctured car tonneaus or tires, smashed a few office windows, and pockmarked the Standard Oil Building. The audacity of the attack staggered the public. Back-alley brawls and saloon battles were now as quaint and old-fashioned a notion as Victorian postcards. The gangsters of the Twenties seemed to care little if the law-abiding community witnessed or suffered injury during their fights. Fred Pasley noted that the battleground at Michigan Avenue and Ninth Street was only slightly less crowded than the bustling intersection of Fifth Avenue and Forty-Second Street in New York.

On August 15, five days later, the Capone mob struck again. Weiss, Drucci, and one of their legal advisors were driving south on Michigan Avenue when a car that had been trailing them suddenly surged alongside, forced their vehicle to the curb, and sprayed it with bullets. The attack occurred nearly across the street from the Standard Oil Building. The North Siders sprang unhurt from their ruined sedan and fled into the building, firing back as they ran.

Capone received Weiss's response a month later. On September 20, he and bodyguard Frank Rio were having coffee in the Hawthorne Restaurant, three doors away from Capone's headquarters at the Hawthorne Hotel. It was 1:15 P.M., and West Twenty-second Street was teeming with horseracing buffs from all over America, who had converged on Cicero for the fall meet at the Hawthorne track. Capone, a huge racing fan, was biding his time, waiting for the first race at 2:30.

Suddenly, Tommygun fire rattled in the distance. The street cleared quickly, and the occupants of the Hawthorne Restaurant hit the floor. Rio reacted faster than Capone and pulled his boss down. While they listened, the sound of gunfire grew louder, passed by the front of the building, and then faded away.

Thinking that the danger was over, Capone got to his feet and approached the door. Rio's mind worked more quickly, and he realized the street outside was a little too tidy and tranquil—no shattered windows or bleeding victims—to have been the scene of a machine-gun assault. Sensing a ruse, he yanked Capone to the floor again. Less than thirty seconds later, ten sedans rolled leisurely down West Twenty-second, their occupants opening fire as the first car drew even with the Anton Hotel next to the Hawthorne. The vehicles stopped in front of the café, and machine-gunners fired hundreds of rounds into it, shattering the windows and virtually demolishing the interior. The Anton and Hawthorne Hotels and the neighboring shops also were badly damaged. Locals and visitors in town for the races scrambled for safety, shocked and terrified.

A man in overalls and a khaki shirt stepped out of the ninth car and knelt on the sidewalk in front of the Hawthorne Restaurant while men in the tenth vehicle covered him with their weapons. The lone figure aimed his machine gun at the café interior and emptied a hundred-round drum in less than ten seconds. The café fixtures that had survived the first onslaught splintered and shattered under this more concentrated attack. His mission accomplished, the gunman returned to his car. Someone in the motorcade honked his horn three times, and the lethal procession rolled off to the east, back toward Chicago.

Police investigators who surveyed the wrecked thoroughfare estimated that over a thousand rounds had been fired. In their opinion, it was a miracle that only four people had been hurt. They included Clyde Freeman, a racing buff from May, Louisiana, whose knee was grazed by a bullet; his son, whose scalp was lightly scraped; and Freeman's wife, who was struck in the eye by a piece of glass from their car's shattered windshield. The fourth person injured was Louis Barko, who had participated in the August 9 assault on Weiss and Drucci. He suffered minor shoulder and neck wounds, having been caught in the fusillade as he was entering the Hawthorne Hotel. The police hauled Weiss, Moran, Drucci, and Peter Gusenberg down to the station for Barko's inspection, but he denied that he'd seen them taking part in the Cicero attack.

Capone took some responsibility for the disaster, having been its intended target. He paid for repairs to the damaged shops, compensated the owners of riddled vehicles, and shelled out five thousand dollars to save Mrs. Freeman's sight.

Something had to be done about Hymie Weiss, whose assaults had been escalating in ferocity since the blasting of Capone's car at Fifty-fifth and State in January. The *Herald and Examiner*'s lead editorial the day after the Cicero siege summed up the situation (in case anyone needed to see it in black and white) succinctly, crying: "THIS IS WAR!" Past attempts to kill the Polish gangster had resulted in failure, and the continuation of the battle could only result in police pressure applied to both sides, ruining their businesses and bringing on harassing arrests.

Remembering Torrio's past example of diplomacy, Capone proposed a peace conference. He sent word via an emissary to Weiss, who agreed to a sit-down at the Hotel Sherman on October 4. Tony Lombardo, president of the Unione Siciliana since Samoots Amatuna was killed, represented Capone, who had authorized him to offer Weiss any peace terms within reason. The North Sider had only one term that had to be met: He wanted Scalise and Anselmi, who had pulled the triggers in O'Banion's murder, to be executed. They were still in Joliet at that time, but Weiss knew executions could be arranged just as easily inside prison as on the outside. When Lombardo telephoned Capone for an answer, Scarface Al's response was an indignant, "I wouldn't do that to a yellow dog!"

It was obvious at that point that there could be no peace. Weiss was not willing to settle for anything less than bloodshed; he wanted his friend avenged. A strong friendship had bound Weiss and O'Banion together, and no extra beer concessions or additional business territory would set matters right in Weiss's mind. Capone's refusal to meet the North Sider's terms guaranteed that the war would continue.

At 740 North State Street, directly next door to Schofield's flower shop, stood a three-story rooming house. The somber stone building belonged to crime writer Harry Stephen Keeler, whose fifty-plus books included such bestsellers as *The Spectacles of Mr. Cagliostro* and *Sing Sing Nights.* Long before the October 4 meeting between Weiss and Lombardo, a young man who gave his name as "Oscar Lundin" showed up on the front step and requested a room overlooking the street. When told that all front rooms were occupied, he amiably agreed to take a hall room until a one in the front became available. While Lundin was moving in, a pretty young woman who gave her name as Mrs. Thomas Schultz rented a third-floor bedroom at

1 Superior Street. Her window overlooked both the front and rear entrances of the flower shop.

October was turning out to be a busy month for Weiss. In addition to his regular duties of running the North Side Gang, he had the Hotel Sherman conference on the fourth and, on the eleventh, was to oversee the jury selection for Joe Saltis's upcoming murder trial. On August 6, Saltis had killed Sheldon beer runner John "Mitters" Foley as part of a general assault in a long-running war with Ralph Sheldon. Unfortunately for Saltis, two witnesses saw him do the deed, and he was indicted. With his vicious partner, Frank McErlane, in jail and battling extradition to Indiana for a May 1924 murder, Saltis had been in dire straits.

Hymie Weiss came to his rescue. The North Sider had been cultivating an alliance with the Saltis–McErlane Gang, realizing that he needed allies in the war with Capone. When McErlane was arrested for the Indiana murder, Mary Weiss, Hymie's mother, had signed the bail bonds. Now that Saltis was in trouble, Weiss himself offered assistance.

Special prosecutor Charles McDonald knew that he was up against formidable odds when several of his witnesses lost their memories or left town. Even his files were rifled at night. Weiss shelled out one hundred thousand dollars to ensure Saltis's acquittal, and that kind of money bought frustrating results for the law.

On October 8, landlady Anna Rotariu told Oscar Lundin that the front bedroom he had wanted was now available, and the boarder gratefully moved into it. The room was dismal, containing only a battered oak dresser, tarnished brass bed, a few straight-backed chairs, a gas ring, tin food box, and a few sorry specimens of plates and cutlery. For Lundin, the shabbiness was offset by the outside view it offered. Standing at the window, one could see the front entrance of the Schofield flower shop, as well as anyone approaching it.

After paying a week's rent in advance, Lundin and Mrs. Schultz moved out of their rooms, never to be seen again. Two men whom Mrs. Rotariu recognized as friends of Lundin took over the room at 740 North State. She later described one as being in his mid-thirties and wearing a gray overcoat and fedora, and the other as being much younger and wearing a dark suit and a light hat. Down the street, at 1 Superior, two men of apparently Italian descent took over Mrs. Schultz's room.

On October 11 Weiss spent most of the day in the Criminal Court Building, watching the jury selection for the trial of Saltis and his driver, Frank "Lefty" Koncil, who also had been indicted. At 3:30 P.M., the twelfth juror, Philip Chynard, was sworn in. Chynard, when questioned, said that he did not "believe in capital punishment where the proof of murder was based on circumstantial evidence." The prosecution, knowing that two witnesses had actually seen Saltis kill Foley, accepted Chynard after he added, "I'd vote to hang my own brother if he committed a cold-blooded murder."

When court recessed for the day, Weiss and his party piled into two cars and headed for Schofield's. His companions included his bodyguard Patrick "Paddy" Murray, a minor bootlegger and brother of Jimmy Murray, who was serving time for the Rondout train robbery, and Sam Pellar, a Morris Eller associate and former drifter who had a criminal record in both Indianapolis and Alabama. Also in the party was Benjamin Jacobs, another Eller lieutenant, who had been charged with manslaughter in 1915 in a gang-related killing, and attorney W. W. O'Brien, who was on Joe Saltis's defense team and had retained Jacobs as an "investigator."

When Weiss and his associates reached their destination, they parked one car, a Cadillac coupe, in front of Holy Name Cathedral and left the second vehicle on Superior Street. As the five men started across State Street, heading for the flower shop, the two men in Lundin's room poked a shotgun and machine gun out the window. They fired, filling the street with thunderous noise and peppering their targets with lead. Paddy Murray fell to the ground with seven bullets in his body, killed instantly. Weiss was struck by ten slugs and collapsed in the gutter. O'Brien was hit four times but managed to crawl to safety in a basement stairwell, and once the shooting subsided, struggled to a doctor's office at 748 North State. Pellar was hit in the groin, Jacobs in the foot. Like O'Brien, the two men ran for cover, and later made it to a doctor's office at 720 Cass Street, where police picked them up.

The two gunmen, their mission completed, hurried out of their room, ran down the building's back stairs, and exited via a rear window. They navigated a maze of alleys, pausing once to throw their Tommygun on top of a dog kennel a block south of Superior Street, until they reached Dearborn Street, where they melted into the afternoon crowd.

A group of priests from Holy Name, led by Father Francis A. Ryan, hurried to Weiss and Murray after the smoke cleared from the street. They did not immediately notice the damage the fusillade had done to the church building. The stone exterior was chipped, and the cornerstone, which had originally read, "A.D. 1874—AT THE NAME OF JESUS EVERY KNEE SHOULD BOW—THOSE THAT ARE IN HEAVEN AND THOSE ON EARTH" (from St. Paul's Epistle to the Philippians), now appeared as:

EVERY KNEE SHOULD
HEAVEN AND
ON EARTH

Squad No. 1 of the Chicago Fire Department was returning from an alarm when it came upon the scene of the shooting. Fireman Louis Diana later testified that Weiss, although unconscious, was still breathing, so he was removed to Henrotin Hospital. At the hospital, a search of his bloodied clothing revealed a loaded .45 automatic tucked in his belt. A stack of letters removed from his coat pocket revealed his identity. Weiss died on the examination table without regaining consciousness.

In addition to the letter, Weiss's pockets yielded fifty-three hundred dollars in cash, a check for six thousand dollars, and correspondence with Terry Druggan, who was vacationing in Miami. Only one piece of paper excited police interest: a list of the veniremen for the Saltis–Koncil murder trial. If there had been any doubts that the North Sider had been attempting to bribe the jury, they were dispelled.

Officers sought further clues in Weiss's offices on the second floor of the flower shop. Remnants of food on a table indicated that the North Sider had enjoyed a last meal not long before his death. His safe yielded a list of the witnesses scheduled to testify against Saltis, among other pieces of personal correspondence. A note signed T.E.D from Miami (Terry Druggan) told of a rum-running boat that had been seized by the government. He requested five hundred dollars to secure its release. The boat in question was most likely the *Half Moon*. Apparently Weiss failed to respond in a timely manner, for the *Half Moon* ended up at a federal auction. W. E. of Quebec wrote a cryptic note, claiming that he "couldn't do a thing about the motors until Congress was again in session." W. E. also thanked Weiss for "having adjusted that mater for Joe."

The letters proved the existence of an alliance between Weiss and the Druggan–Lake Gang. They also confirmed that the North Side Gang's influence had expanded beyond Chicago. The safeblowing gang organized by Charles Reiser in 1917 had evolved into a huge, efficient organization that took in thousands, if not millions, of dollars in bootlegging and gambling revenues. By 1926, almost every gangster in Chicago was either a "Weiss guy" or a "Capone guy." Had Weiss not been killed, one can only speculate whether he eventually might have eliminated Capone and taken over Chicago completely.

The mantle of the North Side leadership now rested on the shoulders of Vincent Drucci. Drucci was in his suite at the Bentmere Hotel on Diversey Parkway when news of the attack reached him. He rushed out of the hotel in a rage, leaped into his car, and drove toward the scene of the shooting. An acquaintance recognized him and flagged him down at the entrance to Lincoln Park. The man told him that Weiss had been killed, and to avoid State Street. Drucci sped back to the Bentmere, cleared his room of personal effects (except for a framed photo of Weiss, which occupied a place on honor on the dresser, and a small cache of weapons), and went into hiding. Reports from police informants indicated that Drucci was being held in restraint by his followers, his grief and fury maddening him to the point of incoherence.

The police caught up with him five days later while he, Potatoes Kaufman, and Harry Sorg, a Druggan–Lake associate, were watching a football game at Cubs Park. When Lieutenant John Sullivan told him he was wanted for questioning in connection with the Weiss murder, Drucci initially protested but finally gave in. By the time Chief of Detectives Schoemaker arrived at the detective bureau to question him, he had calmed down. "I don't know anything about any rum warfare," he insisted, earnestly yet respectfully. "I'm a real estate man, with offices in the First National Bank Building. You can come and see me anytime."

In an adjacent office, Deputy Chief John Stege and Potatoes Kaufman were having a battle of words. When Stege threatened to run the gambler out of town if his association with known gangsters continued, Kaufman reminded him that two could play the same game. Sorg, who had been arrested in San Francisco with Terry Druggan two years previously, initially tried to hide his identity but was soon found out.

The three men were ordered held in the basement for further questioning, but the police, lacking the necessary evidence to do otherwise, released them by the end of the day.

No one doubted that Al Capone had orchestrated Weiss's murder. In one of many interviews that he gave on the subject, Capone told a *Herald and Examiner* reporter, "What makes them [rival gangsters] so crazy to end up on a slab in the morgue, with their mothers' hearts broken over the way they died, I don't know. I've tried to find out, but I can't. I know I've tried since the first pistol was drawn in this fight to show them that there's enough business for all of us without killing each other like animals in the street, but they don't see it.

"I read in the papers that Hymie Weiss's mother was coming here from New York for his funeral. I know that sweet old lady. She's a wonderful mother. When Hymie was in business with us, many's the night I slept in his house and ate at his table. Why didn't he use some sense and keep out of this shooting stuff?"

The murder investigation was clouded at the beginning by conflicting witness reports. Charles McKibbon claimed that he saw Sam Pellar shoot at Weiss. He said that Pellar and Jacobs fired from the curb in front of the cathedral and rushed into the street after Weiss fell. One shouted to the other, "Come on, I got the ——!" They ran down Cass Street, firing over their shoulders as they went. Weiss, said McKibbon, returned their fire before he fell. After Pellar and Jacobs disappeared, another man dressed in a black suit and hat stooped over Weiss's body.

Pellar and Jacobs denied being armed, which seems unlikely. Deputy Chief of Detectives Stege said, "McKibbon's story seems entirely plausible to me. In checking up, we find that Weiss's body and the body of Murray both contained lead bullets along with the steel-jacketed machine-gun slugs. . . . Pellar may have been a trusted friend, but from our experience, friends mean nothing in gangland. They're friends one minute and killing each other the next."

Captain Daniel Murphy of the East Chicago Avenue station, who had been the first police officer on the scene of the O'Banion murder, was not so sure. "I'll grant," he said, "that Pellar lied about carrying a gun, for we have it. Pellar was probably shooting at Weiss's assassins."

While the validity of McKibbon's statement was being determined, the police contended with the new theory of a drive-by shooting. Al Thomas, a musician employed at the Oriental Theatre, and a friend were driving north on State Street when, as Thomas put it, "a dark car ahead of us that looked like a Lincoln suddenly shot across the west side of the street. Several men dashed out of it, one carrying a machine gun. In a second there was a blaze of shots, but I kept on going."

Thomas's story was given little credence, as the evidence proved that the fatal shots were fired from the boarding-house window at 740 North State. As for McKibbon, investigators concluded that he misinterpreted what he had seen, and that Pellar and Jacobs had been firing in the general direction of the machine-gun onslaught, not at Weiss.

Chief Collins stated the obvious when he told reporters that Weiss's successors would carry on the battle. "It isn't over. I fully expect that there will be a reprisal, then a countereprisal, and so on. These beer feuds go on in an eternal vicious cycle. I don't want to encourage the business, but if someone has to be killed, it's a good thing that the gangsters are murdering themselves off. It saves trouble for the police."

The inquest, headed by Coroner Oscar Wolff and Deputy Coroner Charles Kennedy, yielded little except the fact that the Weiss family had not been a harmonious one. Frederick Weiss, the youngest brother, was called to the stand to give his notorious sibling's personal history. He proved both ignorant and hostile. He did not know or care about where Hymie Weiss had lived, and "Not known" was written into almost every blank on the death certificate.

The rest of the family did not harbor such dark sentiments. Mary, his mother, and his sister Violet Monahan remained in a state of near collapse until the funeral. Mrs. Monahan's home at 224 South Humphrey Avenue in Oak Park had also been Mary's address, and Hymie had been a frequent visitor. Only a couple of years before, the Monahans, Mary Weiss, Walente Wojciechowski (who was estranged from, but on friendly terms with, his wife) and Hymie Weiss had all lived under the same roof at 3808 West Grand Avenue. It appeared as if Frederick, not Earl, was the black sheep of the Weiss family.

The funeral of Hymie Weiss on October 15, 1926, was a much less spectacular affair than the O'Banion funeral two years before. Less than two hundred people visited Sbarbaro's to view the body. Boyhood classmates from St. Malachy's school carried his modest bronze casket to the hearse, where it was conveyed to a plot in unconsecrated ground at Mount Carmel Cemetery. Eight magnificent carloads of flowers accompanied the cortege, but the crowds and the pomp and flash were missing. Those who affixed placards to the sides of the cortege vehicles calling for the election of Sbarbaro as municipal judge, Joseph Savage as county judge, and Morris Eller as Sanitary District trustee must have been hoping for a turnout rivaling O'Banion's, but it did not happen.

The only impressive spectacle throughout the entire affair was petite, lovely Josephine Simard, who went under the stage name Josephine Libby. She claimed to be Weiss's widow, telling a story of meeting him in Canada when he had made a trip there in September. She said it had been love at first sight and that they had married soon after they returned to Chicago together.

"Earl was one of the finest men in the world," Josephine told reporters, "and I spent the happiest time of my life with him. You'd expect a rich bootlegger to be a man about town, always going to nightclubs and having his home full of rowdy friends. But Earl liked to be alone with me, just lounging about, listening to the radio or reading. He seemed to be pretty well-read. He didn't waste time on trash but read histories and law books. If you hadn't known what he was, you might have mistaken him for a lawyer or college professor. He was crazy about children. 'I like 'em, Jo,' he said. 'I want a boy of my own some day. I don't amount to much, but maybe the youngster would turn out all right.'"

The dead gangster's family had suspicions about the truthfulness of the story. When the young woman failed to produce a marriage license after the funeral, Mary Weiss had herself named administrator of the estate. Josephine had been demanding the return of Weiss's large sedan, which she insisted he had bought for her, but when she was unable to furnish proof of ownership, Probate Judge Henry Horner awarded permanent custody of the two-thousand-dollar car to Mrs. Weiss. The gangster's estate was valued at nearly eleven thousand dollars, a minute fraction of his actual financial worth, and it ultimately was divided equally among his parents and siblings.

Unlike O'Banion, Weiss had been hostile to the press and never gave them the fuel to construct any kind of a popular or positive legend around him. His stony silence led the press and public to judge him by his actions alone, and he came out as an ugly killing machine. It was not until Edward Dean Sullivan published the last of his memoirs in 1929 that the Weiss legend was softened with a human aspect.

Sullivan recalled that a boyhood friend had approached the gang leader and asked to be cut in on the bootlegging money machine. Weiss replied, "Kid, I won't do it to you. I wouldn't let you have a part of it. I hope no one else will either. You want it till you've got it, and then what is it? Trouble. I wish I could trade places with you right now. But I wouldn't do it to you."

"I was sad when I heard about Weiss, even though I didn't exactly like the guy," E. Barnett said. "He was smart, more so than Dean in a lot of ways. He could have taken the boys far. But he had the revenge thing on his mind, and his health was just not good. The headaches were always knocking him out, and I heard some people say that he had something seriously wrong.

"Vince Drucci took over after Weiss. I ran into him coming out of the Belmont that Christmas, and he asked me if I wanted to come back to work for them. He said a lot of guys had gone in with Capone, and that a good guy you could trust was something he needed just then. I felt bad for turning down his offer, but I knew where it was all heading. That was why I quit after Dean died.

"Things were changing. The guys like Weiss and O'Banion, who ran their own shows, were being squeezed out in favor of these bigger Italian mobs who were connected and organized. It was bigger business, and the guys running it would kill anyone to protect it. I didn't want my mother reading about me being found beside some country road downstate. So I didn't want any part of it."

16

From Mayhem to Massacre

When his alliance with the North Siders become public knowledge, Joe Saltis was scared—and with good reason. He knew that Capone had assumed him to be an ally as well as a regular customer for the Italian gangster's beer. The witness and jury lists found in Weiss's possession spelled out his treachery, and Saltis also knew how Capone dealt with traitors. At the moment, Capone was occupied with deciding how to establish peace with Drucci and Moran, now the joint leaders of the North Side Gang, but sooner or later that issue would be settled, and then Saltis would get his.

Terrified, Saltis approached his friend Dingbat O'Berta, who was also being tried in connection with the murder of Mitters Foley. O'Berta knew right away who could avert bloodshed: Maxie Eisen, erstwhile friend of Dean O'Banion. Eisen had returned from a round the world trip with his wife and son in time to act as an honorary pallbearer at Weiss's funeral, and was appalled by how much conditions in Chicago had deteriorated during his absence. Although informally affiliated with the O'Banions, he managed to command the respect of Chicago's other gangs, making him an ideal mediator. He told O'Berta that, in his opinion, Capone needed friends more than enemies and would be in more of a forgiving mood now than ever. He offered to try and arrange a general armistice.

"The idea is to call the war off," he explained. "You're a bunch of saps, killing each other this way, and giving the cops a laugh. There's plenty of jack for everybody, as long as Prohibition lasts. I'll talk to the boys."

First, he approached Tony Lombardo, who he knew had Capone's ear. Lombardo reported the next day that Capone was more than willing to talk peace. Two meetings in the office of underworld bail bondsman and scrap-iron dealer Billy Skidmore followed. On October 20, thirty underworld figures converged on the Hotel Sherman, where the failed pow-wow with Weiss had occurred. They came without weapons or bodyguards, as previously agreed. Capone's representatives, besides himself, were his brother Ralph, Lombardo, Jake Guzik, and Eddie Vogel, Cicero slot-machine king and co-defendant with Hymie Weiss on the bootlegging charge of 1925. Drucci and Moran were accompanied by Potatoes Kaufman, Frank Foster, and vice operator Jack Zuta. Myles and Klondike O'Donnell also attended, as did Billy Skidmore and Barney Bertsche, a former safecracker and O'Banion associate who now derived a sizable income from gambling.

"We're making a shooting gallery of a great business," Capone told everyone present. "It's hard and dangerous work, aside from any hate at all, and when a fellow works hard at any line of business, he wants to go home and forget about it. He doesn't want to be afraid to sit near a window or open a door."

Having lived with similar fears themselves since the warring began, the others nodded. The inter-gang treaty that they proposed and discussed called for a general amnesty, and total forgiveness for any shootings or killings that had taken place in the previous months. No more ribbing (challenges to follow up violently on perceived slights) or gossip, most of which was perpetrated by journalists and policemen, would be heeded. Every gang would stay within assigned territories, and any who broke the rules would be punished either by their own people or, in the case of freelancers, by the wronged parties.

The territories assigned differed little from the boundaries suggested by Torrio when the very first inter-gang alliance took place.

Drucci and Moran retained the North Side, while Capone took the South and the suburban territories to the south and west of the city proper. The West Side O'Donnells were left with less power in Cicero than they'd had before, but their domination over a generous chunk of territory West Side was confirmed. Jack Zuta, Billy Skidmore, and Barney Bertsche, loosely affiliated with the North Siders, carried on as before. Ralph Sheldon and the Saltis–McErlane forces kept their stockyards and Back of the Yard territories.

Once the meeting broke up, everyone retired to Diamond Joe Esposito's Bella Napoli Café, where they indulged in a high-spirited celebration dinner that a reporter later described as "a feast of ghouls." Former killings and attacks were relived and laughed over, even to the victims' friends.

"Remember that night eight months ago when your car was chased by two of ours?"

"I sure do!"

"Well, we were going to kill you that night—but you had a woman with you."

When Joe Saltis and Lefty Koncil were acquitted of Foley's murder on November 7 (Dingbat O'Berta's trial was removed from the court calendar completely), they beheld a different Chicago gangland, the direct result of Saltis's desire to avoid punishment for defection. Spike O'Donnell and his crew attempted one final rebellion, but after two of Spike's brothers ended up badly wounded, the South Side Irishman backed off for good. He never made another bid for supremacy.

The peace continued even after a Ralph Sheldon beer runner, Hillary Clements, disappeared on December 16 and was found facedown in a shallow grave on December 30. No retaliation took place for the killing; everyone, Sheldon included, was too anxious to put the violent past behind them. "Just like the old days," Capone told a reporter with whom he was friendly. "They [Moran and Drucci] stay on the North Side and I stay in Cicero, and if we meet on the street, we say hello and shake hands. Better, ain't it?"

Big Bill Thompson had been a busy man during the years after he relinquished office to William Dever. He constructed a sailing ship at the staggering cost of twenty-five thousand dollars, called it the *Big Bill*, and had his bust attached as its figurehead. He announced his intention to sail it to the South Seas to capture specimens of tree-climbing fish. The ship made it as far as New Orleans, with Thompson speechifying at almost every community that bordered the Mississippi.

In April 1926, a year before the scheduled mayoral election, Thompson put on a bizarre performance at the Cort Theatre. He presented two caged rats to the audience, and called them Fred and Doc, after his former campaign manager Fred Lundin and Lundin's new protégé, Dr. John Dill Robertson, who once had been city health commissioner under Thompson. "This one on the left here is Doc. I can tell because he hasn't had a bath in twenty years," Thompson told the chuckling onlookers.

Robertson ended up withdrawing from the February 1927 primary, leaving Thompson to run against Dever in April. Big Bill's campaign was just as colorful as any of his previous runs for office, and once again, he accused his opponents of being a threat to American patriotism in Chicago. He claimed that Dever's superintendent of schools was "King George's stool pigeon." Even the Volstead Act was apparently a royal plot. "I wouldn't be surprised," he told all who would listen, "if the king had something to do with slipping the Volstead Act on us so that all their distillers can make fortunes selling us bootleg liquor. . . . If George comes to Chicago, I'll punch him in the snoot."

Dever's campaign slogan, "Dever and Decency," was a lot less showy than Thompson's rowdy "America First" appeal to the masses, and the gangsters supported Big Bill for an obvious reason. "When I'm elected," Thompson promised, "we will not only reopen places these people [the Prohibition agents spurred on by Dever] have closed, but we'll open ten thousand new ones." The underworld was all for that. Capone donated an estimated $260,000 to Big Bill's campaign chest, and North Side ally Jack Zuta added $50,000 to the pile, proudly proclaiming, "I'm for Big Bill, hook, line, and sinker, and Big Bill's for me, hook, line, and sinker."

George Brennan, who handled patronage under Dever, tried to discredit Big Bill to the law-abiding voters by warning them that all of Chicago's hoodlums were backing Thompson. Always the opportunist, the former mayor drew chuckles from his audiences by addressing them as "my fellow hoodlums." A group of society matrons giggled at the reference, secretly thrilled.

Drucci worked as diligently for the Thompson cause as any of his brethren. Under his direction, a gang of North Side sluggers broke into the Forty-second Ward office of Alderman (and Dever man) Dorsey R. Crowe, beating up the night watchman and destroying the premises. Chief Collins ordered the immediate arrest of all known North Side Gang leaders.

On April 5, a detective squad spotted Drucci and two companions, Albert Single and Henry Finkelstein, coming out of the Hotel Bellaire, and stopped them. A search of all three revealed a gun tucked in Drucci's waistband. As the officers escorted the men into a nearby squad car for a trip to the Criminal Court Building (Chief Collins had ordered that all gangsters arrested be taken before Judge Lindsey), Drucci objected to one of them, Danny Healy, holding his arm. The North Sider cursed him, and Healy responded by drawing his own gun and saying, "You call me that again and I'll let you have it."

Danny Healy was one of the force's toughest officers, a man who hated criminals and did not hesitate to let them know it. He had killed a bandit during a shootout on Armitage Avenue in early 1927, and he nearly killed Joe Saltis in November 1926, when Saltis was captured in a raid on a South Side saloon. When the hulking gangster berated him, Healy drew his pistol, stuck the muzzle against his prisoner's side, and threatened to shoot him. Only the intervention of Lieutenant Liebeck, who headed Healy's squad, prevented bloodshed.

Drucci, who likely knew of the young officer's tough reputation, was only too happy to let him know what he thought of police officers in general and Healy in particular. As the gangster got into the squad car, he snarled, "You kid copper, I'll get you. I'll wait on your doorstep for you."

Healy told him to shut up.

"Go on, you kid copper," Drucci taunted. "I'll fix you for this." When Healy repeated the order to keep quiet, Drucci challenged, "You take your gun off of me and I'll kick hell out of you."

Despite the hostile exchange, Healy got into the back seat of the car with Drucci, Albert Single crouching nervously between them. Sergeant Daniel Keough sat in the collapsible seat in front of them with Henry Finkelstein, and Lieutenant Liebeck sat up front with his chauffeur, Sergeant Matthew Cunningham. The car proceeded east on Wacker Drive. As it neared the Clark Street Bridge, the quarrel between Drucci and Healy intensified. The police officers later testified that the North Sider, beside himself with rage, punched holes in the side curtaining before leaping at Healy with a cry of "I'll take you and your tool!" The police officer drew back and shot him.

Henry Finkelstein told a different story. He claimed that Healy threw the first punch while in the car, initiating the scuffle, and that Sergeant Keough pulled over as the car came into Clark Street. Healy got out, turned, and shot Drucci while the gangster sat with his hands on his lap. Albert Single said that both cop and gangster had struck each other before the fatal shots were fired, and that Drucci had challenged Healy to "Take off your gun and we'll get out and fight it out."

Whichever way it happened, Drucci fell to the floor of the squad car, bleeding heavily from gunshot wounds to his arm, leg, and belly. The squad car immediately drove to the nearby Iroquois Hospital, but the attending doctor there said that the gangster's condition was too serious and ordered him sent to the county hospital. Drucci died just before arrival.

His lawyer, Maurice Green, was waiting at the Criminal Court Building with a writ of habeas corpus; he'd been notified of the initial arrest. When Green learned of his client's death, he telephoned Cecelia Drucci, the gangster's blonde wife, immediately. After identifying her husband's body that night at the morgue (she took one look and sobbed, "My great big baby!"), she demanded that Healy be charged with murder, to which Chief of Detectives Bill Schoemaker responded, "I don't know anything about anyone being murdered. I do know that Drucci was killed trying to take a gun away from an officer. We're having a medal made for Healy."

Chief Collins was a little more apologetic, verbally at least. "I am sorry that Drucci was killed in police custody. Drucci was temperamentally erratic and ready to fight at the drop of a hat. A great deal depended on who handled Drucci."

A coroner's jury ruled the killing a justifiable homicide. Officer Healy went on to serve on the Chicago police force for thirty-seven more years. Upon his retirement in 1964, he became chief of police of Stone Park, a West Side suburb where several motels, cocktail lounges, and gambling houses were backed by Syndicate money. It is interesting to note that Healy, whose disdain for gangsters motivated him to kill Drucci, did not inconvenience the Stone Park operations in any way.

Drucci's family and friends continued to view his killing as murder. Charles Wharton, who represented Cecelia Drucci at the inquest, responded to the verdict by telling reporters, "We never did figure out how an unarmed man in a police squad car surrounded by armed policemen can be shot to death without the act being called murder."

On Thursday, April 7, Drucci, a navy veteran, was buried in Mount Carmel Cemetery with full military honors. His ten-thousand-dollar aluminum and silver casket was draped with an American flag and surrounded by thirty thousand dollars' worth of flowers, most of which had been provided by William Schofield. Viola O'Banion consoled the widow. As Cecelia Drucci left Mount Carmel after the burial, she managed to smile at reporters. "A policeman murdered him," she said, "but we sure gave him a grand funeral."

Now Bugs Moran was head of the North Side Gang. He had not looked favorably on peace after Weiss's murder, taking the killing personally. Drucci had overruled him. Now he would act.

Election Day in Chicago was remarkably peaceful, thanks to the numerous and heavily armed police squads sent out by Chief Collins. Dever assigned an extra five thousand men to oversee the polls with the aim of preventing the intimidation of voters and related violence. Two bombs were thrown and a few miscellaneous beatings of election workers took place, but on the whole, the entire event was a pale shadow of its predecessors.

While the counting was taking place, Big Bill Thompson held court in the Louis XIV Ballroom at the Hotel Sherman. At one point, fortified by a succession of stiff drinks, he leaped onto a chair, waved his gigantic cowboy hat, and bellowed, "The lead is now fifty-two thousand! I thank you one and all, I thank you. Tell 'em, cowboys, tell 'em! I told you I'd ride 'em high and wide!"

Thompson won the election by a majority of more than eighty-three thousand votes. He celebrated by leading a festive crowd to the Fish Fans clubhouse, an inactive vessel moored off the coast of Lincoln Park. The caretaker warned that the old hulk would not be able to stand the guaranteed abuse from fifteen hundred drunken revelers, but the Thompson party persisted, and sure enough, the clubhouse sank six feet into the water, touching bottom. No one was hurt, and most of the celebrants who sheepishly disembarked did not even get their feet wet.

One of Thompson's first acts in office was to transfer Michael Hughes from his isolated post with the Highway Patrol Department and appoint him chief of police. His former chief, Charles Fitzmorris, became city controller. Daniel Serritella, a Capone agent, was made city sealer. The Thompson family doctor, Arnold Kegel, received the post of health commissioner. Four years of Dever and Decency were undone in a matter of weeks.

Capone, anticipating a long term of forthcoming prosperity, expanded his quarters at the Hotel Metropole (where he had moved in 1925) to fifty rooms. The area became a beehive of activity, with police and politicians coming in for payoffs (the Metropole was convenient to city hall and the police department), and gangsters and their women prowling through the halls at all hours. A blind pig in the lobby and service bars in the rooms kept the liquor on tap. As Capone's notoriety grew, the building became a local tourist attraction, with tour bus conductors referring to it as "Capone's castle."

While Capone's flamboyant presence kept him in the public eye like an insect specimen pegged to a display board, Moran went quietly, furtively about his business. He was seldom seen, rarely spoke to reporters, and in general defied description, unlike the exuberant O'Banion, the lethal Weiss, and the energetic Drucci. One Chicago citizen whose notice he did not escape (although the acknowledgment had a few negative consequences) was Judge John H. Lyle.

Lyle was the bane of Chicago gangland. He railed against criminals from his position on the judicial bench, and any bootlegger, murderer, or gangster unfortunate enough to appear before him was practically guaranteed a one-hundred-thousand-dollar bail order for an offense that would warrant five thousand dollars anywhere else. Before becoming a lawyer, Lyle had been a professional boxer, which some opponents found to their detriment years later when he brawled with another politician on the floor of the Chicago City Council.

His fists were secondary weapons to his determination. All a Chicago law enforcement officer had to do was ask, and Lyle would issue search and arrest warrants for gangsters and their property. He also conceived the idea of issuing vagrancy warrants against known public enemies. To evade such a warrant, a gangster would have to prove that he did indeed have means of support, and Lyle was sure that no taxes had been paid along the way. Defense against a vagrancy warrant was a foot in the door that any Treasury agent might make use of later on.

Although the judge hated gangsters as a species, Lyle admitted to a reluctant liking for George Moran. The feeling seemed to be mutual, although both men were in adversarial positions. Moran knew that Lyle would throw the book at him on principle whenever he appeared before the crusading jurist, so he always requested a change of venue.

"What's the matter?" Lyle asked from the bench during one appearance, after Moran asked once again to be heard by another judge. "Don't you like me, Moran?"

The North Sider cracked a nervous smile. "I like you, Your Honor. . . . But I am suspicious of you."

Gangster and judge ran across each other outside the courtroom one day, while both were attending a Cubs baseball game at Wrigley Field. Noticing a brilliant ring flashing on Lyle's finger, Moran said with a straight face, "Judge, that's a beautiful diamond ring you're wearing. If it's snatched some night, promise you won't go hunting me. I'm telling you right now I'm innocent."

John Lyle and George Moran had other such unconventional encounters. One day, the judge's courtroom was interrupted by a terrific racket coming from the direction of the bullpen. Investigating, Lyle found Moran in the cell, battling three bailiffs. They had spotted him in the building when he arrived to sign papers related to another charge, and thinking that he'd escaped from custody, grabbed him. They managed to snap one cuff on his wrist before he pulled free, clutched the other steel cuff in his fist to emulate brass knuckles, and began fighting like an enraged bear.

"Sorry, Judge," he gasped when Lyle appeared, "but these clowns were trying to throw me back in the can."

The judge asked that he be freed, a courtesy for which Moran warmly thanked him. Reporters followed the gangster outside, where an attractive brunette waited for him in an expensive car.

"Gentlemen, my wife," he said. "If anyone asks for me, you can tell them that this is our wedding anniversary and we're going roller skating."

Lucy Moran, a Sioux Indian, had been a showgirl who wowed customers under the stage name Alice Roberts. Soon after their marriage in 1926 the Morans moved to a fancy Belden Avenue apartment, which they occupied briefly before moving to the Parkway Hotel at 2100 Lincoln. George and Lucy, by all accounts, were an extremely happy couple, and neither was known to stray throughout their many years of marriage.

Moran made little secret of his hatred for Capone. When the Reverend Elmer Williams interviewed him for a social reform magazine, *Lightnin'*, he was quick to portray Capone as a subhuman, greedy monster with a conscience that obviously tortured him.

"The Beast," he said, using a favorite sobriquet for his archrival, "uses his muscle men to peddle rotgut alcohol and green beer. I'm a legitimate salesman of pure beer and good whiskey. He trusts nobody and suspects everybody. He always has guards. I travel around with a couple of pals. The Behemoth can't sleep nights. If you ask me, he's on dope. Me, I don't even need an aspirin."

Although Capone coveted the North Side territory, ethnic prejudice was against him, allowing Moran to maintain a solid customer base and ongoing source of income. Captain John Stege summed up the situation to Judge Lyle in a conversation Lyle recounted in his memoirs:

> The North Shore millionaires, businessmen, and country clubs buy their liquor from Moran. On the South Shore they do business with Ralph Sheldon. These people don't trust Capone. They're afraid that if they open the door to him the Mafia will be after them with blackmail and shakedowns.

Despite the battering that the North Side leadership had taken since O'Banion's death, George Moran still commanded a loyal and ferocious crew.

His ace killers were the Gusenberg brothers, Pete, Frank, and Henry. Pete, the oldest, appeared on a police blotter for the first time in 1902, when he was arrested for larceny. Found guilty of burglary in 1906, he did a three-year stint in Joliet. Released in 1909, he was returned to prison the following year for violating his parole. Released again in 1911, he evaded further incarceration until 1923, when he was arrested along with Big Tim Murphy for the Dearborn Station mail robbery. He served three years in Leavenworth, completing his sentence in time to ply his shooting talents in the service of the North Side Gang.

His younger brother Frank was just as brazen, in his personal as well as criminal life; Frank was married to two women at once. His police record dated back to 1909 when, under the name of Carl Bloom, he was arrested and fined for disorderly conduct. In 1911 he did thirty days in the Bridewell for the same type of offense. In 1924 he was tried on a burglary charge, but by that point he was an active member of the North Side Gang and shared in their general immunity from prosecution. The third Gusenberg brother, Henry, was considerably younger than Frank and Pete and had a much less illustrious record. The gang had secured him a no-show job as a $175-per-week movie projectionist.

Adam Heyer was Moran's answer to Jake Guzik and served the North Side Gang as a business manager and accountant. He did a year in jail for robbery in 1908 and served a minor sentence in Joliet seven years later for directing a confidence game. He violated his parole twice, returning to Joliet each time, and finally walked free in February 1923. A sharp dresser with a keen mind, he lent his name to many property leases that the North Siders took out, such as the SMC Cartage Company warehouse at 2122 North Clark Street, which, along with an office at 127 Dearborn Street and the Wigwam bar in the Marigold Hotel, was a gang hangout.

Albert Kachellek, otherwise known as James Clark, a native of Krojencke, Germany, worked with the Gusenbergs as an enforcer. His first arrest was in 1905 for running a confidence game and committing a robbery, for which he drew a four-month sentence. He went to trial on robbery charges again, in 1910, but was found not guilty. The same year he was found guilty on another robbery charge and sent to Joliet, from where he was paroled in 1914. He had only been free for a matter of months before racking up three more charges, two for robbery and one for murder. He must have made himself useful to someone since his last court appearance, for the state's attorney ended up striking the charges from the record. To spare his mother, Anna Kachellek, grief because of his growing notoriety, he changed his name to James Clark.

Albert K. Weinshank was of Russian descent, a club owner, and a former associate of O'Banion and Weiss. He stayed on with the North Siders under Drucci and then Moran. When Moran moved the North Siders into the cleaning and dyeing unions, he installed the tough and shrewd Weinshank in the vice president's post.

John May, the thirty-five-year-old son of a Canadian immigrant, had a minor record as a safecracker and robber. By 1928 he was serving the Moran gang as a fifty-dollar-a-week mechanic and backup muscle when necessary. He had an ill wife and seven children who relied on him as their sole support.

Even with such an experienced and formidable crew behind him, Moran followed Hymie Weiss's example and cultivated allies. Like Capone, he recognized the Unione Siciliana for the large source of revenue and muscle it could provide, so when one aspirant to the presidential throne approached him and proposed partnership, he agreed immediately.

Sicilian-born Joseph Aiello was the head of a large family of brothers and cousins who had assumed control of Little Italy's alky-cooking industry after the Genna Gang experienced a minor civil war and disintegrated. He had been partnered with Tony Lombardo for years in a variety of businesses, including alcohol, cheese, bakeries, and olive oil, but when Capone helped Lombardo attain the presidency of the Unione, a position that Aiello coveted, the personal and professional relationship between the two men deteriorated. Aiello, realizing that he needed backing if he hoped to take on the Capone interests, formed an alliance with Moran's North Siders, West Side vice lord Jack Zuta, gambler and former safecracker Barney Bertsche, and Billy Skidmore, a professional bail bondsman and gambler.

Moran stood ready to back him up as Aiello struck out against both Capone and Lombardo. Aiello offered the chef at the Bella Napoli Café thirty-five thousand dollars to put prussic acid in Capone's soup, but the chef informed Capone. The Aiello interests put out the word that fifty thousand dollars was there for the taking by anyone who could kill Capone. Several hitmen, mostly from other American cities, attempted to collect and ended up dead themselves, Tommygunned to death and left with a nickel in their lifeless palms, the signature card of ace Capone gunner Jack McGurn. When a handful of Aiello adherents were murdered, Chief of Detectives William O'Connor, who had arrested Dean O'Banion for hijacking three years previously, announced that he was forming a special armored-car force to do battle with gangsters. Eleven murders had been committed as a result of Aiello's offensive, and O'Connor felt he had to make a gesture to show the agitated public that the situation was being handled.

"It is the wish of the people of Chicago that you hunt these criminals down and kill them without mercy," he told the squad once it had been assembled. "See to it that they don't have you pushing up daisies. Make them push up daisies. Shoot first, and shoot to kill."

Unknown gunmen shot and killed Tony Lombardo on September 7, 1928, as he was walking in the Loop with two bodyguards. Before Aiello could seize the coveted Unione position for himself, Pasqalino "Patsy" Lolordo (whose brother, Joseph, had been one of Lombardo's bodyguards on the day he was killed) was elevated into the spot with assistance from Capone. Undeterred, Aiello and Moran resolved to deal with Patsy Lolordo the same way they had taken care of Lombardo. On January 8, 1929, via arrangements that remain a mystery, Lolordo received a group of men in his home, two of which were later suspected to be James Clark and Pete Gusenberg. Mrs. Lolordo heard the guests drink a toast to her husband seconds before shots rang out. Although she could not or would not identify the killers, she did say that they were not Italians.

These murders were on O'Connor's mind when he issued his brutal directive to the Chicago police officers. His men didn't shoot anyone, but they did catch Joe Aiello, two of his cousins, and a young Milwaukee gunman in a room at the Rex Hotel when they raided it on a tip from an informant. When the group was brought to the detective bureau, a flood of taxis arrived less than an hour later and disgorged a small crowd of men whom a police onlooker recognized at once as Capone gangsters.

The gunmen surrounded the building in a maneuver that the press later dubbed "the Siege of the Detective Bureau." Three of the men were seized and placed in a cell adjacent to Aiello's. A policeman who understood the Sicilian dialect overheard them warn Aiello of impending doom. The terrified gangster, the moment he was released, collected his family and, together with his brothers Tony and Domenic, left Chicago for Trenton, New Jersey, for almost two years.

Moran and his North Siders did not let Aiello's departure weaken their resolve; they harried and challenged Capone as incessantly as ever. They hijacked inbound liquor trucks consigned to

South Side customers and once stole an entire cargo of whiskey meant for Capone from a Canadian ship anchored in Lake Michigan. They made two attempts on the life of Jack McGurn. The second time, the Gusenberg brothers trapped "Machine-Gun" Jack in a public phone booth at the Hotel McCormick and nearly finished him off with pistol fire.

Moran also challenged Capone in the dog-racing field. He built a track in downstate Illinois and backed his business manager, Adam Heyer, in the construction of the Fairview Kennel Club in Cicero, a Capone stronghold. When a fire destroyed the Hawthorne Kennel Club, a competing track run by Capone, no one had to guess who was responsible.

In addition to gambling and bootlegging, the North Side Gang under Moran made further inroads into the unions. The thirty-five-million-dollar-a-year clothes-cleaning industry had long been the fiefdom of the Master Cleaners and Dyers Association, which controlled all of Chicago's cleaning and dyeing plants. It operated in conjunction with two associate unions, the Retail Cleaners and Dyers Union and the Laundry and Dyehouse Chauffeurs Union. They forced shopkeepers and business operators to pay such high subsidies that the latter had to raise their prices. The public rebelled, either by doing their own cleaning and dyeing work at home or giving their business to operators in the suburbs. Many small cleaning shops, facing continuing operating costs and required union kickbacks that were not lowered to compensate for the loss of trade, went out of business. Others turned desperately to men tough enough to take on the unions, namely the gangsters.

Morris Becker, a South Side businessman, took on Capone as a partner, and his troubles with the Master Cleaners and Dyers ceased. An independent cooperative plant, the Central Cleaning Company, followed suit by approaching Moran and offering to pay him eighteen hundred dollars a week to protect it from the sluggers, guns, and bombs of the Master Cleaners and Dyers.

Moran accepted the assignment and installed two of his men, Albert Weinshank and Willie Marks, as vice presidents of the Central Cleaning Company. But the arrangement soured when Ben Kornick, the president, became convinced that the North Siders were trying to muscle him out. He tried to back out of his deal with them, and when that failed, he approached the Master Cleaners and Dyers

Association for help, a high irony since he'd aligned himself with the gangsters to combat that organization. Kornick knew that he would first have to unionize his help if he expected any assistance from the Master Cleaners and Dyers, and approached John G. Clay, who had a reputation for honesty, in organizing a union.

When Moran learned of Kornick's intention, he sent Willie Marks to see Clay with a preemptive offer: Clay could unionize the company's drivers. Clay asked Marks to show him proof of his authority from Central Cleaning's president, Kornick, to negotiate an agreement. When Marks failed to produce it, Clay refused to go any further with the deal, suspecting that the gangsters would try to talk their way into his good graces, then muscle him out and seize control of his drivers union and its three-hundred-thousand-dollar treasury.

Moran would not be dissuaded, however. On the night of November 16, 1928, Clay was sitting at his desk at his union headquarters. A car pulled up outside and discharged two men, who walked up the building's steps and paused at the stone landing. One was armed with a revolver, the other with a sawed-off shotgun. They fired through Clay's office window, killing him.

The murder did not yield the expected results. Organized labor was so enraged that the North Side Gang retreated and kept a low profile. Once the heat died down, Moran ousted Kornick as Central Cleaning Company president and replaced him with Al Weinshank. The incident would be one of many factors taken into account by law enforcement agencies when they attempted to solve the most sensational gang murder of all time three short months later.

There was nothing about the outward appearance of the squat, one-story brick building at 2122 North Clark Street that could possibly attract suspicion. It crouched between two three-story rooming houses, which were a fixture of that stretch of Clark Street. The storefront measured about twenty-five feet wide and ran about 150 feet deep. The upper half of its huge double window had been painted black, to conceal activities inside from curious eyes, and a dirty placard bearing the inscription "S.M.C. Cartage Company" covered the lower half. The words "MOVING" and "EXPRESSING" ran vertically down either side of the street door.

Anyone entering the place casually would not have been impressed. A threadbare office, separated from the rest of the building by a battered partition, occupied the front section and contained only a couple of desks, chairs, and a counter with telephones. The rest of 2122 North Clark was garage space, with large double doors that opened into the alley at the rear. There were always a couple of trucks parked on the premises. The SMC Cartage Company was, outwardly, a small moving company that operated as business flow permitted.

One Frank J. Snyder, which was an alias used by Moran associate Adam Heyer, had leased the premises in October 1928, and thenceforth it had served the North Siders as a liquor storage depot and garage, where John May worked on the gang's small fleet of trucks. A storage space hidden in the building's rafters was regularly stacked with cases of liquor brought in from Detroit by Paul Morton, brother of Nails. Once in a while a freelance hijacker's stolen plunder could be found, for Moran, like O'Banion, was only too happy to handle hijacked merchandise and even pay for tips.

In early February men arrived at the rooming houses managed by Mrs. Michael Doody (at 2119 North Clark) and Mrs. Frank Arvidson (2135) and applied for streetfront rooms. They told the landladies that they were cab drivers and would be coming and going at all hours, although they mostly worked nights.

According to the legend surrounding the event that was soon to unfold, a freelance hijacker contacted Moran about the same time the mysterious lodgers appeared in the neighborhood. The party in question told the North Side Gang leader that he had a huge load of Old Log Cabin whiskey available at fifty-seven dollars per case. When Moran agreed to buy, the hijacker promised to deliver the load personally at about 10:30 A.M. on February 14.

That morning, the "cab drivers" watched the front door of the SMC Cartage Company intently. Mechanic John May was the first to arrive at the garage, having work to do on some of the trucks. He brought along his Alsatian dog, Highball, attaching the animal's leash to the wheel of one of the trucks. Soon after, Adam Heyer, Pete and Frank Gusenberg, and James Clark showed up. They were joined by someone whose fascination with gangsters was about to prove fatal.

Reinhardt Schwimmer had been a friend of O'Banion, who'd been much more open than most of his peers about socializing with those outside gangland. An optometrist, he had inherited his father's eyeglass-fitting business ten years previously, but had failed at it and was currently supported by his mother. Schwimmer had already been divorced twice, and both personal and financial success eluded him. He attempted to compensate by boasting that he shared in the North Side Gang's profits and could arrange executions if someone crossed him the wrong way. On the morning of February 14, he was dropping by for a quick chat, and had plans to meet his mother at two that afternoon.

Al Weinshank arrived last and was wearing a tan hat and gray winter coat. His attire made Weinshank resemble George Moran more so than usual, and this may have served as a signal for the carnage that followed.

Elmer Lewis, a driver for the Beaver Paper Company, was peering about for the address of his next delivery as he neared the intersection of Clark and Webster. Suddenly, a seven-passenger Cadillac swerved left from Webster onto Clark and collided with Lewis's truck, its left-rear fender hitting the delivery vehicle's left front.

Both vehicles pulled over in front of 2156 North Clark Street. When Lewis saw that the Cadillac was equipped with a police siren, gong, and rear gun rack, he was sure that he was in trouble. Two uniformed policemen were among the vehicle's five occupants. To his surprise and relief, the man who got out to inspect the damage—an American-looking individual wearing a blue suit and, strange for a law enforcement official, a chinchilla coat—smiled and waved him on, suggesting that no harm was done. Lewis was only too happy to get back into his truck and carry on.

The Cadillac carried on as well, finally rolling to a halt in front of the garage at 2122 North Clark. All five occupants climbed out and entered the building. Minutes later, Moran and Ted Newberry arrived, but they stopped when they saw the police vehicle. Willie Marks and Henry Gusenberg came upon the scene at roughly the same time. All four men drew the same conclusion: a police raid was in progress. More annoyed than concerned, all four retraced their steps and left.

The events that followed indicated that the seven men inside the garage also believed that they were receiving a nuisance visit from the law. If they had suspected that anything other than a raid was in progress, Pete and Frank Gusenberg, and James Clark in particular probably would have ensured that the outcome was quite different than what actually transpired.

All seven men were lined up against the garage's rear wall, patted down, and relieved of any weapons (Frank Gusenberg's loaded pistol was later found on the floor). It is not known how soon it was before they figured out that this was no police raid, but their hands were still raised when the first spray of bullets from two Thompson submachine guns brought by the raiders mowed them down. Two subsequent shotgun blasts blew away the left side of May's skull and tore into Schwimmer's chest.

When the smoke cleared, a horrible scene existed in what had been a dingy, nondescript garage minutes before. May, Schwimmer, and Weinshank lay on their backs, blood from their gaping wounds trickling in thick rivulets across the floor toward a drain. James Clark lay facedown along the wall. Pete Gusenberg had fallen sideways onto a chair and slumped over it. Frank Gusenberg lay among the human wreckage, so still that the assassins did not realize he was still breathing.

A housewife, Mrs. Joseph Morin, was glancing out of her front window at 2125 North Clark when she saw two men emerge from the garage at 2122 with their hands raised. Two men in police uniform followed them, carrying "long guns which they were pointing at the backs of the men," she later recalled. Sam Schneider, a tailor with a shop at 2124 North Clark, heard no shooting but did see the four men depart. Like Mrs. Morin, he assumed a raid had occurred and took no further notice.

Only Mrs. Jeanette Landesman, who was ironing in the third-floor back room of 2124, heard the gunfire. She hurried to her front window in time to see the party leave, and her curiosity was further heightened when she saw the Cadillac swing out of the congested lane it had entered, swerve around an oncoming trolley, and make a hasty departure. They had certainly seemed in a hurry to leave the scene. Mrs. Landesman decided to investigate and went downstairs to the SMC Cartage Company's front door. She tried to open it, but when it wouldn't budge, enlisted the aid of one of her building's other roomers, Charles McAllister. He forced the door open, walked warily through the front office, and edged down a corridor formed by a line of parked trucks. The anguished barking of a dog somewhere on the premises assailed his ears, and his nose burned with the pungent smell of gunpowder and smoke.

The sight of the bleeding collection of humanity piled against the wall made him sick to his stomach. When he heard the weak voice of Frank Gusenberg call from the heap of bodies, "Who's there?" he rushed out and reported his findings to Mrs. Landesman, who called the police.

Lieutenant Thomas Loftus was the first to arrive. When he saw Frank Gusenberg crawling toward him, he said urgently, "Do you know me, Frank?"

"You're Tom Loftus." The two men had known each other for years.

"Who did it? What happened??"

"I won't talk."

"You're in bad shape, Frank—"

"For God's sake, get me to a hospital!"

Loftus called for an ambulance. While riding with the dying gangster to the hospital, the officer tried again to get the identities of the shooters and reminded Frank that Pete was dead. "I'll never tell," Gusenberg insisted. He died at Alexian Brothers at 1:40 that afternoon without ever naming his killers.

When he learned of the mass slaying, Moran supposedly shouted, "Only Capone kills like that!" His outburst made the front pages of newspapers in Miami, where Capone was vacationing at the time. In actuality, Moran had sent word to Chief of Detectives John Egan that "We don't know what brought it on. We're facing an enemy in the dark."

Theories as to the reason for such a slaughter abounded. Moran's muscling in on the Central Cleaning Company was proposed as a motive for revenge by organized labor; other theorists suggested that Detroit's Purple Gang was tired of losing shipments consigned to Capone. Most investigators cast suspicious eyes toward Miami—Capone more than anyone else stood to profit from Moran's murder. The North Side Gang was Scarface Al's only real opposition in the city of Chicago by 1929, and removing them would put an end to the dog-track fires, the shootouts, and other problems the North Sider had been inflicting on Capone's interests since 1925. The proof was lacking, however.

The resulting outcry and publicity was huge. Dubbed the "St. Valentine's Day Massacre," papers everywhere held up the event as proof that the gangster element had gone unchecked for too long. The *New York Sun* declared, "Crimes like this constitute the underworld's supreme defiance of society."

State's Attorney Swanson responded to intense public pressure and ordered the police to crack down on speakeasies, brothels, gambling joints, and handbooks—in short, all of the enterprises that channeled money to the underworld. Chief of Police William Russell directed his men to be meticulous in their searches, going into garages, barns, backyard sheds, anything that could house a single still or more.

Their thoroughness aroused fear in the right person. On the night of February 21, the smoking remains of a seven-passenger Cadillac sedan was found in a garage at 1723 North Wood Street. It matched the description of the murder car as provided by witnesses. Assistant State's Attorney Ditchburne earned the gratitude of the Chicago police force when he said that the car had been found, and that it definitely was not police issue. "The detective squads are freed from suspicion," he said.

In tracing the person who had rented the Wood Street garage two days before the massacre, the police found that whoever it was had given the garage's owner a home address that was right next door to the Circus Café, which was the hangout of Capone associate Claude Maddox. Witnesses who viewed Maddox claimed to have seen him around the Wood Street garage two days before the mangled car was found, but there being no law against trashing cars, and Maddox was never charged.

All leads and clues were followed rigorously. A St. Louis gang called Egan's Rats was known to have worn police uniforms in order to approach and disarm their victims before killing them. A witness who had seen the Valentine's Day killers leave the garage claimed that one of them had a missing front tooth, and a prominent member of the Rats matched that description. While that angle was being followed, Machine-Gun Jack McGurn, who had dispatched so many of Joe Aiello's hitmen and barely survived an attack by the Gusenbergs, was picked up as the suspected mastermind of the massacre, but his alibi was too good. He had been in bed with lovely blond Louise Rolfe the entire day, and she unashamedly swore to it.

Ten months after the murder car was found, the machine guns used in the massacre turned up. A police officer was killed in St. Joseph, Michigan, when he interfered in a quarrel between two motorists who had suffered a minor collision. One of them shot him but was forced to abandon his car and run when its wheel broke. Papers found in the vehicle led police to an address south of town, where they located two machine guns. Tests performed on the guns by ballistics expert Calvin Goddard proved that they had fired the bullets that killed James Clark and Reinhardt Schwimmer. To top off the string of coincidences, the bungalow was the home of none other than Fred Burke, the Egan's Rats suspect.

Burke never stood trial for complicity in the massacre, having received a life sentence in a Michigan prison for murdering the Michigan policeman. Whether he was actually one of the St. Valentine's Day executioners is a matter of debate (he could have gotten the guns long after the massacre), as is almost everything else about the case.

E. Barnett, although he had not worked for the North Siders since 1924, had his own questions, not about who had killed the seven men in the SMC garage but precisely what so many of the gang's key members were doing there at once.

"That's something that never made sense to me," he said. "I read that they were there to receive some hijacked whiskey, but come on! All of those guys? It was never that way with O'Banion. And if you've ever known a Chicago winter, you'd know that a freezing garage is the last place where you'd want to hang out, so I think they were gathered there for a more important reason than to be social. I remember looking at the pictures published in the papers and thinking, *Those guys were too well-dressed to be receiving hijacked stuff. What if they had to help unload?* Those clothes were a little too fancy for work. If you want my honest opinion, I think they were waiting for someone. Someone important, from the looks of it."

Although the careful planning and masterful execution of the St. Valentine's Day Massacre suggested that it was a Capone operation, to this day no one knows for sure who the killers were. Among those suggested were John Scalise, Albert Anselmi, Joseph Lolordo (brother of the murdered Patsy), Fred Burke, Claude Maddox, and some Detroit gangsters. If Barnett's hunch is right, and the North Siders had been in the Clark Street garage that frigid morning to meet someone or something more consequential, then an additional mystery presents itself: the reason for the meeting.

"The Tommygunners in the garage were historians of a sort," wrote John H. Lyle. "With .45-caliber bullets they wrote *finis* to the legend of as spectacular a crew of outlaws as any city or any era has known. Dion O'Banion, Nails Morton, Three-Gun Louis Alterie, Schemer Drucci, Hymie Weiss—each left his stamp, black though it was, on his day and age. In the end there was left only Bugs Moran, mobster without a mob. Capone—Moran's "Beast"—had won, but [he] didn't get full value for his ten-thousand-dollar investment in massacre. Moran cheated him by showing up late for his own murder."

Moran continued to operate in Chicago, despite the popular assumption that his power died in the massacre along with the best of his troops. Immediately after the bloodbath, he fled to Windsor, Ontario, to collect his wits and regain the nerve he had lost as a result of his close brush with death. After lying low for a year, he moved to repair the damage done to his small empire.

In the spring of 1930, Moran, Julian Kaufman, and professional gambler Joey Josephs made plans to re-open an elegant casino, the Sheridan Wave Tournament Club, at 653 Waveland Avenue. During its 1928–29 heyday, the club ranked as one of the most fashionable and prosperous in the city, but it ended up closing in the wake of the massacre. Kaufman went to an old friend, *Tribune* reporter Jake Lingle, for assistance in relaunching the enterprise.

Lingle had powerful connections with high-ranking police officials and city politicians, and had paved the way to similar establishments opening in the past. The shylock reporter supposedly demanded 50 percent of the Sheridan Wave profits in exchange for obtaining unofficial consent to open, but Moran, Kaufman, and Josephs refused. Lingle allegedly told them, "If this joint is opened up, you're going to see more squad cars in front ready to raid it than you ever saw in your life." The Moran interests went ahead anyway and advertised an anticipated June 9, 1930, grand opening in sporting newspapers. It didn't happened on schedule, for that day Jake Lingle was assassinated in the Loop, his double-dealing past having finally caught up with him.

Moran and his partners were among those questioned during the crusade-style murder investigation (the *Tribune*'s publisher took the killing of one of his reporters personally). Although one Leo V.

Brothers, a St. Louis racketeer, was eventually convicted for the slaying, the rumor persisted that Brothers was a highly paid fall guy, and that Lingle's murder had been ordered by Moran ally Jack Zuta and carried out by longtime North Side associate Frank Foster.

Two months after the massacre, in May 1929, Capone added to the gangland body count. He had discovered that John Scalise and Albert Anselmi were plotting with the current president of the Unione Siciliana, Joseph Guinta, to kill him, take over his businesses, and, according to one version of the story, grant the North Side franchise to the still-rebellious Joe Aiello in exchange for his support. Capone was especially livid because he had also turned down the chance for peace with Hymie Weiss when he refused to sanction their execution.

The Big Fellow, giving no outward indication that he knew of their treachery, wooed the three men to a roadhouse near Hammond, Indiana, telling them they were to be the guests of honor at a banquet. After the last toast had been drunk, Capone seized a sawed-off baseball bat and battered all three plotters to death. Their bodies were left in an isolated spot outside Hammond, scattered in and around a stolen car. The remote killing spot was chosen because the outcry over the North Clark Street massacre had not yet died down in Chicago. A pathologist who examined the deceased trio commented in awe that he'd never seen such badly beaten bodies.

Few things brought out the rabid animal in Capone more quickly than betrayal. In 1927 he'd learned that his old Brooklyn mentor, Frankie Yale, who had killed Big Jim Colosimo and Dean O'Banion for Johnny Torrio, had been double-crossing him. Yale had originally favored Joe Aiello to become Unione President after Samoots Amatuna was murdered, but Lombardo had acquired the position with Capone's help. When Lombardo began showing more independence and remitting less Unione money to Yale, the Brooklyn gangster made up for the deficit by hijacking Chicago-bound liquor trucks consigned to Capone. When an old Brooklyn friend confirmed the double-cross to Capone, Yale had the man murdered. On July 1, 1928, Yale was shot and killed while driving home—Capone's response to the death of his friend.

Joe Aiello followed Yale, Scalise, Anselmi, and Guinta to the grave in October 1930. Fifty bullets from a machine-gun nest tore him to pieces as he was leaving the house of a friend on Kolmar Avenue, where he had been holed up for several days.

Another worry for Capone was the federal government's interest in his source of income. He had never filed a tax return and owned no property in his own name, yet his high standard of living did not suggest a man who had no income whatsoever. The government began to dig and eventually uncovered enough evidence to take him to trial. Its persistence was due in part to the massacre, which turned Capone into a national embarrassment. As writer Robert Schoenberg put it, "If Chicago would do nothing about Capone — and clearly Chicago, even after the Massacre, would not or could not—others would."

The bane of Moran's existence after the St. Valentine's Day Massacre was a series of vagrancy charges. In April 1930 the Chicago Crime Commission issued a list of twenty-eight Chicago criminals whose very existence warranted prison sentences and called them all "Public Enemies." Capone topped the list; others included Moran, Ralph Capone, Terry Druggan, Frankie Lake, Spike O'Donnell, Ralph Capone, Joe Aiello, Jake Guzik, Jack McGurn, Frank McErlane, Jack Zuta, and Ralph Sheldon's successor Danny Stanton. Many of them were targeted by Judge Lyle's vagrancy warrants, as proving their source of income would require them to open the door to possible tax-evasion charges.

Not long after Aiello was killed, Moran was resting up at Elizabeth Cassidy's resort at Bluff Lake, near Waukegan. He was lounging on his bed, clad in pajamas and reading the Sunday paper, when Constable George Stried and a private detective, George Hargrave, walked in. They were looking for Leo Mongovern, one of Moran's bodyguards, who was wanted in connection with the June 1930 murder of *Tribune* reporter (and Capone lackey) Jake Lingle.

"We didn't expect to find you back in Lake County," Stried said sternly. Earlier that month, Moran had been arrested on a vagrancy warrant and ordered to leave. "Come along."

Moran refused. "I'm out on bail now," he retorted. "I've got some rights as an American citizen. You can't pinch me."

Stried and Hargrave took the protesting gangster before Justice of the Peace Harold Tallot. He stood accused of harboring Mongovern, and a vagrancy charge was thrown in for good measure.

"What are you trying to do, pull some Lyle stuff?" Moran demanded to know. "This is double jeopardy or something. You can't do it."

Justice Tallot warned him that indeed he could, and he would add a contempt-of-court charge if the gangster challenged him further. Moran fell into a sullen silence.

"You're going to be taught to stay out of this county," State's Attorney A. V. Smith said. "You'll be arrested every time you're found here."

Moran protested that he was only in Waukegan for some duck hunting. When asked what he knew about Aiello's slaying, he said, "That double-crosser? I haven't seen him for eight months. I haven't been in the rackets for four years. I'm a respectable guy." He laughed when asked about his efforts to reorganize the North Side Gang after the massacre. "I'm out of it all. I'm not after anybody, and no one is after me. Don't get me wrong, though. I'm not afraid of anyone, Capone or whoever it is."

For the next couple of years, until the repeal of Prohibition, Moran and what was left of his gang attempted to retain and defend their North Side stronghold, but Capone's outfit had become so large and so diversified that Moran's resistance amounted to little more than weak shots in the dark. After Capone was found guilty of income tax evasion in 1931 and sent to prison, the North Sider continued to operate, first in Chicago and then after Repeal, in Wisconsin and both Lake and McHenry Counties in Illinois. In 1938 he and nine associates were indicted for running off a half-million dollars' worth of counterfeit American Express Company checks. He affiliated himself with the Bookie Gang, a minor-league crew specializing in the robbery of Syndicate handbooks. While working with them, he met two men with whom he clicked especially well: Virgil Summers and Albert Fouts, both bank robbers. When the Bookie Gang's activities subsided during the early 1940s, the merry trio struck out on their own.

George "Bugs" Moran, once the overlord of the North Side, became one of many wandering outlaws who enlivened and colored the Depression years in the United States. Even after the economic climate improved, he continued to survive by robbing banks and doing low-key fencing. On June 26, 1946, he, Summers, and Fouts stole ten thousand dollars from a bank messenger in Dayton, Ohio.

The police traced them to Henderson, Kentucky, and arrested them on July 6. All three were found guilty of bank robbery and sent to the Ohio State Prison for ten years.

By all accounts, Moran was a model prisoner during his years in the Ohio penitentiary. Domenic Marzano, an inmate barber at the time, recalled, "I worked on the psych range for seven years with old George Moran and Yonnie Licavoli [a hoodlum from Toledo and Detroit who arrived at the prison during the Thirties with associates Joe "the Wop" English and Sarafina Sinatra]. We were there to keep them [psychopaths] from getting hurt . . . so the guards wouldn't get to them." Marzano explained that gangsters like Moran and Licavoli, because of their histories, commanded respect among the guards and inmates alike. "They didn't bother anyone, and no one bothered them."

Warden Marion Koloski agreed with Marzano. "There were no more perfect gentlemen than the Wop, Joe Sinatra, and Bugs Moran. When they were in charge of the psych range, you didn't have inmates diddling anyone."

Moran completed his prison stretch in 1956, only to be arrested by the FBI for the 1945 robbery of a bank in Ansonia, Ohio. The ageing gangster was sent to the federal prison at Leavenworth, Kansas, to serve another ten-year sentence. He died there on February 26, 1957, of lung cancer.

When Judge John Lyle read of Moran's death, he recalled the gangster's interview with the Reverend Williams in his courtroom more than thirty years before, during which Moran admitted that he would rather die from bullets than cancer. He had survived countless gangland assassination attempts, only to meet the end he feared most. His funeral was a mere shadow of the extravagant sendoffs he had helped to give Dean O'Banion, Hymie Weiss, and Vincent Drucci. He was buried in a cheap wooden coffin on the prison grounds, clad in a prison-made wool suit, and attended only by six convict pallbearers and a priest.

Lyle had dealt with numerous gangsters over the years and remembered all of them bitterly except for Moran. "As a man, Moran had interested me," Lyle wrote in *The Dry and Lawless Years*. "In the many times he had been before me in court I had discerned contradictions in his makeup. He was guilty of many wicked acts. But also he was sharp-witted, had a keen sense of humor, and at times was highly emotional. I had long thought that of all the gangsters I had observed, Moran was most likely to repent before he died and seek God's forgiveness."

Lyle expressed his thoughts in a letter to Father O'Connor, the chaplain at Leavenworth. The priest's reply confirmed that Lyle's predictions were correct.

"George Moran died a very peaceful death and was strengthened with the full Last Rites of the Catholic Church while he was fully conscious," Father O'Connor wrote. "This happened some days before he died and was not a 'last-ditch' stand. Your theory certainly proved out very satisfactory in his case. I am sure that God in his mercy was very kind to him in judgment."

EPILOGUE

ALTHOUGH AL CAPONE WAS the Chicago gangster who achieved permanent nationwide celebrity, spawning dozens of books and movies either about him or based on his likeness, the North Side Gang and its succession of colorful leaders captured the public attention and imagination during their day. Soon after Dean O'Banion's murder, a young woman showed up at the detective bureau and claiming that she had information on the killing. After giving a fragmented interview, she said suddenly, "Take me to see Louis Alterie!" She had used the information as a ruse in an attempt to get a peek at her "favorite gangster." Reinhardt Schwimmer's fascination with O'Banion and the North Siders eventually resulted in his dying among the men he idolized.

Each North Side leader had a public image that could have been written for him by a skillful press agent intent on giving his clients eternal notoriety: O'Banion, the cheerful but deadly three-gun florist, who walked with a limp but shot with as steady an arm as any; Earl "Hymie" Weiss, the cerebral successor, who died because of his refusal to let a friend's murder go unpunished; Vincent Drucci, the aggressive Italian who appeared to "turn on his own kind" in fighting for the Irish O'Banion's cause; and George "Bugs" Moran, the last of the North Side generals, whose David-versus-Goliath stance against Capone inspired admiration and sympathy among those who read about the Chicago gang wars from a safe distance. One writer commented, "Most of the citizens of Chicago were openly rooting for Moran to win the war against Capone."

The North Side Gang as a whole appeared to be tolerated by a citizenry who knew that there would always be gangsters in Chicago and preferred good old Irish-style terrorism to the secretive, stiletto-in-the-back tactics attributed to the underworld's Italian element. As Johnson and Sauter wrote in their colorful, witty history, *Wicked City*, "If O'Banion had not succeeded so well in his endeavors, he could be dismissed as just another low-level hoodlum, but he did succeed, and with an Out-of-my-way! Élan that appealed to native Chicagoans. He's a rascal all right, our Deanie is, but he's our rascal, not some damn foreigner, by God! At least he can speak English!"

In 1931, seven years after his death, Warner Brothers released *Public Enemy*, the gangster melodrama said to be loosely based on O'Banion's life. The likeness is feeble enough to be hazardous; the bloody rise and deadly fall of hoodlum "Tom Powers" (played by James Cagney) bore only a passing resemblance to O'Banion's story. The horseback riding accident suffered by "Nails Nathan" (Morton's cinematic counterpart) and the execution of the guilty horse (an act allegedly committed in retaliation by Louis Alterie) were recognizable components of the North Side Gang's history, but everything else was pure Hollywood. "Schemer Burns," Drucci's namesake, was Tom Powers's nemesis instead of ally, as Drucci had been. The character of "Bugs Moran" bore no resemblance to the real Moran at all. Dean O'Banion and Tom Powers did die as a result of their livelihoods, but under different circumstances.

In retrospect, one wonders whether O'Banion's name was used in connection with the film to give it an allure to a public that remembered the O'Banion days with fascination. *Scarface*, starring Edward G. Robinson, had been released a year earlier and had drawn crowds who anticipated it as a thrilling insight into the life of Al Capone. O'Banion, dead for many years, still captured the popular imagination.

"It's tough for anyone who wasn't around back then to know just what a big shot Dean was," Barnett said. "If anything big went down in Chicago, he was the first one that the cops came looking for. His funeral was better attended than the 1919 World Series. When he died, *all* the papers covered it. My mother was in Canada when it happened, and she wrote me right away to tell me that it was page-one news in the little town where she and my sister were staying."

In addition to James Cagney, O'Banion has been portrayed on the silver screen by such accomplished actors as Robert Gist and John Agar. Even a popular science-fiction book series saw fit to ascribe an imaginative cause to his death: Terrence Stamp's *Blood Harvest,* a Dr. Who novel, suggested that aliens in gangster form killed Dean O'Banion to ensure that one of the Earth's biggest cities would be torn apart by a violent gang war. The short-lived television series *Young Indiana Jones* featured one episode in which the lead character joins his college roommates Eliot Ness and Ernest Hemingway in solving a murder, only to be captured by O'Banion, tied up in the gangster's flower shop, and threatened with death if they interfere further.

Weiss and Moran have had their cinematic and literary counterparts as well. The one North Side boss who hasn't is Vincent Drucci, but the omission is hardly surprising. A core ingredient in the O'Banion legend is his supposed hatred of Italians, and Drucci presents an opposition to that cherished theory. When he is mentioned at all in Chicago histories or crime almanacs, writers call Drucci "O'Banion's faithful Italian" or "the only Italian whom O'Banion ever liked and vice versa."

"I'll bet a lot of these writers wish Vince never existed," Barnett said. "It makes it so hard for them to pass Dean off as some bigoted wop-hater. I read one newspaper article where they called Drucci a Spaniard. Go figure. It's not surprising, but it's sad to see the lengths some people have gone to in order to make sure Dean's remembered as something other than he really was."

The florist shop where O'Banion died passed into the hands of William Schofield's sons, who managed it until August 1960, when it was razed to make way for a parking lot. The business then moved to 731 North State. Five years later, forty-eight-year-old Steven Schofield was arrested for illegal gambling activities and sentenced, along with two co-defendants, to six months in jail. The judge, who called professional gambling a "national calamity," refused a thirty-day stay of sentence so that Schofield could train a temporary replacement in the shop.

Holy Name Parochial School, where O'Banion attended classes from 1904 until 1907, still stands, as does the cathedral where he attended Mass and in whose towering shadow Hymie Weiss breathed his last.

For years there was a bar in Chicago called O'Banion's, a rough spot that catered to the gay leather trade. In the mid-1970s it became the city's most popular punk hangout, offering live bands and an uninhibited atmosphere. It closed around 1982.

O'Banion's grave at Mount Carmel Cemetery remains a popular destination for tourists in the Hillside area, and the tall, obelisk-shaped monument that stands atop it is rarely without some kind of floral adornment. The mausoleums containing the remains of Hymie Weiss and Vincent Drucci are nearby, but in equally close proximity is the Genna family crypt. Sworn enemies in life, O'Banion, Weiss, and Drucci lie near the Sicilian gangsters in death. The irony was not lost on one veteran Chicago cop who shook his head and said to a reporter, "When Judgment Day comes and those graves are opened, there's going to be hell to pay in that cemetery."

BIBLIOGRAPHY

BOOKS

Allsop, Kenneth. *The Bootleggers and Their Era.* London: Hutchinson, 1961

Asbury, Herbert. *Gem of the Prairie.* New York: Knopf, 1940

Bennett, James O'Donnell. *Chicago Gangland.* Chicago: Chicago Tribune, 1929

Burns, Walter Noble. *The One-Way Ride.* Garden City, N.Y.: Doubleday, 1931

Callahan, Bob (ed). *The Big Book of American Irish Culture.* New York: Penguin Books, 1987

Heise, Kenan, and Ed Bauman. *Chicago Originals.* Chicago: Bonus Books, 1990

Helmer, William J. *The Gun That Made the Twenties Roar.* New York: Macmillan, 1969

Kobler, John. *Ardent Spirits.* New York: Putnam's, 1973

Kobler, John. *Capone: The Life and World of Al Capone.* New York: Putnam's, 1971

Landesco, John. *Organized Crime in Chicago: Part III of the Illinois Crime Survey 1929.* Chicago: University of Chicago, 1929

LaVell, Mark, and Bill Helmer. *The Quotable Al Capone.* Chicago: Mad Dog Press, 1990

Lewis, Lloyd, and Henry Justin Smith. *Chicago: the History of its Reputation.* New York: Harcourt, Brace, 1929

Lundberg, Ferdinand. *Imperial Hearst.* Connecticut: Greenwood Press, 1970 (reprint)

Lyle, John H. *The Dry and Lawless Years.* Englewood Cliffs, N.J.: Prentice-Hall, 1960

McPaul, Jack. *Johnny Torrio.* New Rochelle, N.Y.: Arlington House, 1970

Murray, George. *The Legacy of Al Capone.* New York: Putnam's, 1975

Nelli, Humbert S. *The Business of Crime: Italians and Syndicate Crime in the United States.* New York: University of Oxford Press, 1976.

Pasley, Fred. *Al Capone: The Biography of a Self-Made Man.* Ayer, 1987 (originally published 1930)

Schoenberg, Robert. *Mr. Capone.* New York: William Morrow and Company, 1992

Sullivan, Edward D. *Chicago Surrenders.* New York: Vanguard, 1930

Sullivan, Edward D. *Rattling the Cup on Chicago Crime.* New York: Vanguard, 1929

Wendt, Lloyd, and Herman Kogan. *Big Bill of Chicago.* New York: Bobbs-Merrill, 1953

Zorbaugh, Harvey Warren. *The Gold Coast and the Slum: A Sociological Study of Chicago's Near North Side.* Chicago: University of Chicago Press, 1929.

PERIODICALS

Magazines

"Chicago, the American Paradox," Samuel Merwin. *The Saturday Evening Post,* Oct. 26, 1929.

"Getting Away with Murder," Justin Miller. *The Survey,* vol. 62, July 1, 1929.

"Modern Pirate Walks the Plank" William Slavens McNutt. *Collier's,* Jan. 24, 1925.

Newspapers

The Chicago Daily News

Chicago Herald and Examiner

Chicago Tribune

Columbus (Ohio) Dispatch

Decatur (Illinois) Daily Review

The New York Times

Rocky Mountain News

Official Documents

Federal Court Records

The United States vs. Dean O'Banion et al., Criminal Case 12475, U.S. District Court for the Northern District of Illinois, 1924

The United States vs. Dean O'Banion, Dan McCarthy, and Earl Weiss, Criminal Case 12363, U.S. District Court for the Northern District of Illinois, 1924

The United States vs. Earl Weiss, Frank Foster, and Edward Vogel, Criminal Case 14678, U.S. District Court for the Northern District of Illinois, 1926

Criminal Court of Cook County Records

Indictment 23893–*Burglary charge against Dean O'Banion,* March 1921

Indictment 24784–*Procuring Explosives charge against Dean O'Banion,* June 1921

Indictment 28982–*Robbery charge against Dean O'Banion, Vincent Drucci, and Harry Hartman,* July 1922

Circuit Court of Cook County Records

Probate documents for the estates of Dean O'Banion and Earl J. Weiss

Additional Resources

U.S. Census for the State of Illinois: 1880, 1900, 1910, 1910.

World War I Draft Registration Records

Archdiocese of Chicago: Marriage, baptismal and parochial school records for Dean O'Banion

INDEX